REFORMING METROPOLITAN SCHOOLS

REFORMING METROPOLITAN SCHOOLS

Allan C. Ornstein, Loyola University of Chicago
Daniel U. Levine, University of Missouri—Kansas City
Doxey A. Wilkerson, Mediax Associates, Westport, Connecticut

Goodyear Publishing Company, Inc.,
Pacific Palisades, California

L C
5 1 3 1
. 0 7 6 3

Library of Congress Cataloging in Publication Data

Ornstein, Allan, C.
    Reforming metropolitan schools.
    (Goodyear education series)
    Includes bibliographies.
    1. Education, Urban—United States—Addresses,
essays, lectures. I. Levine, Daniel U., 1935–
II. Wilkerson, Doxey Alphonso, 1905–
III. Title.
LC5131.0763   3.70.19′348′0973   74-3721
ISBN 0-87620-780-8 (pbk.)

Library of Congress Catalog Card Number: 74-3721

ISBN: 0-87620-780-8

Y-7808-2

Current printing (last number):

10 9 8 7 6 5 4 3 2 1

Printed in the United States of America

Contents

68014

Preface:
The Setting

In his *Age of Reform*, Richard Hofstader pointed out that the United States was born in the country and moved to the city. From its beginning, the nation's social and political values were shaped by rural life. It was only after the turn of the twentieth century that the United States became a metropolitan society. (In simple terms, a metropolitan area consists of a city and its surrounding suburbs.)

Few can disagree with this appraisal. In 1790, at the time of the first census, more than 90 percent of Americans lived in rural areas. As late as 1860, 75 percent of the populace lived in rural settings. Forty years later, approximately 40 percent lived in metropolitan America, and 60 percent still lived in rural America. After the 1919 armistice, the popular slogan was "How're you goin' to keep 'em down on the farm after they've seen Paree." Hence the social circumstances, coupled with the increased emigration of Europeans to America, resulted in a large growth in the cities, and the cities began to expand outward toward the suburbs.

We are now a metropolitan society. By 1970 the census estimated that 75 percent of Americans lived in metropolitan areas, and the census projections of this figure to the year 2000 bring the percentage almost to totality. At present, there are 33 metropolitan centers with a population of a million or more, compared to the turn of the century when there were only two metropolitan areas with one million or more people. According to present trends, by the end of this century, there will be between 50 to 75 metropolitan areas each with a minimum of one million people.

As the metropolitan setting develops, and especially as the cities grow, there is increasing doubt whether it is worth living in the cities of America; furthermore, the tides of dissatisfaction and alienation run high in America today throughout the metropolitan area. For some groups, the problems are growing population and pollution, racial discrimination, deteriorating houses, crowded slums, unrepresentative governments, and tax loopholes for big business and the rich. For others, the most important problems are of law and order, crime and violence, riots and reverse discrimination, growing welfare rolls and increased taxes, and neglect of white ethnics. Manifestations of growing dissatisfaction and alienation are keenly reflected in black-white confrontations in various institutions, in the rise of black power currently followed by the fever of white ethnicity, in the increasing demands of have-nots versus the increasing expectations of the have-littles.

Just how the schools can alter the social order, or how the rest of society can alter the schools, is not yet clear; nevertheless, educators should be aware of the nature of the social setting. For the most part, the schools do not change society, they reflect it, and the ills of society usually affect the schools. Many schools, today, seem burdened with black-white confrontation, crime, violence and drug addiction, students' rights and teacher militancy—a general rage and anger which reflect the ills of society.

While we focus in this book on the problems of inner-city schools, we also allude to other metropolitan schools and we do not want to minimize the needs and concerns of outer-city and suburban groups. While we pay close attention to the poor and racial minorities, we also recognize the need to be concerned with the nonpoor and white groups. After presenting an overview of metropolitan schools, we have selected for discussion four of the major issues facing metropolitan schools; they are (1) compensatory education, (2) accountability, (3) administrative decentralization and community control, (4) and desegregation. We hope the book will encourage thought and clarify some of the important issues and challenges descending on city (inner and outer) and suburban schools and metropolitan education in general.

For readers who are curious, Mr. Ornstein was responsible for chapters 3 and 4. Mr. Levine was responsible for chapters 1 and 5 and Mr. Wilkerson was responsible for chapter 2. As may be noted in these chapters, the authors are not in complete agreement on all issues. Portions of this book appeared in the September 1973 issue of *Today's Education*, the NEA Journal, and in the May and June 1973 issues of *Phi Delta Kappan*.

A special word of thanks goes to Ted Hipple of the University of Florida and to David Grady of the Goodyear Publishing Company for their advice and encouragement in designing this textbook. Finally, we wish to extend our sincere appreciation to Ms. Valerie Kiegelis and Mrs. Marjorie Thoelke, who typed the final draft of the book.

Allan C. Ornstein
Loyola University, Chicago

Daniel U. Levine
University of Missouri,
Kansas City

Doxey A. Wilkerson
Mediax Associates, Inc.
Westport, Conn.

Chapter 1

METROPOLITAN PROBLEMS IN EDUCATION

Much has been written about the "crisis" in urban schools, but in reality there are several crises.

More properly stated, public education in metropolitan areas is not in "crisis" in the sense that some critical component is going to explode and bring the whole structure down with it in the next few years. Rather, a number of important components are facing problems that are "critical" in that few if any satisfactory solutions are in sight and there is little agreement concerning directions to move to correct them in the future.

If no one possesses *the* answers for solving these problems, why study—or write a book about—critical issues in metropolitan education? The answer, of course, must be because we are unlikely to find solutions, or even workable responses, unless we understand what the problems are and where we stand with respect to existing proposals and efforts aimed at solving them.

The major purpose of this book, then, is to assess where the public schools stand with respect to critical issues in metropolitan education. Unfortunately, it is not possible in a work of this length to review all the important issues in very much depth; to do so would require a veritable Encyclopedia of Metropolitan Education. For this reason, we have selected several of the issues that are most critical in terms of severity of the problems they involve and of the amount of attention being given

1

them in efforts to improve the quality of metropolitan schools. These issues, each of which will be treated in a separate chapter, are:

> Compensatory Education
> Educational Accountability
> Decentralization and Community Control
> Desegregation

One can readily see that each of these issues involves the education of economically disadvantaged children and youth in big cities; that is, community control of schools, accountability of educators to their clients, compensatory education, and desegregation are topics bearing relatively directly on the problem of providing more effective education for disadvantaged students in poverty and/or racial ghettos in big cities. These issues do not exhaust the list of important alternatives one might propose for improving the education of disadvantaged students; but they do delimit, to a degree, the major alternatives now being utilized in attempts to find a solution to the most pervasive and formidable educational problem in large metropolitan areas.

The situation, simply put, is that the schools are not succeeding in providing an adequate education for many millions of economically disadvantaged students who live and go to school in predominantly low-income areas in big cities. It is not necessary to agree with the prevalent emphasis on "achieving" in the public schools and then "going" to college in order to perceive the national disaster inherent in the low achievement levels found among economically disadvantaged students in big city schools. Whether or not committed to combatting employment practices that too often require irrelevant educational credentials, most observers will admit that far too many disadvantaged youngsters are not acquiring the minimal skills in reading and computation needed to compete for skilled or even semiskilled jobs. From this point of view, improving educational programs for disadvantaged students certainly must be viewed as a central, overriding concern in metropolitan education.

On the other hand, the issues we are concerned with in this book should not be viewed as having implications only for economically disadvantaged students in big-city school districts. Discussions on "accountability" and "decentralization," for example, generally are applicable to schools throughout the metropolitan area, because they deal with problems that are of serious concern in middle-class and affluent sections of big-city and suburban school districts, as well as low-status, inner-city sections. Problems and trends involving desegregated education, similarly, in a sense may originate in the fact that disadvantaged students in the inner city are deprived of equal opportunity when forced to attend neighborhood schools that do not provide adequate education, but such problems immediately assume city-wide and/or metropolitan dimensions when one seeks to give inner-city students an opportunity to attend more functional schools. For these reasons we view the themes in this book as being "metropolitan" rather than simply "inner city" in their scope and implications.

The situation in metropolitan education is thus analogous, in many respects, with that which exists regarding other metropolitan issues such as housing and community development. The present stage of metropolitan evolution in the United States, that is to say, poses sharp dilemmas for which attractive-sounding solutions can easily be delineated on paper but which often seem largely insoluble and intractable in practice.

In housing, for example, policy makers who truly want to help citizens living in decaying, low-status neighborhoods in the inner city are baffled by the institutional obstacles to progress which characterize metropolitan areas segregated by social class and race. Does one pour millions of tax dollars into new housing, code enforcement, rehabilitation, and other housing services in inner-city ghettos despite the fact that such expenditures typically accomplish little in slowing down the decline of neighborhoods in which investors will not invest and landlords do not earn enough profit to maintain existing properties? Or, rather than making seemingly futile attempts to "gild the ghetto," does one attempt to eliminate the ghetto by designing programs to disperse its inhabitants to more livable neighborhoods? A dispersal strategy would seem to be the more prudent and less wasteful course of action, but many question whether dispersal is either feasible, given the political and legal obstacles to its realization, or desirable, given its tendency to fragment the political influence of disadvantaged minorities.

Policies regarding employment opportunities embody a similar dilemma. Should government attempt to stimulate employment and business in inner-city ghettos where the market for products is inherently limited and the costs of transporting goods are often high, or should jobs be created elsewhere where travel time and costs function as a disincentive for inner-city residents? Is one throwing good money after bad by sinking it into an inner-city community where conditions do not favor capital investment, or does a greater waste of resources occur when subsidies are provided to help transport inner-city employees to suburban locations?

In education, "compensatory" programs represent the "gilded ghetto" approach, while integration plans, which in one way or another take disadvantaged students out of inner-city schools, are equivalent to the dispersal strategy in housing. As we shall see in later chapters, compensatory education generally has been, if anything, less successful than large-scale public-housing projects in the inner city, and truly integrated education may prove almost as difficult to achieve as is dispersal in housing. (This does not mean, of course, that it necessarily is impossible to carry out either strategy but only that future programs would have to be far more effective than existing ones.) Because compensatory education has not accomplished very much and integration has hardly been tried at all in large metropolitan areas outside the South, educators and parents have been forced to look toward other alternatives even though these alternatives also pose problems and are selected more out of either faith or despair than on the basis of empirical evidence concerning their value and workability.

Two of the most widely discussed and advocated alternatives of this kind are being pursued in the interrelated movements toward "accountability" to the public on the one hand and "community control" of local public schools on the other. These movements in education have their counterparts in other aspects of urban and metropolitan affairs, as in efforts to make municipal departments (for example, trash collection, street repair, police) and private agencies (for example, medical and banking) more accountable to their clients either by working out ways to evaluate and monitor their effectiveness or by placing them wholly or partly under the control of local communities, or both. In the inner city, they represent almost a last-ditch effort to find a way out of the terrible dilemma associated with the gilded ghetto and the dispersal approaches.

Whether movements toward community control and accountability in education will prove any more successful than compensatory education remains to be seen. We assess the current status of these movements in subsequent chapters, because they do offer some promise for the future. But there is no assurance this promise will be fulfilled, and there are many reasons for being skeptical about their potential for overcoming the ineffectuality of schools and other social institutions in the inner city. Thus we are not able to conclude that community control and accountability provide reliable "answers" to the difficult problems of inner-city education, any more than we could argue convincingly that these movements are bound to be successful in improving other institutions in the inner city. Our aim is much more modest: to help readers understand the reasons for believing that these movements may be of some help, as well as the reasons for believing they may prove to be temporary diversions within a larger dialogue between those who emphasize reforming inner-city schools by other means (for example, change in instruction and school organization) and those who believe that desegregation is necessary before there can be much improvement in the achievement of economically disadvantaged students in the inner city.

Before turning to these issues, however, it is useful to discuss several fundamental considerations which should be kept in mind when evaluating policies and proposals regarding desegregation, compensatory education, community control, and accountability. These considerations may be paraphrased into two questions of special underlying importance in reviewing proposals to improve inner-city education: (1) Why is it so frustratingly difficult to provide effective education in inner-city schools, even when expensive "compensatory" services are provided to improve teaching and learning conditions in the classroom? and (2) How can instruction be made more effective in inner-city schools? The position an observer takes on these questions is likely to condition, though not completely determine, his stance regarding desegregation, compensatory education, community control, and accountability.

DIFFICULTY OF PROVIDING EFFECTIVE
EDUCATION IN THE INNER CITY

Entire books have been written about the difficult circumstances students and teachers encounter in inner-city schools. There are many reasons for low achievement in the inner city, some of which we examine at more length in chapter 2. At this point, however, we want to draw attention particularly to two of the most important ones: the sense of *hopelessness* people experience in an inner-city environment, and the feeling of *illegitimacy* many students experience in inner-city schools.

Behavioral psychologists have labored for years to show that man, like other animals, generally tends to repeat behaviors that are reinforcing and to cease behaviors that are nonreinforcing. From this point of view it is justified to conclude that behavior patterns are strategies for obtaining rewards and avoiding punishments.

Something unexpected happens, however, when an animal's responses to threats in its environment bear little consistent relationship to whether it is rewarded or punished. It has been shown, for example, that dogs placed in a conditioning apparatus and given electric shocks regardless of what they do to avoid this punishment rapidly learn that their responses have little to do with what happens to them later. In essence, they have been taught that they are powerless to control their environment and that outside forces determine their fate. Afterward, they tend either to respond in a stereotyped way to later stimuli (that is, to repeat the same response again and again), or not to respond at all except when forced to, even when experimental conditions have been changed to provide immediate rewards for a new response (Seligman, 1969).

Human beings, too, can be taught that hostile forces are at work to ensure their defeat and that stereotyped responses at least have the virtue of relieving frustration by providing something to do. This response pattern is exactly what is being taught to—and learned by—many hundreds of thousands of disadvantaged children confined by social stratification and racial segregation to inner core sections of the metropolitan area.

How is this frustration-avoidance pattern developed among children in the inner-city? For a substantial proportion this outcome is brought about by living in an environment in which:

1. A large number of people have few economic resources even though many work very hard and some have acquired a good deal of formal education. In this way children learn that people like themselves are destined to fail no matter how hard they may work. From this point of view the inner city is a geographic-social environment which tells a child that people like himself (for example, those who are poor, or dark-skinned, or are from a minority ethnic background) are destined to be placed apart. It is only a small jump from this perception to the invention of excuses which a child can use to justify withdrawal from a difficult competition for which he suspects he is not adequately prepared in the first place.

2. Chances to engage in activities much more exciting than those in the classroom are near at hand. With thousands of people packed into a small patch of land so that a large peer group is present, and with gambling, narcotics, and other "adult" activities an immediate part of the environment, it becomes difficult and sometimes impossible for parents to maintain control of children against the competition of the streets. As a result, many parents are unable to protect their children from deleterious influences in their neighborhoods, and both parents and later young people begin to behave as if it is hopeless to try.

In sum, if one set out to encourage behavior patterns characterized by hopelessness and frustration, the goal would be achieved by placing young people in an inner-city environment in a large metropolitan area. It is hardly surprising that many of the people who grow up or live in the inner city come to believe that they have little control over their environment or their future. As a consequence, many do not see much point in trying to achieve goals that seem unattainable and unrealistic. In turn, this sense of powerlessness means that many will not take much advantage of opportunities that do become available, and the situation will tend to persist as long as the environment itself teaches hopelessness and despair.

Viewing the school as being not "legitimate" to many economically disadvantaged students does not mean that it necessarily is perceived as having no right to function in an inner-city neighborhood. Nor does it mean that education in the abstract is seen as undesirable or useless. As a matter of fact, inner-city families—especially black families—usually place high value on obtaining an education and strongly believe that educational attainment is the best route to social mobility. What it does mean is that the inner-city school typically is not well attuned to the problems and characteristics of the children it serves. In part, this is why commitment to education often does not carry over in a practical sense to the school itself and why youngsters who agree that education is a means to escape poverty frequently act as if this applied more to others than to themselves.

There are many respects in which existing schools (that is, schools as they generally are organized and operated today) are foreign elements in the lives of inner-city students and the affairs of inner-city neighborhoods. The language used in the school, for example, usually is standard English, but many inner-city students speak nonstandard dialects or languages other than English at home and have not been prepared to understand and utilize relatively abstract concepts in the standard dialect. Curriculum materials, too, still tend to deal primarily with concepts and phenomena that are outside the range of immediate experience of the inner-city child; thus they violate one of the best established principles of psychological research, namely, that material is likely to be learned much more rapidly and adequately if it is meaningful and practically important to the learner than if it is foreign and insignificant to him. In addition, to function successfully in existing schools generally requires a good deal of independent activity on the part of the learner, but inner-city students frequently have not learned how to work this way in the classroom.

These examples of lack of fit between the school and inner-city realities are obvious and well known, but surprisingly little has been done to modify curriculum and instruction in the inner-city school. For the most part the curriculum in inner-city schools and the instructional methods used to teach it are not fundamentally different from what they were ten or twenty years ago. In most instances, curricular and instructional changes to reduce the illegitimacy of the school in the inner city have been superficial and piecemeal.

Part of the reason is that effective change on a wide front costs money, and big-city school districts have not had the financial resources to underwrite massive reform. (Federal aid has been helpful, but it has not been nearly enough to make an appreciable difference.) Part of the reason is that hunger, poor housing, and other environmental conditions which obviously hamper learning in many subtle as well as direct ways are still allowed to exact a heavy toll in the lives of residents of the inner city. An equally important reason, however, is that reform proposals more often than not have been based on a one-sided frame of reference. For various reasons involving particularly the bureaucratic organization of school districts and the defensiveness of teachers who work in frustrating circumstances, school officials frequently have limited themselves to asking how the child can be helped to adjust to the school, not how the school can be changed to help the child. School critics, for their part, often have been wedded to one or another simplistic prescription calling only for change in the institution: if the school would recognize and respect the human worth of the child, the academic deficits of disadvantaged students would be largely overcome. Neither of these one-sided positions is likely to prove helpful in itself. That is, if disadvantaged students are to succeed in our schools, the schools will have to undergo comprehensive change at the same time that much more is done to prepare the child to function successfully in the classroom. Even then, it is not completely certain that large numbers of inner-city schools can be made very effective given the sense of powerlessness which pervades the inner-city environment. Whether inner-city schools can succeed in anything like their present form is particularly problematic at the secondary level, where peer influence becomes very strong and—to our knowledge—there are no really successful "regular" inner-city schools to be found anywhere. Accordingly, we will limit the following discussion on improving the effectiveness of instruction in the inner city to the elementary level.

IMPROVING THE EFFECTIVENESS OF INNER-CITY ELEMENTARY SCHOOLS

Few schools in the United States have been very effective in the sense of motivating and guiding pupils to learn a fraction of what most are capable of learning. Students who have come to school well prepared for existing programs and highly motivated to succeed in them have tended to learn a good deal, and students for whom the school has seemed foreign and artificial have learned very little. Because social class and family background are highly correlated with motivation and preparation to succeed in existing school programs, it is possible to make accurate predictions concerning how well a group of students will succeed academically without knowing anything at all about the characteristics of the schools they attend (for example, amount of money spent per pupil, class size, new or old school building).

For example, information about parental occupations, incomes, levels of education, or other global indicators of social class generally accounts for 25 to 40 percent of the variation in achievement scores among a large group of students (Lavin, 1965). Information about conditions in students' families (for example, "orderliness" in the home) and neighborhoods (for example, extent of poverty), raises the proportion of variation explained to between two-thirds and three-fourths. Unless it is assumed that youngsters from lower-status families or from homes low on indicators associated with school achievement are born with fewer of the intellectual and attitudinal resources needed for success in the schools, the only possible conclusion that can be drawn is that the schools simply have not been sufficiently powerful to affect substantially the social and educational advantages and disadvantages which accrue to individuals as a result of their social class and family background.

Approached from this perspective, the problem of educating disadvantaged students reduces itself partly to that of trying to overcome the obstacles that have made the public schools as a whole—not just the inner-city school—generally impotent in the sense described above. This requires, in turn, that instructional practices and organization be radically improved to achieve goals that educators have constantly reiterated in slogans for at least fifty years but have seldom come near to accomplishing in practice: "Individualized instruction"; "Start with the child where he is"; "Make learning meaningful," and the like. The challenge in the inner-city school is to live up to ideals that until now have received plenty of verbal affirmation in American education but precious little real implementation. A brief listing of some of the most important and/or promising practices for doing this should include the following:

1. *Curriculum and instruction.* To enable teachers to work effectively with individual students, schools can be reorganized in a variety of ways. Working with aides and volunteers, teams of teachers can take responsibility for groups of students which are subdivided and regrouped as necessary to allow for individual and small group instruction focused on definite instructional objectives particularly appropriate for the individual learner. A wide range of materials and resources can be made available in skills centers (for example, reading, creative arts) and subject matter centers (for example, mathematics laboratories) in which students carry out prescribed assignments and pursue voluntary studies that especially interest them. Teachers can be given easy access to many appropriate resources for individualization and to equipment and supplies to prepare materials on their own. Emphasis can be placed on diagnosis of individual learning needs and on immediate evaluation of whether they are being fulfilled, and teachers working in teams can become specialists in diagnosis, evaluation, or other highly skilled roles.

2. *Technology.* Educational media and technology have an important place in the "effective" school. Sophisticated machines such as the Edison Response Laboratory ("talking typewriter") or the Bell and Howell Language Master (a semimanual machine that helps pupils relate things to concepts) may be used for tasks that machines can perform better than the average teacher because they have infinite patience and they enable a student to learn more nearly at his own rate. Technology can be used to "store" in easily retrievable form a much greater amount of instructional resources than otherwise would be available, as well as to diagnose the learning status and difficulties of each student.

3. *Organization and administration.* As implied in the preceding paragraphs, both the school schedule and the school staffing pattern can

be changed to facilitate appropriate individualization of instruction, and teachers can be given adequate time every day to work with other staff members in planning instruction for the pupils for whom they are responsible. To learn to utilize complex equipment and to perform specialized functions, teachers can be given much more adequate training—and continual retraining—than they heretofore have received on college campuses or in occasional in-service training sessions. Sharing decision-making authority with staff members who are in a position to know what is working or not working in the classroom, the principal or head administrator can be granted (or can seize) authority to organize the school and to determine how resources will be deployed within it. One important implication here is that administrators must be chosen more for independence and initiative than for characteristics (such as unwillingness to rock the boat) which too often have been the basis for selection in the past—particularly in large, hierarchical, urban districts.

Beyond these emerging approaches for making schools more effective regardless of whether their students are low or middle or high in social status, inner-city schools must place special emphasis on activities that might counteract the isolation and powerlessness of their clients and the illegitimacy or "foreignness" of the school. Among the most potentially important school responses to these conditions are the following:

1. *Careful structuring of learning experiences leading to increasing independence and self-control on the part of disadvantaged students in the classroom.* Inasmuch as requirements for self-directed activity constitute one of the critical factors that make the school a foreign setting for many inner-city students, it is not surprising that most special programs that have reported some success in educating the disadvantaged have provided a high degree of initial structure in learning requirements and instructional sequences. Carefully structured or prescribed activities and expectations not only can help disadvantaged students learn to function successfully in the school environment but also can help reduce psychological insecurities bred by the uncertainties of life in the slums and can facilitate identification and correction of specific skill deficits (Levine and Doll, 1972).

2. *Parent involvement.* Parent and citizen participation in education in the inner city can take a variety of forms ranging from involvement as an aide in the classroom to full participation in school decision making. Although the current stress on parent involvement in many big-city school districts is too new to determine which forms will turn out to be most productive, there is some reason to believe that parent participation will prove to be an indispensable element in the reform of inner-city education. Probably the most important function parents can help perform is to "watchdog" the school to make sure that school programs are properly implemented and do not provide merely paper promises of

improvement in curriculum and instruction. Another is to increase parents' knowledge of realities in the classroom in order to counteract the commonly held view that repression and physical coercion can be effective in "making" children learn. A third important purpose of parental involvement in the inner city is to show pupils that the people who live in their neighborhood are able to exercise influence over the institutions they are taxed to support.

Many of the goals of parent involvement can be realized through an approach usually labeled "the community school." A community school is a school kept open afternoons, evenings, and weekends to provide a variety of courses and services for residents of its neighborhood. Particularly when combined with parental participation in making decisions on major policies regarding a school's organization and operation, the community school approach provides an opportunity to make the school a more legitimate part of an inner-city neighborhood (Levine, 1968).

3. *Minimization of failure.* Failure can be minimized by giving children better preparation for the classroom. Head Start, television's "Sesame Street," and other special programs for very young children have been designed explicitly for this purpose, as are the widespread efforts now being undertaken to teach low-income parents how to provide good learning environments for their preschool children. When we say, after all, that existing schools are foreign to the inner-city child, we are also saying that the child is foreign in many ways to the culture of the school, thus indicating that action should be taken to prepare him for success in the institution. Although the evidence is still fragmentary and somewhat inconclusive, it appears that parent education activities in conjunction with preschool classes emphasizing intellectual development can make a difference in preparing inner-city youngsters for success in school—provided that there are concomitant improvements in regular classrooms as pupils enter the primary grades (Lopate et al., 1970). Available evidence also suggests that carefully planned reinforcement schedules emphasizing extrinsic rewards may be particularly useful in motivating disadvantaged youngsters until they internalize good learning habits.

4. *Nurturing positive self-definition.* Whether a student makes good use of opportunities for learning or other social and economic opportunities which may be available to him depends partly on whether he perceives himself as having the ability to take advantage of opportunities as well as on whether he thinks it is realistic for persons like himself to hold high aspirations in any given type of activity. Such aspects of self-concept depend not just on the unique personal experiences that contribute to a positive or negative self-image but also on a person's self-definition as a member of a racial or ethnic group. Because the isolation of an inner-city ghetto generates crippling feelings of personal

and group powerlessness which in turn detract from achievement, educators working with disadvantaged students must do all they can to foster improvements in self-concept and sense of control of the future.

In addition to minimizing failure, which is an obviously potent element in creating a negative self-concept in a learner, educators must use a variety of other approaches aimed at nurturing positive self-images among students in inner-city schools. Reforms that are particularly promising and are being widely adopted for this purpose include: (a) placing systematic emphasis on the history and achievement of minority groups heavily represented in the student composition of a particular school; (b) the language experience approach in which instruction initially utilizes the language and concepts students already know in order to provide a basis for verbalization and conceptualization in the classroom; and (c) bilingual programs in which students from homes in which little or no English is spoken learn to communicate more satisfactorily in their native language before or at the same time they learn to handle standard English. Each of these approaches has important and legitimate purposes besides building positive self-definitions among economically disadvantaged students in the inner city, but their convergence on this particular goal suggests that they might be woven into a comprehensive strategy for counteracting some of the pernicious results of socioeconomic and racial stratification in the metropolitan area.

The importance of insisting that any plan for improving inner-city education must be comprehensive and systematic is difficult to overemphasize. Despite large expenditures, compensatory education programs generally have not had a fair testing. In most instances, for example, teacher retraining programs have provided only a fraction of the amount of training required to bring about a substantial change in classroom methodology. Where substantial retraining programs have been conducted, training often has concentrated *either* on improving teachers' understanding of disadvantaged students *or* on developing skills useful for teaching in the inner city; neither approach by itself can be expected to result in much improvement in the performance of disadvantaged students. Where adequate training has been provided for some teachers, its effects usually have been dissipated in a few classrooms without changing the norms and expectations held by a majority of students and teachers. In the few cases where a unified faculty effort has been made to introduce instructional materials and curricula especially appropriate for disadvantaged students, little has been done to involve parents in school programs and school decision-making as part of an effort to unify the school and the home. Such piecemeal attempts at reform offer little hope for making the school a more legitimate and influential institution in the lives of children who are isolated within metropolitan society.

The purpose of the preceding sections has been to describe the most critical actions and changes required to improve the academic performance of disadvantaged students in inner-city elementarysschools. For a substantial and possibly growing minority of inner-city youngsters, however, alienation from the school already is so great that even the best-conceived and most comprehensive plans for institutional reform may make little difference. For students who have long since psychologically dropped out of school after repeated failure or who are so hostile toward the institution that its expectations hold virtually no meaning for them, what is called for is not so much institutional reform as new institutional settings. Because the problem of socializing for educational growth in these cases is due to the existence of an almost unbridgeable gap between the institution and its clients, the only way the goals of the institution can be achieved is by transforming the institution to reduce or eliminate the chasm. Examples of such change are described in a later section of this chapter on metropolitan secondary schools.

OTHER MAJOR PROBLEMS IN METROPOLITAN EDUCATION

Because we believe that the ineffectiveness of schools enrolling economically disadvantaged students in inner-city sections of the metropolitan area constitutes the single most important problem in metropolitan education, most of the material in this book is devoted to critical issues more or less directly related to the question of what should be done to improve the academic achievement of inner-city students.

However, depending on one's point of view, other problems in metropolitan education can be viewed as equally serious in terms of their implications for metropolitan development and the long-range difficulties educators are likely to encounter in trying to solve them. Three of these problems will be described briefly in the remainder of this chapter, partly in order to illustrate some of the ways in which problems in metropolitan education are related to or arise from the differing circumstances of various social groups which tend to be separated or concentrated in differing parts of the metropolitan area. Here, too, we have had to be very selective in choosing topics for examination and do not wish to imply that those included begin to exhaust the list of possible problems and situations that deserve consideration and discussion.

Alienation in Upper-Middle-Class Schools

Many reasons might be given to account for the discontent that has become widespread during the past ten years among upper-middle-class students in outlying parts of the city, as well as in the more affluent suburbs. Although social scientists do not fully agree about all the reasons alienation has become so marked among students in predominantly middle-class schools in these communities, any attempt to sketch out the fundamental causes should include at least the following considerations:

1. *Unreality of the suburban environment.* Whatever else one may think about the socializing environment of the middle-class community, it often fails to provide much sense of reality for the young people who grow up in it. By definition, relatively homogeneous middle-class neighborhoods constitute only a small slice of modern urban society, and it is a slice that is designed to achieve placidity, security, and domesticity —exactly the qualities young people must learn to transcend as part of their struggle to make their way in the larger society. If it is a youthful oversimplification to capsulize the homogeneity of middle-class communities as being simply "plastic" and "one-dimensional," at least these terms aptly communicate the aura of unreality and inauthenticity which institutions in these communities apparently are generating among middle-class youth. Just as the inner-city family is at a competitive disadvantage in raising children attracted to life on the street, upper-middle-class families (and schools) predictably are losing out to a youth culture which, despite its drugs and fantasies, paradoxically seems more real ("It's what's happening!") than protective suburban cocoons that reflect the fears of adults more than the interests and motivations of young people.

2. *Relative affluence.* Another factor that is tending to detach young people from established institutions such as the school is the effect that relative affluence[1] has on perceptions of social reality. Because most middle-class youngsters no longer have to take part in a desperate struggle to earn the necessities of life, schooling is less likely to be valued primarily as a means to acquire material possessions. For this reason the school must become expressively important and meaningful in its own right rather than assuming, as it has till now, that an economy of scarcity will invest it with unquestioned importance.

3. *Surfeit of opportunities.* Whereas the problems faced by inner-city youngsters are associated first and foremost with unequal and insufficient opportunities, the difficulties experienced by middle-class youngsters are more closely tied to the surfeit of opportunities available to advantaged young people in a highly developed postindustrial society. Because a limitless range of career and vocational opportunities seems possible in this type of society, which provides instantaneous exposure to a bewildering variety of life styles and cultural patterns, it has become more difficult for youth to work out a stable and personally rewarding identity (Klapp, 1969). At the same time, the empiricism that flourished in Western culture during the past five hundred years developed an openness to experience which makes it conceivable—indeed, for some,

obligatory—to try out a large variety of roles and identities which are available in the culture and are accessible to the individual. About all that is certain for a growing proportion of middle-class youth is that a person need not automatically assume the roles and identities of his parents and that individuals now have a real opportunity to become what they most want to be. The identity confusion which results is inextricably tied, of course, to what happens in the school, since it is not possible for a person to function very successfully within an institution unless he securely knows who he is and why he is there.

4. *Intellectual acuity*. Another obvious reason upper-middle-class students increasingly question the credibility of major social institutions is simply that they are better informed and more knowledgeable about the immense gap between social ideals and social realities in the United States than any large group of middle-stratum young people has been in the past. To a degree, awareness of this gap is a function of the relatively high level of education and cultural awareness which has been attained in the middle class, but it also reflects the development of national and international mass communications, as well as unique historical events such as the movement of black Americans to cities where oppression is less invisible than it had been in the rural South. Possibly the most important result of these and other related developments in the evolution of American society is that upper-middle-class youth constitute the first sizable subculture in the United States to realize that science and technology by themselves not only do not guarantee but in some ways block social progress and the fulfillment of human needs. With science, technology, and the concept of progress no longer sufficient to serve as guides for daily behavior, youth faces a dilemma similar to that which confronted Western society hundreds of years ago when the church had lost its central influence over people's decisions about how they would live —except now the dilemma is more excruciating because the forces of modernity which discredited religious world views no longer provide a plausible alternative to replace what was discarded.

5. *Prolonged adolescence*. One of the frequently noted causes of dissatisfaction among middle-class youth in the United States has been the emergence of career patterns that require ten or more years of attendance in high school, college, and graduate school. Some observers believe that prolonging adolescence through a decade or more of educational training makes neither economic nor psychological sense of any kind; others point out that definite social functions are served by keeping young people out of an economy with limited capacity for absorbing and rewarding workers who possess relatively little formal education or specialized intellectual skills. Neither point of view negates the rather obvious truism that postponing employment not only encourages experimentation with a variety of shifting identities and roles but also reduces the salience of, and

causes to be taken for granted, the educational institutions established to prepare youth for a receded future. Particularly when schooling becomes a highly competitive struggle to prepare oneself for still more rigorous competition in abstruse future tasks at which only a small percentage of competitors are likely to truly excel, educational institutions are more likely to be questioned and rejected by participants whose commitment to their goals and traditions is less than total.

6. *Socialization for independence.* It is no accident that many middle-class youth tend to value independence and to articulate if not always adhere to philosophies favoring individuality in judgment and idiosyncrasy in personal expression. As Melvin Kohn (1969) and other social scientists have been painstakingly demonstrating in a series of studies carried out over the past decade, middle-class parents explicitly set out to raise children who can handle the initiative and independence required to make the sophisticated decisions that are the essence of upper-middle-class professions.

Yet, the very same forces which require that young people be socialized to think and act independently also tend to place them in institutions in which they are expected to be conforming and dependent. Just as the fundamental dilemma of professionalism within complex organizations appears in industrial societies which place creative specialists within large hierarchical organizations, so too the educational dilemma is posed by the tension created when schools try to treat students simultaneously as individuals and as clients of a complex bureaucracy. On the one hand, it is apparent that learning is always ultimately individual and that the educational process depends on providing experiences that are appropriate in terms of the motivation and capability of each individual involved in it. On the other hand, it is also apparent that schools utilize standardized procedures to coordinate large amounts of resources drawn together to educate large numbers of students. Technological change and complexity require that students master more advanced and abstract bodies of knowledge (which requires successful individualization of instruction) while simultaneously creating larger and more bureaucratic educational institutions which treat clients impersonally and interchangeably (thus causing students to question the plausibility and hence the legitimacy of the institution). The inherent contradictions between these two opposing trends are responsible for no small part of the alienation now becoming increasingly acute in middle-class schools.

This necessarily sketchy description of forces that lead middle-class students to question and, frequently, reject the education they are receiving has drawn attention to the similarity in outcomes which urban schools have been producing among economically disadvantaged students in the inner city and economically privileged students in the suburbs. The alienation of many upper-middle-class students in the suburban or suburban-type high school is an unprecedented mixture of earnestness and playfulness, of individuality and identity confusion, or moral relativism and social commitment. In particular, much of what is central in the situation of middle-class youth can be summarized by noting the shift that has been occurring from concern for *product* to concern for *process*. When religious and scientific belief-systems lose much of their power to generate unquestioned acceptance of predetermined goals, when technological productivity lifts the burden of fear that the future will bring recurrent famine and starvation, when social change uproots people from primary communities and places them in impersonal bureaucratic settings, and when mass media provide images and knowledge of a new universe of diverse activities and pleasures to be sampled and indulged in, instrumental preoccupation with the future gives way to expressive concern for the quality of experience in the here and now. Although the schools traditionally have provided opportunities for expressive as well as instrumental behaviors, institutional emphasis on the instrumental (for example, academic competition looking toward college admissions) historically increased just when middle-class students were becoming less willing to ignore or forego expressive satisfactions. Students in the middle-class school, in such circumstances, tend to view the school as a repressive force rather than an institution authentically concerned with their interests and motivations.

The alienation of middle-class students obviously has somewhat different roots than does discontent among disadvantaged students in the inner city, but the two resemble each other in producing students for whom the traditional high school is largely inauthentic and meaningless. For both groups, alienation from traditional high school programs has been turning into open rebellion on the part of a substantial proportion of students. For neither group is there much prospect that the traditional high school will be perceived as providing valid and worthwhile educational experiences. For both groups, urban high schools must become very different institutions than most are today if they are to be much more than custodial facilities in which students are confined until old enough to withdraw or graduate. Among the fundamental changes without which there is little hope that urban high schools will serve a useful purpose in the lives of alienated disadvantaged and middle-class students are the following:

1. *Debureaucratization.* Bureaucracy is a social invention designed to coordinate rationally human and nonhuman resources in order to accomplish the goals of an organization. But to function effectively, bureaucracy presumes that its clients generally understand and accept both its rules and regulations and the purposes for which rules and regulations are codified in the first place. That is, bureaucratic organiza-

tion is ineffective unless its clients believe it is legitimate to learn its rules and operate within its parameters.

For reasons summarized above, growing numbers of both disadvantaged and middle-class youth either are unable to function well within bureaucratic school settings or openly reject the goals and expectations of the traditional bureaucratic school. Urban high schools will have to become considerably less bureaucratic if they are to educate students who consciously or implicitly question their legitimacy. One possibility along these lines is to group perhaps one to three hundred students and five to fifteen teachers in semipermanent "subschools" where personal, face-to-face relationships are increased and social distance between students and staff is minimized. Another possibility is to expand greatly student participation in all types of decision-making in order to bring about more of a coincidence between the goals of the institution and those of its clients.

2. *Pluralism.* Briefly considered, pluralism in the composition of the school can be a vital element in helping economically disadvantaged students for whom attendance at an inner-city school reinforces the debilitating isolation of big-city slums and in overcoming the isolation of middle-class students for whom relatively homogeneous suburban-type environments seem unreal and inauthentic. Urban educators who understand what pluralism can contribute in these respects must take affirmative action to bring students of varying economic, racial, and ethnic groups together in working teams to pursue educative activities in a truly pluralistic context.

3. *Identity building.* Students who are confused or negative about who they are or what they should aspire to be cannot be expected to function well in schools which assume that other socializing institutions already have enabled youth to work through problems of identity with which they otherwise would be preoccupied. Even assuming that the family, the church, and other institutions once performed this function fairly satisfactorily (a big assumption), it would be hard to make a defensible case that they are doing so today. Particularly with respect to adolescents from low-status, inner-city families and from relatively high-status suburban families, whatever forces previously may have operated to produce a secure and stable sense of identity for the young clearly have been weakened if not wiped out by the exigencies of metropolitan stratification. Urban high schools that ignore the resulting psychological havoc created in the lives of their students are all but asking for chaos in their classrooms and corridors.

At present it must be admitted that very little is known with certainty about how the school can help students acquire positive and satisfying identities appropriate for industrial societies in the latter part of the twentieth century. (This is not surprising, inasmuch as the schools have been almost totally unconcerned with identity-building.) The first priority in the inner city probably should be to build pride in ethnic and racial heritages. For middle-class students, the school probably should concentrate first on systematically providing opportunities to test a variety of roles and identities. In the long run, however, the dissolution of traditional tribal subcommunities and the discrediting of prelunar philosophies make both functions important for all students.

4. *Utilization of community resources.* Another possibility for reducing the (perceived) artificiality and inauthenticity of traditional schools —particularly high schools—is to tie education closely to the world outside the classroom. Whether this is done by introducing what some educators call a "survival curriculum" that concentrates on the major problems of contemporary society, by taking advantage of opportunities for academic as well as work-related study in cultural, business, and other institutions throughout the metropolitan area, or by arranging for students to play an active part in solving community problems and providing community services, utilization of the community as a resource for learning offers obvious potential for helping to solve major problems in metropolitan education.

5. *Voluntarism.* Another important step urban high schools can take to modify traditional programs for alienated disadvantaged and middle-class students is to allow much more choice in deciding what to learn and how to learn it. Providing students with an opportunity to select topics for study and to participate or not participate in given activities may be the surest way to reduce feelings of powerlessness and dependency arising from prolonged bureaucratic processing of students. It certainly is a necessary though not sufficient prerequisite to restoring the legitimacy of schools which students feel are not their own and do not automatically deserve their allegiance and commitment. Observers as diverse as social critic Paul Goodman (1964) and educational psychologist J. M. Stephens (1967) have pointed out that formal education dealing with abstract subject matter is in itself an artificial and alienating activity in the sense that many if not most youth have little intrinsic interest in abstractions studied in the classroom. Forcing students who are viscerally preoccupied with the task of growing up to study continuously prescribed abstract subject matter is more a prescription for trouble than for learning. Voluntarism in the selection of learning experiences does not mean that every student is always completely on his own in choosing what to study, but rather that topics of study are chosen individually or in groups from within broad subject headings such as humanities, language arts, social sciences, and natural sciences. It means that educators admit that prescribed curricula and curriculum guides have little utility in educating students for whom the traditional school has become a fundamentally meaningless experience.

There is nothing startling about the foregoing outline of general possibilities for alleviating the festering and explosive crisis that exists in so many metropolitan high schools. Most of these imperatives have been advocated so often by one or another group of educational or social reformers, as well as by students themselves, that they would be *ad nauseum* platitudes if much of consequence had been done to modify urban schools in accordance with their logic. Unfortunately, nothing of the sort has occurred in the great majority of metropolitan high schools. Here and there a school may have become slightly less bureaucratic or marginally more voluntary than it was before. A few schools have made gestures toward freeing learning from the tight confines of the classroom, and occasionally efforts have been made to provide a more pluralistic context for education. But in general urban high schools are constituted and operated very much as they were forty years ago when few of their students contested the legitimacy of their goals and programs.

What would high schools which strike out in new directions responsive to the metropolitan environment of the 1970s look like? Rather than following one or two standard "models," they probably will draw inspiration from a variety of sources, each school devising its own eclectic combination of programs and concepts. For example, aspects of the School Without Walls projects already under way in Philadelphia and Chicago could be incorporated into the regular program of the high school, particularly their arrangements for independent study of student-selected courses taught by craftsmen, businessmen, and other lay citizens and for cross-age grouping of several hundred students guided by teams of certified teachers and a host of neighborhood and preprofessional volunteers. For alienated inner-city youth, wider use could be made of the "street academy" approach in which a few instructors work with a small number of students in informal programs that reject predetermined curricula but retain an emphasis on mastery of basic skills. Whether conducted as adjunct "outposts" located at a distance from existing schools or established as "in-school" academies and "free" schools within a high school proper, these approaches provide a way to reduce the bureaucratic and custodial character of the traditional high school.

Leadership Drain in Inner-City Schools

Because the sense of powerlessness and frustration characteristic of inner-city schools is generated partly by the fact that economically disadvantaged students are segregated within predominantly low-income inner-city neighborhoods, proposals for improving the achievement of inner-city students frequently raise issues involving the possibility that change may make matters worse overall by draining away the positive leadership that does exist in these neighborhoods.

For example, if an integration plan is largely or partly voluntary, inner-city parents who choose to put their children in a better school environment are likely to be mobility oriented persons whose children stand the best chance of succeeding in whatever school they attend. In this case, the inner-city school might lose not only its best pupils but also the affiliation of parents who tend to be most active in P.T.A.s. Thus it is possible that an integration plan could do as much harm as good in the long run, even though it did offer better educational opportunities for a limited number of inner-city students.

Similarly, proposals to encourage the establishment or maintenance of private or parochial schools in the inner city also could result in the draining off of potential or actual leadership from inner-city schools. In this regard it sometimes is argued that public support (financial aid, books, equipment) should be given to inner-city parochial schools because students in these schools appear to be achieving better than their counterparts in the public schools. It may or may not be true that parochial schools tend to have more effective instructional programs (as a result of more systematic emphasis on discipline, more stable faculties, and the like) than do nearby public schools. But it also is possible that inner-city parents who send their children to parochial schools are above average in providing support and supervision for learning and that achievement differentials which may be found between public and parochial schools are due more to differences in parent background than school quality. In one study in Kansas City, for example, evidence was found that the parents of students at a highly rated inner-city parochial school scored much higher on a home environment scale that correlates closely with school achievement than did parents whose children attended a nearby public school, even though parents of students attending the two schools were similar in occupational status (Levine et al., 1972). If achievement differentials between two such schools can be attributed wholly or largely to differences in students' family background, one is justified in worrying whether the parochial school was not attracting the most talented and ambitious students in the neighborhood and in so doing possibly helping perpetuate inferior educational opportunities in the public school.

The issue is not trivial. If inner-city public schools lose their potentially most successful pupils through voluntary integration plans, private school competition, or for some other reason, it will be more difficult to conduct effective instructional programs there than it would otherwise be. This is particularly likely because of the possibility that "threshold effects" may be an important factor in accounting for the ineffectiveness of instruction in inner-city schools.

Threshold phenomena can be defined as situations in which problems in an institution are multiplied exponentially once they pass a point at which staff members are prepared and able to handle them satisfactorily. For example, a teacher probably can work successfully with two or three very slow learners in a regular classroom because he can find enough time to give them extra help. If there are five or six such students, however, the teacher may not be able to provide individual help, and the situation in the classroom may deteriorate very fast because failing students may become disruptive. Similarly, the problems in a class with four disruptive students may be many times as difficult as in a class with two, because disruptive students tend to egg each other on and at some point the teacher may give up trying to teach when he becomes frustrated trying to work with three or four disruptive students at once.

When the best motivated and potentially most successful children are "creamed" out by private schools or voluntary integration plans, it is possible that threshold points in inner-city public schools may be exceeded more rapidly than would otherwise happen. Conversely, the loss of students who might provide various kinds of leadership in an inner-city school may make it that much more difficult to establish a constructive learning environment no matter how much in additional funds is spent to provide extra services.

It does not follow, however, that inner-city parents should be deprived of the rights to enroll their children in private schools or to have every opportunity for sending their children to integrated schools outside the inner city. In many instances, for one thing, these alternatives may offer parents the only real chance to give their children a decent education. In addition, such alternatives also may have the effect of enabling families to remain in the inner city and contribute to efforts toward its revitalization without having to sacrifice the education of their children at the same time. Thus it is no easy matter to decide—assuming it can be decided at all—whether the possible damage to inner-city schools associated with the draining off of their best students may outweigh the possible benefits associated with other alternatives in any given situation. About all we can conclude on the overall question is that it is an important issue which deserves explicit attention from persons interested in metropolitan education.

Schools in White Working-Class Communities

Most large metropolitan areas contain a number of white working-class neighborhoods located either in or near the inner core part of the central city or in the suburbs, or both. In many respects educational problems in these communities resemble those in working-class neighborhoods inhabited primarily by black or other minority groups. That is, dropout rates at schools in these communities are relatively high, academic achievement is low, and the influence of neighbors and peers operates to depress rather than stimulate educational achievement. Just as in black working-class neighborhoods, parents may express high educational aspirations for their children, but for one or another reason these aspirations are not translated effectively into actual performance in the schools.

Recognizing this, it should be clear that the extensive research literature which "explains" low educational achievement in terms of family social status is as applicable to white working-class schools as to inner-city schools attended primarily by black, Puerto Rican, or other racial and ethnic minorities. Indeed, more often than not research which has established the correlation between educational achievement and family background has been conducted largely or primarily with samples of white schools because it is easier to find a wide range of white schools than of minority schools at differing social class levels (Wilson, 1959).

Because there generally is not nearly as much of an overt and visible demand for educational reform and improvement from parents of students in white working-class schools as from their minority counterparts in inner-city schools, it may be thought that the "problem" of low achievement in these schools is phony or nonexistent. Because parents do not generate much overt demand or pressure for serious reform in white working-class schools, it might be argued, they are basically satisfied with the output of their local schools even though the latter are educationally ineffective and academic achievement is very low.

From one point of view, this conclusion may be justified, but from other points of view, it is not. For one thing, many parents in white working-class communities are dissatisfied with conditions and outcomes in their local schools even if they do not express this dissatisfaction publicly or consistently. (We will discuss a few of the reasons for this reluctance to express strong dissatisfaction before concluding this chapter.) Equally important, there is evidence that much of the general dissatisfaction and alienation that exists among white working-class groups in the United States is related to the fact that jobs available to working-class citizens with low educational attainment tend to be boring and repetitious (Upjohn, 1972). We do not believe it is equitable simply to "accept" or tolerate low educational performance in white working-class schools rather than working to improve achievement so that students attending these schools can have as much effective option as possible to strive for high status jobs as adults, any more than it would be desirable to sit back and accept low achievement among low-income minority groups were the latter not so vociferously demanding change.

To a degree, some of the proposed methods for improving the academic achievement of economically disadvantaged minority students also appear to hold promise for improving the educational opportunities available to students in white working-class neighborhoods. Two of the most promising of these approaches are (1) to provide for socioeconomic integration of schools, that is, to remove as many working-class students as possible from predominantly working-class school environments; and (2) to institute reforms in instructional programming and school organization such as those described earlier in this chapter.

Unfortunately, in some ways it may be even less likely that these changes will be made for white working-class students than for inner-city minority students. As regards socioeconomic integration, there is no clear constitutional mandate such as exists in connection with racial integration; without this mandate, it is doubtful whether most school boards will make more than a token effort to eliminate white working-class schools. In addition, the absence of any real demand for socioeconomic integration among white working-class parents suggests that if forced to choose, many actually might prefer ineffective albeit "neighborhood" schools to plans that require attendance (for some students) outside the immediate neighborhoods. (By way of contrast, past polls of black parents generally show that about 50 percent supported busing for integration before a plan was implemented and upwards of 70 or 80 percent tended to support it afterward.)

Similarly, the likelihood of substantial reform within white working-class schools is very limited as long as parents are quiescent and unwilling to challenge local teachers and administrators in order to bring about radical change in school instruction and organization. True enough, parents in white working-class neighborhoods generally welcome additional funds from federal or other sources to "improve" education in their local schools. For various reasons, however, they frequently are reluctant to demand real change in staffing, curriculum, and instructional methods. (The argument that community control might accomplish much to raise achievement in white working-class schools, accordingly, is even more questionable than is true in minority neighborhoods.) The reasons are instructive.

One reason white working-class parents hesitate to take a strong stand on local educational issues is because they do not have a recent tradtition of working actively for school reform and sometimes react as if protest and adversary tactics in education would cause them to be "equated" in the public mind with racial minority groups. Because white working-class groups in the United States historically have been persuaded to accept (to some extent) low status in return for the knowledge that some minorities are still lower in status, it is easy to see why white working-class parents would hesitate to be identified with other working-class groups which are even more depressed, even when their ethnic tradition once included a clear stress on active protest. Thus sociologist Andrew M. Greeley has reported (Zochert, 1969) that the surest way to "assure a steady stream of hate mail" is to point out before an audience of Irishmen that

> There is . . . (hardly) a single accusation that has been made by whites against American blacks that was not previously made against my Irish ancestors. . . . It was said of both groups that they were shiftless, irresponsible, pleasure-loving, violent, incapable of learning American ways, culturally inferior, too emotional religiously, and immoral.

> The only basic difference I can determine is that when the Irish rioted, they did so in a big way. Nothing the blacks have done compares with the antidraft riots of 1863 in New York. Similarly, when the Irish engaged in guerilla warfare, they were far more ruthless and effective. The blacks have not yet, thank God, tried to match the Molly McGuires. (p. 3)

A second reason white working-class demands for change in local schools tend to be relatively moderate is because their neighborhoods and schools generally are not quite as disorganized and unsatisfactory as are those of minority groups in the inner city. Research in Detroit, for example, indicated that working-class respondents in black neighborhoods reported more unstable conditions and more fragmented social ties than did their counterparts in white neighborhoods (Wolf and Lebeaux, 1967). Similarly, where median achievement in some predominantly black inner-city schools runs three to four years below grade level by the seventh grade, reflecting the extremely low social status of today's most "hard-core" slums, average achievement in white working-class neighborhoods tends to be a year or two below grade level in the middle grades. These patterns suggest that on the whole the white working class today tends to be somewhat less depressed—and oppressed—than the black working class.

Exceptions to this generalization certainly can be found in the form, for example, of extremely depressed "pockets" of white poverty in the inner city. (Such pockets often are too small to be referred to as a neighborhood.) Where these pockets exist, social relationships tend to be as disorganized and school achievement as low as is true anywhere in the inner city (for example, see Binzen, 1970); white parents who live there tend to be those "left behind" by the suburbanization process of the past thirty years and seldom play an active part in school or community affairs.

A third cause which might help account for white working-class apathy regarding reform in local schools may derive from an intuitive aversion toward any type of major change in local urban neighborhoods. That is, many white working-class parents may sense (in general) that change in local institutions tends to set young people adrift in an urban wilderness in which social and family bonds are being dissolved without being replaced by institutions and relationships of equal value. If so, lack of enthusiasm for school reform may reflect a useful insight into some of the most serious—though speculative—problems which exist in urbanized societies. While other groups in the metropolitan population (whether disadvantaged or not) may share this insight to a greater or lesser extent, there is evidence that working-class whites tend to be more oriented toward tradtitional social and family ties than other large social groups in the metropolis (Reissman, 1969).

Related to these reasons for the moderation of white working-class demands for educational reform may be a tendency to confuse individual and group dimensions of social change and social responsibility. Many white working-class groups have been coping with urban poverty and hardship for a number of generations, and many parents as a result are deeply, almost intuitively aware that a child does not have much chance to raise his status unless he is taught to take responsibility for what he does or does not do. Corollaries of this understanding are that people are responsible for their success or failure no matter what the obstacles they face and that an individual has only himself to blame if he fails. This is a desirable, maybe even necessary point of view for children to be taught if one wants them to make something of themselves in difficult circumstances. Unfortunately, groups that have learned to stress the importance of individual responsibility sometimes overextend the logic and act as if group insistence on social change somehow violates the tenet that the individual is responsible for what he does. Such a misinterpretation, if it exists among some white working-class groups, would eventuate in reluctance to engage in systematic group efforts to reform community institutions, that is, in a failure of political will and understanding. The probable outcome of an apolitical stance, in turn, would be a tendency to complain about but at the same time fundamentally accept urban deterioration of the kind described by Pete Hamill (1969) in an essay on the "revolt" of low-status whites in New York:

> The working-class white . . . has become a victim. Taxes and the
> rising cost of living keep him broke. . . . The Department of Sani-
> tation comes to his street at three in the morning . . . and slams
> garbage cans around like an invading regiment. His
> streets . . . are now sliced up with trenches that could only be called
> potholes by the myopic. His neighborhood is a dumping ground for
> abandoned automobiles. . . . He works very hard, frequently on a

> *dangerous job, and then discovers that he still can't pay his*
> *way . . . . (p.26)*

As with working-class blacks, the plight of people in working-class white neighborhoods is likely to continue unless they take an active part in city and metropolitan politics. To some extent working-class whites can maintain the stability of their family and neighborhood environments by working to keep the status quo in schools, churches, and other local institutions, but after a point this approach becomes self-defeating because the inhabitants of working-class neighborhoods are victimized as much as any other group by the larger trends of metropolitan evolution (for example, social stratification and segregation; decline of the central city tax base and deterioration of its neighborhoods; urban sprawl and its effects in generating pollution and traffic congestion; and so on). Once this point is reached, whites in central-city working-class neighborhoods must enter actively into coalition politics aimed at preserving and improving neighborhoods throughout the city, reforming local schools, upgrading municipal services, enhancing opportunities available to economically and socially disadvantaged groups, and otherwise joining with others to enhance the quality of life in the metropolitan area.

This course of action is unabashedly political in nature, and is dependent to a large extent on prior political education to develop political consciousness among young people in white working-class neighborhoods. The importance of political consciousness is by no means confined, of course, to the United States, and Sir Arthur W. Lewis (Beeby, 1969) has argued that "the world over . . . the proper context in which to look at what the school does for the working classes is the way in which it provides them with the means for more enlightened and more effective political action" (p.38).

Is it likely that schools in white working-class neighborhoods will take the lead in developing political awareness and understanding which might help preserve and improve these neighborhoods as part of a vital and cohesive metropolis? Can they succeed if they do try? The answer to the first question probably is no; at least, there have been few if any indications that educators in white working-class neighborhoods are willing to stress political education or that parents in these neighborhoods would allow them to try.

The answer to the second question is still more problematic: no one we know of has anything but the vaguest ideas as to how the public schools might effectively encourage and develop "working-class consciousness" even if educators wanted to, and it probably would take years to develop a suitable curriculum for doing this without breeding and intensifying intergroup hostility and chauvinism. Here, indeed, may lie a major challenge to metropolitan education in the years ahead.

ISSUES IN METROPOLITAN EDUCATION REFORM

Generalizing on a topic as complex as metropolitan education tends to imply that an author has more confidence in his diagnosis and prescriptions than the uncertainty of the subject possibly could warrant. For this reason, it is well to conclude by specifying and reviewing some of the most important unresolved and, at this time, unresolvable issues involving the future of metropolitan education.

First, there is a real question whether economically disadvantaged students can succeed in inner-city schools no matter how much money is made available to improve instructional programs there. Because the psychology of being segregated in a poverty environment is itself profoundly linked with the failure of the school and other social institutions in the inner city, it is not surprising that compensatory education has not as yet resulted in substantial gains in the achievement of disadvantaged students in the big cities. Perhaps if funds for inner-city education were doubled or tripled and, more important, were spent to bring about fundamental changes in curriculum and instruction, academic retardation in inner-city schools might be significantly reduced or eliminated. But until it is demonstrated over a period of some years that most youngsters can have a decent childhood and receive an adequate education in an inner-city environment, to place much faith in even the best-conceived program of compensatory education would be reckless and naïve. The current situation with respect to compensatory education is discussed at much greater length in the next chapter.

Second, no one knows for sure whether metropolitan schools can be reformed quickly and thoroughly enough to avoid a "systems break" in existing arrangements for educating the young. Public school systems, for one thing, have been unabashedly organized along bureaucratic lines, and as such they exemplify the rigidities and goal displacements commonly found in large bureaucratic organizations. (Beyond this question, it is possible that social critics such as Paul Goodman [1964] are right in believing that "incidental learning" in natural settings outside the school is the only effective way to educate youth for social and occupational roles after they have acquired some fundamental skills through formal instruction.) A few social scientists and educators are trying to find out how school systems and individual schools might be changed in accordance with new concepts of bureaucracy appropriate for a postindustrial society; but that such changes can be introduced, much less implemented within existing systems, is far from certain. All things considered, reform in the schools may come so slowly that advocates of free schools, no schools, private schools, and other alternatives to the existing system ultimately may carry the day.

Closely related to the issues of whether existing public schools are too rigid to be profoundly transformed is the question of whether reform can be institutionalized on a sufficiently large scale to make basic changes throughout a good-sized school system. Even when intelligent reform is carried out in a few schools, problems will be encountered in attempting to expand promising new programs to serve a significant number of students in a large school system.

It may not prove too difficult, for example, to establish a good School Without Walls program in a large urban community, but it is not at all certain that such a school can be expanded from a few hundred students (their present size) to a few thousand without fairly quickly exhausting the number of truly productive community learning settings available to students. More broadly, exciting new programs in the public schools almost always begin to encounter serious difficulties when they are expanded beyond the pilot stage at which they are staffed by enthusiastic and especially outstanding teachers who volunteer to work in them. It is extremely important to ask how all our schools can develop the flexibility to meet the challenges of a rapidly changing environment, as John Gardner (1961) has done in his writings on self-renewing institutions. But it remains to be seen whether system-wide change is possible in large urban school systems.

Third, it is possible that the cause of urban education reform may suffer more from the efforts of its presumed friends than from the attacks of its avowed enemies. More specifically, some sponsors of educational reform have a rather simpleminded view of what is involved in providing better educational opportunities for metropolitan youth. In experimental high school programs emphasizing independent study, for example, teachers and students frequently have been placed in entirely new educational settings demanding a degree of flexibility, creativity, and individual responsibility they have not been adequately prepared to handle. New programs that emphasize student choice in determining what and how to learn often have floundered because the sponsors of such programs and even the teachers employed in them apparently have believed that all you have to do is give students "freedom" to learn and learning will be assured. Eventually personnel connected with new programs intended to allow for more independent learning realize that teaching in this setting requires even more planning and skilled instruction than does the traditional school—if the program has not by then been destroyed by the new dogmas of a misguided progressivism. From this point of view, one of the gravest threats to educational reform comes from quarters which discredit promising new ideas by attempting to implement them according to the simplistic principle that good intentions are all that is needed to bring about change.

Finally, careful thought must be given to unresolved controversies regarding the role of technology in improving metropolitan education. Technology refers not just to media and machinery used in instruction (for example, computer-assisted instruction), but also to information systems for planning and monitoring new projects, to behavior modification techniques for influencing the attitudes and behaviors of pupils, to evaluation designs for assessing the components of educational programs, and, in general, to any systematic plan for rationally allocating resources to accomplish specific educational goals.

Too often, those who are most aware of the deficiencies of metropolitan education with respect to authenticity, legitimacy, identity, and other concepts discussed earlier in this chapter blindly reject technology as an element which is unnecessary if not actually antithetical to movements for reform in the public schools. This misconception is not generally shared by educators and laymen most directly involved in efforts to improve the schools. For example, many educators deeply concerned with correcting the inadequacies of traditional schools tend to be enthusiastic about management technologies which might increase understanding of what works and what does not work in the classroom. Conversely, behavior modification specialists, for example, frequently are the strongest advocates of new curricula to "humanize" the school. Although it is not now possible to predict exactly how important technology will prove to be in effecting educational reform, it is certain that antitechnological biases carried to an unreasoning extreme will work to the detriment of efforts to improve the quality of urban schools.

CONCLUSION

It is easy to lose sight of the underlying theme that much of the crisis in metropolitan education can be traced to metropolitan stratification. The increasing segregation of social and racial groups within metropolitan society is damaging not just to the obvious victims—the poor and the racial and ethnic minorities— but sooner or later to all other groups in the population as well. When economically disadvantaged youngsters are confined to the unwholesome physical and social environment of the inner city, when economically advantaged youngsters are raised in an antiseptic environment which for many proves boring and alienating, and when masses of lower-middle-class and working-class white youngsters receive an inadequate education while deflecting their status fears and dissatisfactions on an underclass below them, no one can gain.

The results of metropolitan stratification have become easily discernible in all our social affairs. Nationally, stratification within our metropolitan areas generates and fuels polarizations which our political institutions so far have shown little capacity to compromise or moderate. In our educational systems, stratification works in favor of the triumph of tribalism over pluralism, but no one has presented or is likely to present a plausible scenario to explain how a modern industrial social structure can function successfully on a tribal base. If they do not know each other personally, how can economically or socially disadvantaged youngsters and middle-status youngsters perceive each other as individual persons rather than stereotypes? How can high-status youngsters think of the sons and daughters of blue-collar workers without disdain if a status-conscious society keeps them physically separated from one another? How can youngsters of all these differing social backgrounds learn to work in broad-based coalitions for mutually beneficial social progress if they are kept mostly apart by the barriers of metropolitan geography?

Of course, one can say that teachers, parents, and ministers should instruct the young to reject the intergroup prejudices and stereotypes likely to be present in any pluralistic society. Unfortunately, the job cannot be accomplished so easily. People have reasons, whether reasonable or unreasonable, for their beliefs, and one of the best-established findings of social psychology is that verbal exhortation seldom has much effect on intergroup hostilities and mythologies. Sustained face-to-face contact in a setting that requires differing people to work toward a common goal, on the other hand, at least opens up possibilities for building positive intergroup attitudes, though it does not necessarily guarantee them.

There is no inherent reason a student must receive all his schooling all year long in a single classroom or school building. There is no inherent reason every youngster cannot participate in pluralistic educational experiences for at least two or three months a year in special metropolitan learning centers. Better yet, parts of the instructional program in such centers might well emphasize the use of community resources in learning, identity-building, interethnic studies, and other emerging educational imperatives virtually ignored in many existing school programs. Who can doubt that Americans have the ingenuity to provide a pluralistic education for the young even where metropolitan stratification and segregation make it difficult to begin? Whether we have the awareness and commitment to do so is a wholly different matter.

NOTES

1. As used here, the term affluence does not suggest the absence of major financial difficulties and concerns among middle-class families but rather refers to

what Orr and Nichelson (1970) have termed a "state of mind" which has to do with relaxation from primal economic fears and with the belief that a number of satisfying options are financially possible. . . . The middle-class youth may choose to drop out and assume an impoverished style of living, but the mark of his affluence is his ability to drop back in at will" (p. 58).

REFERENCES

Beeby, C. E. (ed.). 1969. *The Qualitiative Aspects of Educational Planning.* Paris: UNESCO. Excerpts reprinted in *Integrated Education* 9 (1971): 35–44.

Binzen, Peter. 1970. *White-Town, U.S.A.* New York: Random House.

Gardner, John. 1961. *Excellence.* New York: Harper & Brothers.

Goodman, Paul. 1964. *Compulsory Mis-education.* New York: Horizon.

Hamill, Pete. 1969. "The Revolt of the White Lower Middle Class." *New York*, April 14, Pp. 24–28.

Klapp, Orrin E. 1969. *Collective Search for Identity.* New York: Holt, Rinehart & Winston.

Kohn, Melvin L. 1969. *Class and Conformity, A Study of Values.* Homewood, Ill.: Dorsey.

Lavin, David. 1965. *The Prediction of Academic Performance.* New York: Sage.

Levine, Daniel U. 1968. "The Community School in Contemporary Perspective." *Elementary School Journal* 69: 109–117.

Levine, Daniel U. and Russell C. Doll. 1972. "Toward a Definition of Structure in the Education of Disadvantaged Students." Pp. 230–278 in A. H. Passow (ed.) *Opening Opportunities for Disadvantaged Learners.* New York: Teachers College.

Levine, Daniel U., et al. 1972. "The Home Environment of Students in a High Achieving Inner-City Parochial School and a Nearby Public School." *Sociology of Education* 45: 435–445.

Lopate, Carol, et al. 1970. "Decentralization and Community Participation in Education." *Review of Educational Research* 40: 135–150.

Orr, John B. and Patrick F. Nichelson. 1970. *The Radical Suburb.* Philadelphia: Westminister.

Reissman, Leonard. 1969. "Readiness to Succeed: Mobility Aspirations and Modernism Among the Poor." *Urban Affairs Quarterly* 4: 379–395.

Seligman, Martin. 1969. "Can We Immunize the Weak?" *Psychology Today* 3: 242–244.

Stephens, J. M. 1967. *The Process of Schooling: A Psychological Examination.* New York: Holt, Rinehart & Winston.

Upjohn, W. E. 1972. *Work in America.* Washington, D.C.: Institute for Employment Research.

Wilson, Alan B. 1959. "Residential Segregation of Social Classes and Aspirations of High School Boys." *American Sociological Review* 24: 836–845.

Wolf, Eleanor P. and Charles N. Lebeaux. 1967. "On the Destruction of Poor Neighborhoods by Urban Renewal." *Social Problems* 15: 3–8.

Zochert, Donald. 1969. "Why U.S. 'Melting Pot' Still Boils." *Chicago Daily News*, August 28, Pp. 3–4.

Chapter 2

COMPENSATORY EDUCATION

During the spring and early summer of 1963, contrasting preoccupations of the black community and public school officials were evident in fifteen large cities, spread coast to coast, which were visited incident to a study of northern school segregation for the National Association of Intergroup Relations Officials (Commission on School Integration, 1963).

On the one hand, Negro organizations were pressing hard for school integration as an approach toward equality of educational opportunity for their children. On the other hand, school officials, highly defensive on this issue, were countering with offers of substantial school improvement in the ghetto—better facilities, extra personnel, smaller classes, and a wide range of special curricular programs to upgrade the academic achievement of black children in their segregated schools.[1] As subsequent developments attest, this latter tendency prevailed.

Most public school systems found it politically more feasible to develop special programs of school improvement in the ghetto than to integrate their schools; and largely as a consequence, compensatory education burgeoned. Begun during the late fifties with support from private foundations and backed with massive federal support in the mid-sixties, compensatory education emerged as the dominant answer of the profession—and of the nation—to the problem of gross academic retardation shown to be endemic among schools serving children of the poor, especially black children in the urban ghetto. By 1974, the federal government was spending about $1.7 billion for compensatory education programs serving more than six million children. In a very real sense, the widespread development of compensatory education during the past decade came as an off-target response to the school-integration demands of the civil rights movement.

Just what "compensatory education" is, operationally at least, depends on who does the defining; the term embraces an extremely varied array of special educational programs extending from preschool to college (see, for example, Gordon and Wilkerson, 1966; McDill et al., 1969; Jabblonsky, 1971; Monacel, 1971). Proportionately, in terms of total population ratios, the main group served, initially and today, consists of black youngsters attending segregated schools. Substantial numbers of Chicano and Puerto Rican youth are also served by compensatory education, as are some Orientals and American Indians, and large numbers of whites.[2] Common to all of these special programs is the avowed purpose of narrowing the gap between the academic performance of well-to-do children and that of children of the poor. They are designed to compensate—to make up for—presumed deficiencies in the learning experiences of socially and educationally disadvantaged young people.

The development of compensatory education has been not only widespread and rapid, but also highly controversial. Contrasting theoretical premises have vied for acceptance as the underlying rationale; varying practices have staked claims to superiority; appraisals of outcomes and their implications have provoked considerable debate; and most of the issues involved are still to be resolved. It is to the summary review and comment on these questions that this chapter is addressed.

RATIONALE

The general problem that compensatory education undertakes to mitigate—the widening gap between the academic achievement of disadvantaged and that of other children as they move through the school grades—has been documented in many studies. It is reflected, but only partly, in the comparison of median scores of white and minority-group pupils[3] at different grade levels on standard achievement tests used in the national survey of *Equality of Educational Opportunity*, the Coleman Report (Coleman et al, 1966). As explained in this report,

> *The minority pupils' scores are as much as one standard deviation below the majority pupils' scores in the 1st grade. At the 12th grade, results of tests in the same verbal and nonverbal skills show that, in every case, the minority scores are farther below the majority than are the 1st graders. . . .*

> *Furthermore, a constant difference in standard deviations over
> the various grades represents an increasing difference in grade
> level gap. For example, Negroes in the metropolitan Northeast are
> about 1.1 standard deviations below whites in the same region in
> grades 6, 9, and 12. But at grade 6 this represents 1.6 years behind;
> at grade 9, 2.4 years; and at grade 12, 3.3 years. Thus, by this
> measure, the deficiency in achievement is progressively greater for
> the minority pupils at progressively higher grade levels. (p. 21)*

These racial and ethnic comparisons cut across social-class lines, and
undoubtedly understate the disparities that would be revealed by comparing the achievement of affluent and poor children. Moreover, they
relate only to those children still attending school at the time of the
survey, and do not reflect the probably even lower achievement levels of
the disproportionately large numbers of minority-group and other poor
children who dropped out before completing twelfth grade.

Such disparities between the school performance of affluent and
poor children have existed for a long time, and were generally accepted as
"natural." They were thrust to the fore of public attention around the turn
of the past decade by the confluence of a number of developments. Chief
among them were the growing concentration of impoverished populations in the inner city, new perspectives for the education of all children
implied by advances in behavioral science theory, a series of progressive
decisions by the Supreme Court on the education of Negroes, and the
mounting pressure of the civil rights movement. Something *had* to be
done. As Riessman (1962) noted in one of the first books on the subject,
here was "one of the most pressing problems facing the urban school" (p.
1).

The main theoretical questions posed for compensatory education
are those of etiology (Why these disparities?), reversibility (Can they be
eliminated or substantially diminished?), and prescription (What principles should guide corrective efforts?). Sometimes elaborate and often
conflicting answers to these questions comprise a vast literature that
cannot even be summarized here.[4] What appear to be the main theoretical
positions advanced are, however, briefly defined and discussed.

Etiology

The cause of gross and increasing academic retardation among children of
the poor is variously attributed to characteristics of the child, either
inborn or culturally induced; to inadequacies of the school, as regards
both professional personnel and curriculum; and to the oppressive
character of our racist and exploitative society. The bulk of theoretical

analysis and experimental investigation, by far, centers around the first of these general positions, presumed "deficits" of children from impoverished backgrounds.

Not many years ago, it was common and fully respectable for educators to explain low scholastic achievement among black children —and, indeed, other disadvantaged populations—in terms of genetic inferiority. As recently as the twenties and thirties, respected and able young instructors with good humanistic values lectured to classes in educational psychology on the "established fact" —however unfortunate—that Negroes were poorly endowed by nature in the capacity for intellectual development. They were conveying a thesis, long used to rationalize slavery and Jim Crow oppression, which was seemingly validated scientifically by recent analyses of intelligence-test data assembled by the Army during World War I. This doctrine of Negro inferiority, unquestionably accepted by the masses of white Americans, had by then been embraced by reputable behavioral scientists and was ensconced in the textbooks of the day.

During the following three decades, however, most of the scientific community reversed its position on this question. The studies of Klineberg (1935, 1944) and many others demonstrated empirically that the race-difference hypothesis was untenable. The work of Piaget (1952), Hunt (1961) and others fostered the now prevailing view that intellectual function, far from being "fixed" by the genes, develops through the interaction of the organism with his environment. And the enhanced influence of blacks in the society during and after World War II eroded the political acceptability of racist theories of intellectual development. By the early sixties, behavioral scientists in all fields overwhelmingly rejected "poor native endowment" as an explanation of educational retardation among Negroes and other disadvantaged groups; and public opinion generally moved substantially toward the same view (Hyman and Sheatsley, 1956).[5] The IQ had lost its scientific aura, and was no longer accepted by most professional personnel—at least overtly—as an index of a child's "capacity" to learn effectively in school.

In any event, the doctrine of inborn inferiority, perforce, could not serve as the rationale for "compensatory education." That role fell to the newly developed hypothesis of "cultural deprivation."

DEPRIVED CHILD

Deutsch's (1960) study of the relationship of minority-group and class status to scholastic achievement probably laid the first systematic, empirical basis for this concept; and it has been further developed since in hundreds of articles and books on the "culturally deprived child."[6]

In brief, the hypothesis of cultural deprivation holds that the academic retardation so common among children of the poor is mainly a function of their early growth and socialization under conditions of poverty and discrimination. They are said to come from homes in depressed areas, where no "father figure" is present, where child-rearing practices are inept and moral values suspect, where language patterns are exceedingly poor, where there are no books, where intellectual discussions —indeed, any sustained discussions—are rare or nonexistent, and/or where uneducated adults are not concerned with the educational progress of their children in school. As a consequence, the argument goes, "these children" enter school lacking the experiential basis for effective cognitive development; and they have little or no academic motivation. As expressed by a school superintendent quoted by Ryan (1971):

> *A victim of his environment, the ghetto child begins his school*
> *career, psychologically, socially, and physically disadvantaged.*
> *He is oriented to the present rather than the future, to immediate*
> *needs rather than delayed gratification, to the concrete rather than*
> *the abstract. He is often handicapped by limited verbal skills, low*
> *self-esteem, and a stunted drive toward achievement. (p. 23)*

This general thesis was quickly embraced by educators, and soon became—and still persists as—the dominant "line" of the compensatory education movement. It has been elaborated by countless studies of the disadvantaged child's many "deficits" —in prenatal nourishment, physical fitness, sensory discrimination, language development, cognitive style, creativity, attitude toward self and school, motivation, and many more. Perusal of a comprehensive bibliography prepared several years ago (Hellmuth, 1967) and a collection of studies published about the same time by Deutsch et al. (1967) suggests the scope of these investigations. This line of thought implies that the task of compensatory education is to overcome, to mitigate, in some degree to make up for these socially induced deficits, widely accepted as the cause of the disadvantaged child's substandard performance in school. The target of change is the child.

As an early and continuing critic of this point of view, one of the authors (Wilkerson, 1964, 1968, 1969b, 1970) continually called attention—as others have done—to serious infirmities in this deficit-correcting rationale of compensatory education.

First, the cultural deprivation thesis is essentially defeatist. It begins with the assumption that children of the poor are so severely scarred by early experiences in home and community that they enter school much less able to learn than other children. It is an easy step from this to the seeming corollary—commonplace in the profession, even among compensatory educators—that whatever potential disadvantaged children may once have had for cognitive development has been almost, if not quite, irreparably damaged. Even the discredited doctrine of genetic inferiority affords no more convenient rationalization than this for ineffective teaching. If you cannot win, why try?

Second, the impressive array of "deficits" that the cultural deprivation thesis posits for disadvantaged children leads to unwarranted and harmful stereotyping. It is almost as if they came from a common mold. The fact is, of course, that the population categories "poor" and "disadvantaged" embrace families and individuals with widely varying characteristics, some negative, others positive. To lump "these children" together as bearers of an enormous burden of deficits negates the pedagogically important fact that children of the poor, like all children, are wondrously varied human beings—in academic ability, self-concept, motivation, aspiration, and probable future. Indeed, as some investigators have pointed out (for example, Davidson and Greenberg, 1967), some from impoverished backgrounds do quite well in school, even without benefit of compensatory education.

Third, many of the "deficits" assumed to be typical of children of the poor are highly suspect and over-generalized. This is suggested by the findings of many studies. For example: Davidson and Greenberg's (1967) study of "severely deprived" children in Harlem found that about one-half of them were living with both parents, and that the presence or absence of "the father or other male figure in the home" did not differentiate between the high and low school achievers among them (p. 143). Zach (1969) reported that apparent deficits in sensory discrimination among poor Negro children she studied just about vanished as they became familiar with test-taking procedures. The alleged unconcern of most lower-class parents for the education of their children is seriously questioned by the findings of Cloward and Jones (1963) and other investigators. Studies of nonstandard English by a number of linguists (Labov, 1968; Dillard, 1972) suggest that speech patterns common among many black children reflect, not deficiency in language development, but competence in a dialect different from that approved by the school.

Fourth, the presumed causal relationship between such characteristics of the disadvantaged child and his ability to learn has by no means been established. Even such associations as have been demonstrated between negative child and background characteristics and performance in school are evidence merely of correlation, not necessarily of causation. As Gordon and Wilkerson (1966) assert: "Although it is probably true that adverse conditions of life do not facilitate academic achievement in most children, we have no firm evidence that such conditions preclude academic success. In fact, there are enough cases of success despite adverse conditions to make untenable the conclusion that difficult life circumstances preclude success in school" (p. 174).

The premise of cultural deprivation has been characterized by Clark

(1965) as a "self-fulfilling prophecy" of academic failure, and by Ryan (1971) as a "savage" illustration of the reality-distorting ideology of "Blaming the Victim." Indeed, they seem to be right. If compensatory education is substantially to enhance the academic development of children of the poor, it must embrace a more valid and fruitful rationale than is afforded by the deprivation hypothesis.

DYSFUNCTIONAL SCHOOL

Recent years have witnessed increasingly sharp criticism of the practice of education in general, and especially in schools serving the urban poor. Many educators and (it seems) even more laymen who write books have reached the conclusion that the schools attended by most children are fundamentally dysfunctional, and that most of those serving the urban ghetto are downright harmful. "Outmoded," "joyless," "insensitive," "stultifying," "racist," "mindless," "tradition-bound," "irrelevant," "alienated," "oppressive"—these are among the characterizations they make.[7]

As expressed by Gordon (1970):

> Public schools as social institutions have never had to assume responsibility for their failures. Only recently have observers begun to view and describe objectively some of the horrors that are perpetrated in the name of public education. We must come to grips with the problem of the utterly stultifying atmosphere of many classrooms, with the way in which rote learning and repetition discourage real learning; and we must also realize that discipline for discipline's sake serves the purpose of creating artificial order, but at the same time produces dull automatons instead of eager students, or turns the inmates of public schools against education, to their lifelong detriment. (p. 4)

Much of this criticism is perhaps valid; and it suggests an explanation for the widespread academic retardation among children of the poor that differs sharply from the one that now prevails in compensatory education circles. The school itself, not the disadvantaged child, is inadequate, ill-adapted to serving his developmental needs. Indeed, the dysfunctional school is the main cause of failure among children of the poor.

This line of thought implies that the appropriate task of compensatory education is to modify substantially prevailing educational practice so as to realize the developmental potential of impoverished children whom schools now serve so badly. The immediate target of change is the school.

Consider several ideas in support of this point of view.

First, prevailing patterns of educational practice developed and crystallized in the service of children far different from those who now predominate in the schools of most large cities. As Jensen (1969) points out:

> *The instructional methods of the traditional classroom . . . evolved within an upper-class segment of the European population, and thus were naturally shaped by the capacities, culture, and needs of those children whom the schools were primarily intended to serve. . . . These methods of schooling have remained essentially unchanged for many generations. (p. 7)*

It is reasonable to assume that however inadequate prevailing school practices are for children in general, they correspond far more closely to the needs of affluent children than to those of poor children. There is a high degree of continuity between the middle-class child's preschool experiences at home and those he enters upon at school. For children from impoverished backgrounds, however, there is gross discontinuity; and the school does little or nothing to help bridge the gap. On the contrary, the predominating stance of the profession is that the school program is essentially valid; and if children from the ghetto do not "fit" into it, the fault is theirs—or their background's—not the school's. With only superficial changes in curriculum and methods, or none, instruction proceeds as if children from a more advantaged social class were involved—and the children of the poor fall behind.

If teaching is to be considered a profession, not merely a craft, educators would do well to implement the long-honored principle that instructional methods and materials should be adapted to the needs of the learners. They cannot excuse the school's failure to do this by the fatuous observation that "these children are different."Rather than fashion self-serving theories about alleged deficits "within" disadvantaged children, they might more fruitfully examine the school environment.

Second, the fact that academic retardation among children of the poor tends to worsen the longer they stay in school suggests an association that is probably more than correlational, especially when viewed in the light of other relevant facts.

Wilkerson[8] once examined what successive teachers wrote in cumulative records about a group of impoverished black pupils in a segregated suburban school, first through fifth grade, and was impressed with the pattern that emerged. In nearly two-thirds of the cases, children assessed by their first- and second-grade teachers as alert, bright, cooperative and promising were seen by their fourth- and fifth-grade teachers as apathetic, failing, and behavioral problems. This apparent metamorphosis probably resulted mainly from these children's negative experiences in a school which was very poor. Deutsch's et al. (1967) observations and interpretation support this inference. Writing about disadvantaged children, they note:

> So often, administrators and teachers say, they are "curious," "cute," "affectionate," "warm" and independently dependent in the kindergarten and first grade, but who so often become "alienated," "withdrawn," "angry," "passive," "apathetic," or just "trouble-makers" by the fifth and sixth grades. In our research at the Institute for Developmental Studies, it is in the first grade that we usually see the smallest differences between socioeconomic or racial groups in intellectual, language, and some conceptual measures, and in the later grades that we find the greatest differences in favor of the more socially privileged groups. From both teachers' observations and the findings of this increasing gap, it appears that there is a failure on some level of society and, more specifically, the educational system. (pp. 41–42)

The common finding that Head Start and other preschool programs have only short-term impact on children's development is relevant to the issue here posed. As Weikart (1973) and many others have noted, disadvantaged children tend to progress dramatically in the preschool programs, but the gains made there tend to vanish soon after they enter the regular school programs. A good part of the explanation probably is that the preschool programs are much more stimulating and relevant to pupils' needs than the programs they enter in the regular grades.

It is quite possible that nonschool influences are to some extent related to the progressive retardation of disadvantaged children as they move through the school grades. It is highly probable that inept school practices, inappropriate to these pupils' developmental needs, are a major causal influence.

Third, there is considerable evidence that the academic performance of disadvantaged children is negatively influenced by teachers' expectations of them. Unrecorded anecdotes that abound among observers of ghetto schools leave no doubt that a large proportion of poor children's teachers really do not expect them to learn effectively, and that, subtly or explicitly, they convey these perceptions to their pupils. Such attitudes among teachers in Harlem were strikingly documented by a survey in the mid-sixties (Harlem Youth Opportunities Unlimited, 1964), and the negative impact of such attitudes on students was revealingly probed in interviews conducted by Fuchs (1966).

There have been some experimental investigations of this problem. Most widely known among them is the Rosenthal-Jacobson (1968) study on the west coast, which reported evidence of association between teachers' expectations and pupils' performance. This study has been criticized for serious technical infirmities, and several efforts at replication have yielded negative results. Nevertheless, the underlying hypothesis it sought to test is so thoroughly consistent with many other observers' field experiences that we have no doubt it will be confirmed by subsequent investigation. This confidence is bolstered by the comparable findings of an earlier study by Davidson and Lang (1960). They demonstrated that pupils' perceptions of themselves, together with their academic behaviors, tended to vary directly with the positive or negative feelings they *perceived* their teachers had toward them.

Several process studies give insight into the manner in which teachers' negative expectations of disadvantaged children color their behavior toward them. Leacock's (1969) four-month observations of four lower-income and four middle-income classrooms, second and fifth grade, white and Negro, showed how individual teachers perceive and behave differently toward the children of different races and social classes.

> *For example, the teacher working with white middle-income fifth-grade children took responsibility for her own limitations and spoke of reacting to their lack of attention as a cue to her, indicating the need for her to arouse their interest. On the other hand, the limitations of the teacher working with low-income Negro children were ascribed to the children, and boredom on their part was attributed to their presumably low attention span. (p. 203)*

Even in low-income Negro classrooms where teachers were "warm" and "friendly," "the children's very being, their existence, as well as their contributions, were being denied or undermined. Albeit pleasantly, lower status roles were being structured for the children, in contrast with the middle-income white classrooms; poorer images of themselves were being presented to them." And the middle-income white and low-income Negro fifth-grade classrooms were "at opposite poles" when compared "from the viewpoint of expectations for children, goals being defined for them, and respect for their ability to learn. . . ."

The relationship between teachers' negative expectations and their behaviors toward lower-class children is even more graphically portrayed in Rist's (1970) longitudinal study of the classroom experiences of "a single group of black children in an urban ghetto school." By the eighth day of kindergarten, the teacher assigned the children to permanent seats at three tables that, it turned out, reflected social-class groupings. These groupings persisted into second grade; and throughout this period, teachers' behaviors tended to favor the more advantaged children over those of lower social class. Rist comments:

> *When a teacher bases her expectations of performance on the social status of the student and assumes that the higher the social status, the higher the potential of the child, those children of low social status suffer a stigmatization outside of their own choice or will.*

> *Yet there is a greater tragedy than being labeled as a slow learner,
> and that is being treated as one. The differential amounts of
> control-oriented behavior, the lack of interaction with the teacher,
> the ridicule from one's peers, and the caste aspects of being placed
> in lower reading groups all have implications for the future life
> style and value of education for the child. (p. 448)*

There can be little doubt that the social-class and racial prejudices that prevail in our society generally are shared in large measure by professional personnel in the schools, and are reflected in their expectations of and behaviors toward children of the poor. There can be little doubt also that the resulting negative experiences of disadvantaged children have a lot to do with their increasing retardation the longer they stay in school.

Two other school influences that limit optimal academic performance among disadvantaged children warrant at least brief mention in this connection. One is the impact of school segregation, ably discussed elsewhere in this volume. Given the racist history and current structure of our society, only the segregated black and/or low-income school with exceptional leadership has much chance to escape the social definition of "inferiority" that tends to pervade its whole life, negatively affecting the behaviors of all personnel involved—pupils and parents, teachers and principals, and the officials "downtown" who run the school system. The other is the typical alienation of the depressed-area school from the community it serves. The principle that community support is essential for effective school programs is almost universally accepted by the profession, at least in theory; but the typical slum school tends to stand aloof from its community, suspicious and defensive. Relationships of hostility and overt antagonism commonly prevail. Probably more than a little of the poor academic performance of disadvantaged children can be justly attributed to the combined influence of racial segregation and the alienation of school from community.

A sound rationale for compensatory education must proceed from the etiological premise that whatever limitations an impoverished environment may impose on the educational development of disadvantaged children, they probably are equaled or exceeded by the limitations imposed by inept school practice. Responsibility for the academic progress of poor children would then be placed on the shoulders of the profession, where it belongs. The central task of compensatory education would be to effect the radical transformation of schools serving children of the poor into institutions that are consciously and effectively adapted to *their* developmental needs.

This calls for a stance we educators have been reluctant to assume. Gordon and Wilkerson (1966) claim that rarely have we said to children of the poor: "We will take you as you are, and ourselves assume the burden of finding educational techniques appropriate to your needs. We have asked of them a degree of change far greater than any that we as educators have been willing to make in our own institutions" (p. 159).

OPPRESSIVE SOCIETY

There is a broader "etiological" frame of reference for interpreting the prevalence of academic retardation among children of the poor. It is that of a social system that creates vast populations of human beings oppressed by poverty and racial discrimination, and maintains public school systems that almost guarantee their continued degradation. The political issue here posed, of course, cannot be resolved through compensatory education; but it is relevant to the ideological orientation of educators as they conceive and develop special programs for the disadvantaged.

From a humanistic point of view, it is patent that most schools serving children of the poor are dysfunctional and oppressive, especially in the urban ghetto; and Greer (1972) has demonstrated effectively that this is by no means a recent phenomenon. Why such schools continue to be tolerated by our society—or by the profession that conducts them —goes to the heart of what our nation deems important.

The main obstacle to effective education for the poor is not, as some assert, that it is not known how to get them to learn. In almost any system there are scores of individual teachers doing it every day; and as Silberman (1970) and others have noted, there are more than a few depressed-area schools where effective education is under way. That such conditions are rare cannot be explained by the unavailability of adequate techniques; more fundamentally, it reflects a lack of purpose, of will, of determination to act on humanistic and democratic values that the society and the profession find controlling.

Our country knows well how to mobilize its unparalled resources for the attainment of priority goals—as in space, or in Indochina; and none can doubt that a real "moon-shot" commitment to the effective education of inner-city children could quickly correct the sordid school conditions that now prevail, developing educational programs more likely to provide young people with the insights and values and skills essential for effective living in a complex society.

Despite considerable rhetoric to the contrary, there is no such national commitment. Not only do allocated financial resources fall far short of need; more important, the confident purpose of making drastic and progressive changes in the education of disadvantaged children simply does not pervade our public school system. The effective development of children of the poor, it seems, is not really important; otherwise we would move vigorously to improve their educational experiences.

More than a few social critics have come to the view that poor education for poor children results not merely from default, but from design, in the sense that it "fits" the social structure. For example, Greer's (1972) historical analysis led him to conclude that "the failure of many children has been, and still is, a learning experience precisely appropriate to the place assigned them and their families in the social order. They are being taught to fail and to accept their failure." Further:

> The fact of the matter is that American public schools in general, and urban public schools in particular, are a highly successful enterprise. Basic to that success is the high degree of academic failure among students. Attitudes and behavior patterns such as tolerance of boredom, learning as memorization, competition, and hostility are learned and reinforced in the classroom. The schools do the job they have always done. They select out individuals for opportunities according to a hierarchical schema which runs closely parallel to existing social class patterns. (p. 152)

One is reminded that, in quite a different context, Parsons (1962) has characterized the school class as "an agency of 'manpower' allocation" (p. 434).

Rist (1970) concludes from his longitudinal observations of classroom procedures "that if one desires the society to retain its present social class configuration and the disproportional access to wealth, power, social and economic mobility, medical care, and choice of life styles, one should not disturb the methods of education as presented in this study." "It appears," he says, "that the public school system not only mirrors the configurations of the larger society, but also significantly contributes to maintaining them. Thus the system of public education in reality perpetuates what it is ideologically commited to eradicate—class barriers which result in inequality in the social and economic life of the citizenry" (pp. 448–449).

Stein (1971) puts the argument most sharply:

> How does it come about that the one institution that is said to be the gateway to opportunity, the school, is the very one that is most effective in perpetuating an oppressed and impoverished status in society? Every oppressive, racist, and exploitative society must use all of its institutions to retain its racist, oppressive, and exploitative character. That is why these institutions were erected. (p. 203)

The inference that seems to flow from these views is that a restructured social system in which humanistic values are dominant is prerequisite to effective education for the masses of poor children. It probably is a valid inference. The school is an integral and interacting unit of the whole culture, highly responsive to prevailing values; and it may be expected to perform differently with now neglected groups only when their interests are backed by social power. As Bruner (1971) has remarked, education "is a deeply political issue" (p. 29).

It by no means follows that individual teachers and administrators and whole school staffs cannot now substantially enhance the effectiveness of their classrooms and schools with children of the poor. Many dedicated and creative professionals are doing it all the time. Even institutional structures negatively biased against the minority-group poor still afford important margins of freedom for those who have the insight and skill and purpose to use them. However, the democratic perspective envisions an educational system in which the effective educational development of poor children is not the exception, but the norm; and this calls for considerable change in the society that shapes the school.

In short, the avowed purpose of compensatory education is to enhance the academic development of children of the poor—to close or to lessen substantially the gap between their achievement and that of more advantaged children. The etiological assumption dominant among practitioners in the field is that widespread retardation among disadvantaged children results from limitations within them, socially induced characteristics that preclude effective cognitive development. Hence, the focus of compensatory education should be toward overcoming their many "deficits" to enable them to fit into prevailing school programs. This deprivation hypothesis is bankrupt—theoretically unsound, defeatist in orientation, and as we shall see, largely fruitless in implementation.

A more valid diagnosis begins with the tenable premise that practically all children, guided in appropriate learning experiences, are capable of doing the work commonly demanded by schools and colleges (Schwebel, 1968), and that dysfunctional school practice is the main cause of academic retardation among children of the poor. On this basis, the focus of compensatory education should be toward radical modification of school programs and practices to make the educational process fit the developmental needs of poor children. The main target of change is the school itself.

Compensatory and other efforts to serve the educational needs of disadvantaged young people are seriously hampered by values and structures that prevail in our oppressive social system, but insightful and dedicated educators who have the will can find the way—and do.

Reversibility

Belief that the gross academic retardation among disadvantaged children can be corrected through appropriate intervention logically inheres in the concept "compensatory education," but there are those who doubt it.

The issues involved are integral to the rationale of special educational programs for the poor, and warrant at least brief discussion.

The biological determinists, of course, reject the principle of reversibility: what the genes have wrought let none think he can undo. They have no confidence in compensatory education.

Skepticism about the reversibility of academic retardation among the poor is also found in other circles. For example, the tendency for gains in Head Start and other preschool programs to "fade out" after children enter the regular school grades is interpreted by some as evidence of nonreversibility. But others offer the explanation that "the public schools may not act to sustain the effects of the Head Start experience" (White, 1970); or, stated differently, that there may be no "fadeout" in situations where "the compensatory input is maintained throughout the educational years" (Campbell and Frey, 1970). Another example is seen in reactions to the widely heralded finding of the Coleman Report (1966) that socioeconomic influences seem far more potent than school and all other influences in determining variability in pupils' achievement, seeming to imply that school efforts cannot make much of a difference. Jenck's (1972) analyses further reinforce this view. But reanalysis of the Coleman survey data by Guthrie and associates (1970) suggests that this finding of minimal school effect may be in part an artifact of the regression-analysis technique—a view supported by Campbell and Erlebacher (1970) in relation to Head Start studies, but challenged by Cicirelli (1970). Still further illustrations are found among neo-sociological determinists presumably in the compensatory education camp—in the cultural-deprivation literature that commonly portrays the "deficits" of disadvantaged children as so numerous and so limiting and so deep-rooted that one senses an underlying doubt that academic redemption for "these children" is possible.

Confidence in reversibility is high, of course, among those who interpret widespread academic retardation among poor children as resulting mainly from dysfunctional school practice. The children can learn effectively if effectively taught. The only doubt is whether needed changes in the school can be achieved.

The findings of research evaluations of compensatory education, subsequently summarized, tend both to support and to question the premise of reversibility. On the one hand, evaluations of many small, carefully conducted programs reveal substantial cognitive and academic growth among children of the poor. For example, IQ gains of 10 or 15 points or more are common, especially on the preschool level—not only in this country, but also in Israel, where problems in the education of disadvantaged children tend to be similar (Smilansky, 1967). Clearly, patterns of retardation among children in these programs are reversible. On the other hand, evaluations of large-scale compensatory programs in big-city systems generally find that they made "no significant difference." Whether this is attributable to characteristics of the children, or of the programs, or of the research evaluations remains a subject of debate.

The empirical evidence needed to resolve fully this issue of reversibility is not yet available. There has been no conclusive demonstration that valid, carefully conducted and sustained programs of compensatory educational intervention involving large numbers of disadvantaged children can or cannot effect substantial and abiding change in their academic performance. Nevertheless, quite ample basis for continuing efforts to this end is afforded by the increasingly accepted developmental theory of learning associated with Piaget (1952).

It is relevant in this connection to recall Skeels' (1966) 30-year follow-up study of orphaned children from impoverished backgrounds who were examined at the Iowa Welfare Research Station in the 1930s. Some of the children remained in orphanages and other institutions, and others were put in foster homes. The enormous contrast between the adult status of the two groups speaks eloquently to the question of the reversibility of early characteristics born of social disadvantage.

Skeels found that not one of the youngsters in the group that remained in institutional settings went to high school; very few went beyond early elementary grades; all of them had institutional care as adults; none of them was married; and hardly any of them were economically self-supporting. Among the comparable youngsters placed in foster homes, however, a few attended college; most of them finished high school; many were married; all were economically self-supporting; and one of them (initially diagnosed as feeble-minded) had two children with IQ's of 120 and above.

Early intervention through adoption, of course, is not directly comparable to intervention through compensatory education; but the findings of the Skeels study should give pause to educators and others who doubt the potential of sustained experiences under favorable circumstances to effect very substantial improvement in the cognitive and other behaviors of children of the poor.

Prescription

The types of educational programs suggested as appropriate for disadvantaged children correspond in some degree to the etiological assumptions of their planners.

The biological determinists eschew all programs aimed at substantial cognitive development, and suggest very limited educational goals for the poor. For example, Freeman (1968) calls unabashedly for differentiation in the types of education available to different social classes, with limited, vocational-training-type programs for "children poorly endowed by nature." Similarly, Jensen (1969), denying a developmental continuum that applies to children generally, posits two more or less

discrete "levels" of learning: "associative," appropriate for the geneti-
cally inferior "Low SES" children; and "conceptual," of which the geneti-
cally favored "Middle SES" children are capable. To all of them, compensatory educational efforts are futile.

The environmental-deprivation enthusiasts would try to prevent or
to correct the negative impact of poverty on the development of disadvantaged children. On the one hand, they would intervene as early as
possible before school entrance, providing the child with educational
experiences designed to forestall or minimize distorted development.
Head Start and other preschool programs are illustrative of this approach.
On the other hand, when the child enters school, they would identify and
try to overcome his "deficits" through psycho-educational diagnosis and
remediation. Programs of "cultural enrichment," counseling, high-
intensity remediation in reading and language arts and mathematics,
together with many more, are illustrative of this approach. The immediate focus is on changing the child.

The dysfunctional-school critics would greatly modify the school
environment in many ways. They would provide disadvantaged children
with an informal and "humanized" classroom climate, "real world"
experiences and materials that are meaningful to them, intrinsic motivation, individualized instruction and progression, black and ethnic
studies, acceptance of nonstandard dialect as legitimate albeit not sufficient, effective teachers who empathize with children of the poor and
appreciate their developmental potential, close home-school relations,
and many other modifications of prevailing structures and practices in
depressed-area schools. As a means to furthering child development, the
immediate focus is on changing the school.

As would be expected, this neat correspondence between etiology
and prescription is far from common in the practical world of compensatory education. Some of the special programs appear to have no coherent
theoretical framework; and many are multifaceted and frankly eclectic,
often including components that seem to reflect diverse orientations.
Moreover, some approaches urged by the deprivationists—for example,
early intervention prior to school attendance—pose no theoretical problem for the school reformists. To an observer in the field, however, and
often from program descriptions, it is not difficult to differentiate between those programs of compensatory education whose main thrust is
to modify the disadvantaged child to fit the school and others whose primary effort is to modify the school to fit the disadvantaged child.

PRACTICE

One of the earliest substantial programs of compensatory education was
the Demonstration Guidance Project in New York City. It began in
1956–57 with an "experimental group" of 717 students in grades seven,

eight, and nine in a depressed-area junior high school, and continued through 1961–62, by which time the three classes of students had graduated from senior high school. A saturation program of compensatory services was developed for these children throughout the period —curricular modifications, small classes, remedial instruction, cultural activities, counseling, clinical services, parental involvement, and others. The staff was enthusiastic about the project and determined to make a difference in these children's academic achievement, other behaviors, and careers. Apparently they did (Hillson and Myers, 1963). Between 1959 and 1962, this program was extended in a somewhat similar Higher Horizons Program, developed in sixty-five New York City schools, third to tenth grade, but with far fewer and less intensive compensatory services, and nothing like the staff dedication in its prototype. This program made no discernable difference in children's academic achievement (Wrightstone, et al. 1964).

In 1960–61, comprehensive programs for disadvantaged children were begun in seven big-city school systems with support from the Ford Foundation's Great Cities–Gray Areas School Improvement Program, and within two years the number of participating systems doubled. These programs varied greatly in goals and emphases; all sought to raise levels of aspiration and achievement among children of the poor. Reports available for a few of these programs suggest that their impact on children's academic achievement was minimal (for example, Philadelphia Public Schools, 1963).

These programs begun during the late fifties and early sixties—and perhaps a few others, for example, the Banneker District Project in St. Louis, started in 1957—mark the beginning of the compensatory education movement. In their wake came many hundreds of small-scale compensatory projects, sponsored by schools and universities and other agencies, comprehensive programs financed largely by city school systems, and several massive programs supported by the federal government. Most notable among the latter are Head Start projects for disadvantaged preschool youngsters, serving some 500,000 children a year at the height of its development; and an extremely varied array of Title I projects, serving an estimated 482,000 disadvantaged pupils in grades one to six at the time of a 1968–69 national survey (Gordon and Kourtrelakos, 1971).[9]

Compensatory educational programs currently operative vary so greatly as regards age-levels of participants, objectives, procedures, and types of learning experiences that any brief summary-description is certain to prove inadequate. None is here attempted. Table 1 summarizes information for eleven illustrative programs on different maturational levels. Beyond this, attention is restricted to a few seemingly valid generalizations concerning the scope and nature of practice in the field.[10]

TABLE 1

ELEVEN COMPENSATORY EDUCATION PROGRAMS

Title, Beginning Date, and Location	Maturational Level of Target Population	Objectives	Methods	Cognitive Gains
Banneker, 1957, St. Louis, Mo.	Preschool through junior high	Achievement improvement; motivation of pupils; improvement of aspirational levels and self-concept; raising of teacher expectations	Exposure to successful adults; teacher in-service training; parental involvement; creation of heightened commitment to school through rallies and interscholastic competition	Three years after program terminated, reading test scores of schools involved were compared first with those of other schools of similar racial and ethnic composition in the same school system; there was no significant gain in achievement between test schools and all-white schools in the same school system
Higher Horizons, 1959, New York City (This program was terminated in 1962.)	Elementary through junior high	Motivation of students and parents for higher achievement and educational plans	In-service teacher training to raise expectations and ability to teach these students; use of curriculum and guidance specialists to increase student motivation; enrichment programs; parental involvement; use of program volunteers; use of special remedial teachers to improve language and arithmetic skills	Data gathered at different times revealed no significant differences in reading and arithmetic scores between (1) experimental and control schools and (2) between experimental and control students matched on IQ and/or earlier achievement test scores

53

TABLE 1
ELEVEN COMPENSATORY EDUCATION PROGRAMS (continued)

Title, Beginning Date, and Location	Maturational Level of Target Population	Objectives	Methods	Cognitive Gains
More Effective Schools, 1964, New York City	Preschool through elementary	Identification and prevention of learning problems; creation of a responsive school climate	Team teaching; reduction of pupil-teacher ratio; teacher training; remedial curriculum features; cultural enrichment; parental involvement	No significant improvement noted in median reading achievement scores for fourth grade students who had been in the program for three years; no appreciable differences in levels of reading retardation between experimental and control schools comparable in ethnic composition
Early Training Project, 1959, Peabody College, Nashville, Tenn.	Preschool	Preparation of the disadvantaged to cope with and gain positively from learning situation in regular school	Summer school program; home visitors during rest of year; parental involvement; reinforcement for "correct" behavior; learning of concepts on abstract levels	Small but statistically significant differences in IQ noted between experimental and control groups after three summers of intervention and three years of home visitation; superiority in reading readiness scores for experimental groups two and a half years after program was initiated (experimental and control groups were formed by random assignment in this program)

54

Program	Level	Objectives	Methods	Results
Bereiter-Engelmann Academic Preschool Program, 1964, Champaign, Ill.	Preschool	Raising of achievement levels in reading, verbal, and numerical skills	Teacher training; special curriculum based on task analysis; parental involvement	Experimental groups showed significantly greater gains in IQ, reading, and arithmetic than control groups at end of first and second years (experimental and control groups were formed by random assignment in this program)
Institute for Developmental Studies, 1958, New York City	Preschool through third grade	Development of language and concept formation skills; prevention of deficiencies	Cultural enrichment: teacher in-service training; parental involvement; special materials and curricula	Inconsistent results obtained on both IQ and reading achievement tests in comparisons of experimental and control groups over time
Perry Preschool Project, 1962, Ypsilanti, Mich.	Preschool	Improvement of language and numerical skills	Parental involvement; cultural enrichment; low pupil-teacher ratio; group teaching emphasizing verbal "bombardment," interaction, and dramatic play; home tutoring of parents	Significant IQ differences between experimental and control groups were noted at end of first year which were not maintained at three later points in time ("fade-out" effect). This pattern held for four other waves of students. Significant differences were seen between experimental and control groups (for all waves combined) in California Achievement Tests (experimental and control groups were formed by random assignment in this program)

TABLE 1

ELEVEN COMPENSATORY EDUCATION PROGRAMS *(continued)*

Title, Beginning Date, and Location	Maturational Level of Target Population	Objectives	Methods	Cognitive Gains
Computer Assisted Instruction, 1964, Stanford University, Stanford, Calif.	Elementary	Improvement of basic reading and mathematics achievement	"Tutorial" and "drill-and-practice" approaches to individualized instruction. The former involves interaction of student and computer, based on a series of levels, each containing several lessons. Each lesson is constructed according to an instructional logic having the capability of "branching" contingent on the student's response. The second approach lacks the branching capability of the tutorial system	Early results showed significant differences in reading achievement and mathematics between experimental and control groups using the tutorial approach. (Experimental and control groups were formed by assigning half the subjects to CAI reading instruction and half to CAI math instruction. Thus the control group for reading was the group receiving math instruction, and vice versa.) Later experiments, however, have produced mixed results with control groups, which sometimes achieved significantly higher than the experimental groups. Evaluation of drill-and-practice approach shows mixed results; positive results were mostly with slow learners

Program	Objective	Level	Method	Results
Diagnostically Based Curriculum for Preschool Deprived Children, 1964, Bloomington, Ind.	Removal of deficits in language, motor coordination, and concept formation	Preschool	Conventional preschool techniques conducted in highly structured settings; frequent field trips coordinated with classroom curriculum; continuous monitoring of each student's progress and needs	Significant differences in IQ and language development were obtained between experimental and control groups at end of one year for three different waves of subjects
Homework Helpers, 1963, New York City	Encouragement of high school tutors of elementary students to remain in school and achieve at higher levels through year-round efforts and economic incentives	High school	High school tutors trained by master teachers, with daily supervision and guidance and frequent workshops using special curriculum materials; year-round efforts using economic incentives for tutors	Selection of tutors and nontutors was on a random basis of eligible participants (97 tutors, 57 controls); experimental group achieved significantly higher increases in reading on Iowa Silent Reading Tests than controls. However, no relationship was found between reading scores and performance in classroom
Small Group Basic Education Program, 1965, Albion, Penn.	Improvement of achievement in reading, mathematics, and writing; increase in school attendance; enhancement of self-esteem	High school	Remedial curriculum; group and individual instruction; individual and group counseling; home visiting	Students selected for low performance in reading and math from low-income families. Experimental group did not increase significantly on Metropolitan Achievement Tests in either reading or math during a four-month period (no evidence of use of a control group)

Source: Edward L. McDill, Mary S. McDill, and J. Timothy Sprehe, *Strategies for Success in Compensatory Education: An Appraisal of Evaluation Research* (Baltimore: Johns Hopkins Press, 1969).

The age range to which programs of compensatory education are addressed extends from infancy to young adulthood. Illustrative at the earliest level is Heber's work with black ghetto children in Milwaukee, beginning tutorial services shortly after birth and instruction in groups by age two (Amerian Orthopsychiatric Association, 1971). Among the many preschool programs for children aged three to five, at least two warrant special note. One is the Perry Preschool Project developed at Ypsilanti by Weikart and associates (1973). It involves a cognitively oriented curriculum based largely on Piagetian theory, and assesses children's growth in many behavioral areas during the two-year program and for several years after they enter regular school. The other is the Academic Preschool developed at the University of Illinois, Urbana, by Bereiter and Engelmann (1966), a tightly structured, high-intensity learning program emphasizing cognitive goals, especially language training. Most programs at this level, including Head Start, follow the child-centered model traditional in nursery-school education. At the upper-age levels are special programs designed to prevent or reverse high school dropouts, and others that seek to encourage and facilitate students' transition from high school to college. Illustrative of the latter is the extensively developed Upward Bound Program supported with federal funds. It involves students in academic study and other experiences during the summer, often on a college campus, and provides follow-up experiences during the school year. There are also many kinds of compensatory programs and services for disadvantaged young people after they enter college (Gordon and Wilkerson, 1966).

Between these age-level extremes is the kaleidoscopic array of school-based programs that almost defy brief description. Probably most common—and least creative—are remedial programs in reading, language arts, and mathematics, on both the elementary and secondary levels. Some exceptional programs of this type are imaginative and innovative, including careful diagnosis, individualized (often programmed) instruction, specially adapted instructional materials, peer teaching, computer and "talking typewriter" techniques, and varied types of reinforcement schemes. It appears, however, that most school-based remedial programs, inluding a large proportion of the Title I projects, involve little more than intensified drill at tasks and with materials previously used unsuccessfully with disadvantaged learners.

Many school systems provide "after-school" programs for retarded learners—most commonly with regular teachers, sometimes with volunteer adults or high school students as tutors. Generally these programs seem to be as humdrum and ineffective as traditional remedial efforts during the school day; but there are notable exceptions, such as the Homework Helper Program in New York City (Cloward, 1966).

Increasing numbers of programs provide bilingual instruction for disadvantaged children with non-English-language backgrounds, especially Spanish. The availability of federal Title VII funds in recent years ($35 million in 1974) has given impetus to this development. A few schools and systems are using bi-dialectical reading programs for black youngsters who speak nonstandard English. Illustrative is the Psycholinguistic Reading Series developed in Chicago (Chicago Public Schools, 1968).

Guidance and counseling services are emphasized in most school-based programs of compensatory education. In addition to their commonplace "trouble-shooting" functions, such services usually undertake to help disadvantaged young people set personal goals and select appropriate courses; and some of them are addressed also to the improvement of self-concept and career orientation.

It should be noted in this connection that developmental goals in the affective domain are characteristic of most programs of compensatory education, and are given major emphasis in some of them. Both the Demonstration Guidance Project and the Banneker District Project, for example, strove hard to develop feelings of self-worth and pride and worthy aspirations among their students, the St. Louis project making extensive use of local role models who "made good." Many programs use black and ethnic studies to help shape positive attitudes toward self and race or nationality. Although there is widespread recognition of the importance of such affective development among disadvantaged children—reflected in the extensive literature on Negro self-concept —relevant and carefully developed curricular and teacher-training materials are extremely meager.

Some compensatory programs addressed to adolescent youth provide modest stipends for participants. Financial assistance of various kinds is also characteristic of compensatory services on the college level. The rationale is not simply that impoverished young people need the money, which they do, but also that it serves as an incentive to improved academic behaviors.

Another component of many compensatory programs is the attempt to involve parents and win their cooperation. Such efforts are almost universal among preschool programs, and widespread on the elementary level; but they are rare on the high school level—as, indeed, are substantial compensatory efforts of any kind.

Generalized descriptions like these necessarily fail to "catch" the concrete and impressive variety of goals and approaches and materials and activities that comprise compensatory education, and several relevant and important developments are not here discussed at all.[11] Even so, this limited overview provides at least a backdrop for a few supplementary comments on practice in the field.

First, as many students of compensatory education have noted, a large proportion of the programs do not have objectives that are defined with enough specificity to guide practice; they conduct learning experiences that seem only slightly related to stated goals; and they seldom include controls to assure efficient implementation of the planned program. This is not true of many small experimental projects, in which careful planning, tight controls, and ongoing evaluation are common. But it is true of very many comprehensive, school-based programs, some of which seem to consist of little more than a flurry of miscellaneous activities expressive of the urge to "do good."

Such vaguely oriented and loosely run programs could hardly be expected to improve substantially the academic performance of disadvantaged children, and usually they do not. The characteristics of compensatory programs more likely to succeed are suggested by the American Institute for Research's comparison of 18 programs shown to be successful in achieving cognitive growth and 25 other programs shown to be unsuccessful on the basis of 91 program components. AIR's analysis led to the following recommendations (Hawkridge et al., 1968 a)[12] for establishing sound programs:

A.   *For preschool programs:*
      1. *Careful planning, including statements of objectives*
      2. *Teacher training in the methods of the program*
      3. *Instruction and materials closely relevant to objectives*

B.   *For elementary programs:*
      1. *Academic objectives clearly stated*
      2. *Active parental involvement, particularly as motivators*
      3. *Individual attention for pupils' learning problems*
      4. *High intensity of treatment*

C.   *For secondary programs:*
      1. *Academic objectives clearly stated*
      2. *Individualization of instruction*
      3. *Directly relevant instruction (pp. 19–20)*

On the basis of a bias reflected through much of this chapter, we would add one other recommendation—for programs on all levels: theoretical-philosophical orientation embracing confidence in the growth potential of disadvantaged learners and commitment to humanistic values.

Second, there probably is no identifiable pattern of curriculum content and learning experiences that represents *the* correct approach to compensatory education. As Gordon (1970) notes: "The search for the best treatment is clearly a futile search" (p. 4). Given such characteristics as those recommended by AIR, he says: "It seems that . . . no matter what the content or method, personal development and content mastery are advanced" (p. 4).

Support for this point of view is found in Weikart's (1973) appraisal of the outcomes of three contrasting curriculum programs on the preschool level: (1) the cognitively oriented curriculum of the Perry Preschool Project (open-framework model), (2) the Academic Preschool's language training curriculum (programmed model), and (3) a unit-based curriculum of the nursery-school type (child-centered model). He concludes that:

(1) On the whole, there are no initial or subsequent differences between the three models on either intellectual or achievement tests with all three models performing unusually well.

(2) The edge that might be expected for the programmed curriculum in regard to later academic achievement does not show up in these data, and the widely reported inability of the traditional child-center curriculum to produce effective results is not supported. (p. 14)

Weikart calls for a shift of focus from "heavy emphasis on curriculum development" to "careful attention to the other components of program operation." His recommendations for successful programs are simple: detailed planning for daily operations and careful supervision to assure effective implementation.

Whether the relationships Weikart found on the preschool level apply generally to programs of compensatory education has not yet been demonstrated empirically, but they probably do. Experience as educators of teachers convinces us that far more important than methods and materials are clarity of purpose and commitment. Teaching is still largely an art, and there are multiple approaches to most learning goals. The purposeful, insightful, creative, and carefully planned implementation of almost any relevant curriculum program is likely to yield substantial improvement in the academic performance of disadvantaged children.

Third, if the criteria for good programs suggested by the preceding two comments are valid, and if they were satisfied by the process of education generally, perhaps there would be little or no need for special compensatory programs. Moreover, if such criteria are not satisfied by these special programs, no matter what their other characteristics, compensatory efforts are not likely to make much of a difference in the educational development of learners from poverty backgrounds.

In this sense, it is quite possible—and perhaps probable—that good educational practice for children is good educational practice for children of the poor.

EVALUATION

In 1965, when systematic evaluation of compensatory education had scarcely begun, a review of ten studies led to the generalization that "currently available research in the field typically reports ambiguous outcomes of amorphous or unknown educational variables" (Wilkerson, 1965). Ten years and scores of investigations later, this generalization is still apt for most evaluations in the field. Also, there is now an enhanced appreciation of the extreme complexity of efforts to assess program outcomes and relate them to program treatments. No adequate description can here be given of the many research evaluations of compensatory education now available. [13] Attention is restricted to a general summary of their findings, several illustrations, and a few comments on this field of inquiry.

As has been noted, most studies of compensatory preschool programs find that there is substantial growth by children during the treatment period, in psychological functions and in academic achievement, but that differences between them and comparable children outside the programs tend to disappear after they enter the regular school grades. This was the general finding of the much-debated study of Head Start by the Westinghouse Learning Corporation and the University of Ohio (Granger, 1969), which compared the performance of nearly 2,000 children in 104 Head Start centers with that of carefully matched nonparticipating children. Similar short-run effects that do not persist are reported by other studies of preschool programs.

This fade-out phenomenon is also reported for a number of small, carefully planned and supervised, experimental projects on the preschool level; but it is not so marked, and some benefits tend to persist. Illustrative is the Early Training Project at Peabody College (Gray and Klaus, 1969). Children in the experimental group participated in two or three summers of preschool and one or two years of weekly home teaching by trained staff. Comparisons were made with two control groups, one 60 miles away, to test the effect of diffusion. Growth was assessed at intervals by measures of psycholinguistic abilities, reading-readiness and reading tests, and achievement tests. During the treatment period, the experimental-group children developed more rapidly than the control-group children. A seven-year follow-up revealed considerable spreading of the program's impact on nearby control-group children, but not on those 60 miles away. By the fourth grade, there was no significant difference in achievement between the experimental and control groups. There was, however, a small, statistically significant difference favoring the

experimental group in Stanford-Binet IQ scores. Weikart (1973) charac-
terizes as a "remarkable achievement" this sustained impact on intellectual development through seven years of the study and four years after
the intervention ended.

This tendency toward both disappearance and persistence of program impact after children enter regular school grades is also evident
in studies of the Perry Preschool Project (Weikart, 1973). Predominantly
black, disadvantaged children in successive experimental groups participated in daily cognitively oriented preschool classes and weekly home-
teaching experiences over a period of two years. Follow-up comparisons
between them and matched control-group children reveal the following:
(1) the experimental groups showed higher Stanford-Binet IQ scores
during the program, but the difference disappeared by second grade;
(2) the experimental groups continued to have significantly higher scores
on achievement tests through first, second, and third grades; (3) the
experimental group received higher ratings on academic, emotional, and
social development by teachers in first, second, and third grade; and
(4) the school seemed to treat the experimental-group children "amaz-
ingly different" from the control-group children. Remaining at grade
level were 72 percent of the experimental group and 60 percent of the
control group. Placed in special education classes were 12 percent of the
experimental group and 27 percent of the control group.

Apparently such small, carefully controlled projects as these have
not only substantial immediate impact on children's development, but
also some beneficial long-term effects. On the basis of studies of several
such programs, Weikart concludes:

> Experimental projects in which the researchers have direct control
> of the curriculum, the operation of the project, and the research
> design seem to offer potential for immediate positive impact in
> terms of stated goals. Such projects can produce significant impact
> on intellectual, academic, and social-emotional growth as long as
> four years after, and on school placement as long as ten years after,
> the preschool intervention. (p. 6)

With a few exceptions, studies of school-based programs of compensatory education commonly find that they do not seem to have even
short-term impact in improving children's academic achievement as
measured by standardized tests, although teachers' assessments tend to
differ. Illustrative are Glass's (1970) analyses of data from the 1968–69
National Survey of Title I projects, comparing both test scores in reading
and teachers' more general ratings for "participants" and "nonparticipants."[14]

Glass reports that analysis of reading-gain scores revealed the following: (1) participants had lower reading scores than nonparticipants;

(2) participating groups in all grades showed negative gain scores, indicating a widening gap between them and nonparticipants; (3) nonparticipants advanced one or more grade-equivalents a year, but participants did not; (4) "increasing the number of hours spent in remedial reading . . . did not reverse the losses suffered by participants"; (5) thus, "in general, for whatever reasons, compensatory reading programs did not yield evidence in terms of performance on standardized tests that the reading deficiencies of participants had been overcome" (p. 193).

However, analysis of teachers' judgments of pupils' development revealed the following: (1) teachers reported a nearly 10 percent greater rate of "some" or "large" improvement in reading proficiency among participants as compared with nonparticipants; (2) similar differences favoring participants were reported for understanding written and oral instructions; (3) there were no important differences favoring participants in mathematical proficiency or independence of learning; (4) two-thirds of the teachers appraised compensatory programs for the disadvantaged as "definitely worthwhile," and one-fourth said they were "generally worthwhile," but had some reservations.

Although the groups compared in this analysis of Title I national survey data were not equivalent, the findings are fairly typical of those reported for most studies of compensatory education programs. On the basis of standardized test scores, most of the programs seemed to have little or no effect on pupils' academic performance; but on the basis of teachers' judgments, the programs seemed to be effective in improving pupils' academic achievement and other behaviors.

There are, however, some school-based programs of compensatory education in which children show significant gains on standardized tests. Probably most of those operative in 1968 are among the twenty-one "exemplary programs," preschool through grade twelve, described by Hawkridge and associates (1968 b). They were chosen from more than 1,000 programs originally surveyed, the criterion of selection being statistically significant larger gains on standardized tests by participating pupils than by controls—a fact that suggests the atypicality of these successful programs.

Although there now are many more careful research evaluations of compensatory education than there were in the mid-sixties, this area of inquiry—as a number of critics have pointed out[15] —is still characterized by serious weakness. Many of them are simple technical weaknesses; others are more basic, some seemingly inherent in the field. Probably most common among the former are inadequate sampling, failure to establish comparable experimental and control groups, and techniques of data-collection that make validity and reliability suspect. Several more fundamental weaknesses warrant brief comment.

First, it is seldom clear what educational interventions are being evaluated in studies of compensatory programs. Few of the school-based programs define precisely what their strategies are; and as Berger's (1969) study of Montessori and "traditional" classes demonstrates, the labels attached to programs are unreliable guides that tend to obscure wide variations in teaching behaviors. Systematic classroom observation is needed to identify just what program inputs are, and this technique is rare in studies of compensatory education.

Second, since most compensatory programs are multifaceted, involving a complex of intervention variables, it is seldom clear from evaluation studies which components are related to measured outcomes. Research in the field has hardly begun to cope with this problem.

Third, the increasing attempt to measure statistically significant differences in standardized test scores has merit, but it tends to ignore qualitative indexes and process variables that may be even more important. On the one hand, positive growth in children's self-perception, social interaction, attitude toward school and learning, career aspirations and the like are important in their own right; but valid and reliable measurement of such qualitative outcomes as these is yet to be achieved by educational research. On the other hand, more illuminating than even reliably measured outcomes may be understanding of the educational processes by which they were fostered; and this calls for research techniques that go beyond standardized testing. There is no way to understand fully the process of education other than by studying it *as a process*; yet, most studies of compensatory education are preoccupied with status measures. Researchers would do well to emulate a few educational anthropologists and others[16] who are conducting process studies in this field.

CONCLUSION

Fourth, most evaluations of compensatory education are short-term appraisals, the main exceptions being a few experimental investigations on the preschool level; but it is quite possible that important effects of the programs not immediately evident may significantly influence children's lives. It may be too soon, for example, to write off the massive compensatory interventions of the sixties as "largely wasted." Only longitudinal studies over many years can yield a "final" assessment, and there are very few such studies in educational research.

Thus far, the predominating findings of research evaluations of compensatory education certainly do not bolster confidence that most of the special programs involved can substantially improve the academic performance of children of the poor. However, what this implies for educational theory and practice—and social policy—is by no means clear. Possibly the children have, indeed, been so scarred by early growth and socialization under conditions of poverty and discrimination that compensatory educational efforts are largely futile. Perhaps the education profession has not yet developed—and implemented effectively!—intervention programs that provide the learning conditions and experiences needed to realize the developmental potential of disadvantaged young people. It may be that prevailing research techniques are not yet able to cope with the complexities involved in appraising the outcomes of compensatory programs. Insofar as empirical proof is concerned, these remain open questions; and policy and practice and evaluation must continue without sure answers.

It is interesting in this connection to note that compensatory education is now pressed by political and other demands to provide "sure answers," to justify itself on the basis of measured outcomes—demands rarely made of public education in general. One wonders whether this insistence is somehow related to the fact that the special compensatory programs are addressed mainly to children of the poor. In any event, as pointed out by McDill, et al. (1969), "those who condemn all compensatory programs out of hand should temper their criticism with the realization of the magnitude of the task confronted, the brief experience in coping with it, and the pitifully small fund of scientific knowledge relevant to the problems of disadvantaged children" (p. 71).

NOTES

1. This trend in the North, following the 1961 antisegregation ruling of the U.S. District Court in the Lincoln School Case in New Rochelle, N.Y., was strikingly comparable to the similar movement in the South in the early fifties, when the segregation cases that eventuated in *Brown* v. *Board of Education* were moving through the federal courts (see, for example, Wilkerson, 1969 a).

2. In absolute numbers, whites predominate by far. Gordon and Kourtrelakos (1971) estimated that more than 5,700,000 children had been served by programs of compensatory education: black, 22.7 percent; white, 69.7 percent; Spanish, 5.6 percent; Oriental, 0.4 percent; and, "Native American," 0.4 percent.

3. Puerto Ricans, Indian Americans, Mexican-Americans, Oriental Americans, and Negroes.

4. Many relevant essays not specifically cited in this discussion are listed among the references. One useful collection of such essays is the *Disadvantaged Child* series edited by Jerome Hellmuth (1967, 1968, 1970).

5. The fact that Jensen (1969) and others have resurrected this once "settled" question for renewed debate reflects no new developments in behavioral science. Coming at a time when the civil rights movement was waning and political reaction emerging, it probably reflects the historical tendency of some intellectuals to "bend with the wind."

6. A term supplanted in time by the seemingly less pejorative "socially disadvantaged child," or simply "disadvantaged child."

7. Relevant titles are legion. For a varied sampling, see: Levine and Havighurst (1971), Gross and Gross (1969), Mayer (1961), Silberman (1970), Kozol

(1967), Rubinstein (1970), and almost any issue of that very useful bimonthly journal, *Integrated Education: A Report on Race and Schools*.

8. The analysis was impressionistic rather than systematic, and was never published.

9. This report by Gordon and Kourtrelakos, *Utilizing Information from Evaluation, Research, and Survey Data Concerning Compensatory Education*, assembles a great mass of information in the field, including program descriptions and analyses and digests of research-evaluation studies. Although unpublished, it is available upon request.

10. Descriptions of a wide range of special programs for the disadvantaged are included in the "Directory of Compensatory Practices," mainly during 1963-64, in Gordon and Wilkerson (1966), and the follow-up "Directory of Selected Ongoing Compensatory Education Programs" by Jablonsky (1971*b*). See also Jablonsky (1971*a*) "Status Report on Compensatory Education."

11. For example: staffing practices in schools with compensatory programs, the education of teachers for effective service with disadvantaged children, and the "Sesame Street" and "Electric Company" programs of the Children's Television Workshop.

12. These recommendations are echoed in *The Report* of the Select Committee on Equal Educational Opportunity, United States Senate (U.S. Senate, 1972).

13. Several "exemplary studies" and more than seventy others are abstracted in Gordon and Kourtrelakos (1971, pp. 144-152, 160-194).

14. "Nonparticipants" included both disadvantaged and other children; hence, the comparisons are not of equivalent groups.

15. See, for example, McDill, et al. (1969) and Gordon (1970).

16. E.G., Leacock (1969), Fuchs (1969), and Rist (1970).

REFERENCES

American Orthopsychiatric Association. 1971. "Heading Off Retardation," *Newsletter* 15, no. 4 (December).

Ausubel, David P. 1964. "How Reversible Are the Cognitive and Motivational Effects of Cultural Deprivation? Implications for Teaching the Culturally Deprived Child." *Urban Education* 1: 16–38.

Bereiter, Carl and Siegfried Engelmann. 1966. *Teaching Disadvantaged Children in the Preschool*. Englewood Cliffs, N.J.: Prentice-Hall.

Berger, Barbara. 1969. *A Longitudinal Investigation of Montessori and Traditional Pre-Kindergarten Training with Inner-City Children*. New York: Center for Urban Education.

Birch, Herbert G. and Joan Dye Gussow. 1970. *Disadvantaged Children: Health, Nutrition and School Failure*. New York: Harcourt Brace Jovanovich, Inc.

Bruner, Jerome S. 1971. "*The Process of Education Reconsidered*." Pp. 19–30 in R. R. Leeper (ed.), *Dare to Care/Dare to Act: Racism and Education*.

Washington, D.C.: Association for Supervision and Curriculum Development.

Campbell, Donald T. and Albert Erlebacher. 1970. "How Regression Artifacts in Quasi-Experimental Evaluations Can Make Compensatory Education Look Harmful." Pp. 185–210 in J. Hellmuth (ed.), *Compensatory Education: A National Debate*, Disadvantaged Child, vol. 3. New York: Brunner/Mazel Publishers.

Campbell, Donald T. and Peter W. Frey. 1970. "The Implications of Learning Theory for the Fade-Out of Gains from Compensatory Education." Pp. 455–463 in J. Hellmuth (ed.), *Compensatory Education: A National Debate*, Disadvantaged Child, vol. 3. New York: Brunner/Mazel Publishers.

Chicago Public Schools. 1968. *Psycholinguistics Oral Language Program: A Bi-Dialectical Approach*. Chicago: Board of Education.

————. 1969. *Psycholinguistics Reading Series: A Bi-Dialectical Approach, Teacher's Manual*. Chicago: Board of Education.

Cicirelli, Victor. 1970. "The Relevance of the Regression Artifact Problem to the Westinghouse-Ohio Evaluation of Head Start: A Reply to Campbell and Erlebacher." Pp. 211–215 in J. Hellmuth (ed.), *Compensatory Education: A National Debate*, Disadvantaged Child, vol. 3. New York: Brunner/Mazel Publishers.

Clark, Kenneth B. 1965. *Dark Ghetto: Dilemmas of Social Power*. New York: Harper & Row.

Cloward, Robert D. 1966. *Studies in Tutoring*. New York: Social Work Research Center, Columbia University.

Cloward, Richard A. and James A. Jones. 1963. "Social Class: Educational Attitudes and Participation." Pp. 190–216 in A. Harry Passow (ed.), *Education in Depressed Areas*. New York: Bureau of Publications, Teachers College, Columbia University.

Coleman, James S., et al. 1966. *Equality of Educational Opportunity*. Washington, D.C.: U.S. Government Printing Office.

Commission on School Integration. 1963. *Public School Segregation and Integration in the North*. Washington, D.C.: National Association of Intergroup Relations Officials.

Davidson, Helen and Judith W. Greenberg. 1967. *School Achievers from a Deprived Background*. New York: City College of the City University of New York.

Davidson, Helen and Gertrude Lang. 1960. "Children's Perceptions of Their Teachers' Feelings Toward Them Related to Self-Perception,

School Achievement and Behavior." *Journal of Experimental Educational Psychology* 29: 107–118.

Deutsch, Martin. 1960. *Minority Group and Class Status as Related to Social and Personality Factors in Scholastic Achievement*. Ithaca, N.Y.: Society for Applied Anthropology.

Deutsch, Martin, et al. 1967. *The Disadvantaged Child*. New York: Basic Books.

Dillard, J. L. 1972. *Black English*. New York: Random House.

Fantini, Mario D. and Gerald Weinstein. 1968. *The Disadvantaged: Challenge to Education*. New York: Harper & Row.

Freeman, Roger. 1968. "Vast Input: Doubtful Output," *Southern Education Report* 4: 10–11.

Fuchs, Estelle. 1966. *Pickets at the Gates*. New York: Free Press.

———. 1969. *Teachers Talk*. New York: Doubleday.

Glass, Gene V., et al. 1970. *Data Analysis of the 1968-69 Survey of Compensatory Education (Title I)*. Boulder, Colo.: Laboratory of Educational Research, University of Colorado.

Gordon, Edmund W. 1970. "Compensatory Education: Evaluation in Perspective." *IRCD Bulletin* 6 (December): 1–8.

Gordon, Edmund W. and James Kourtrelakos. 1971. *Utilizing Information from Evaluation, Research, and Survey Data Concerning Compensatory Education*. New York: Teaching and Learning Research Corporation.

Gordon, Edmund W. and Doxey A. Wilkerson. 1966. *Compensatory Education for the Disadvantaged*. New York: College Entrance Examination Board.

Granger, R. L. 1969. *The Impact of Head Start: An Evaluation of the Effects of Head Start on Children's Cognitive and Affective Development*, vol. 1. New York: Westinghouse Learning Corporation; Athens: University of Ohio.

Gray, S. W., and R. Klaus. 1969. *The Early Training Project: A Seventh Year Report*. Nashville, Tenn.: George Peabody College.

Greer, Colin. 1972. *The Great School Legend*. New York: Basic Books.

Gross, Ronald and Beatrice Gross (eds.). 1969. *Radical School Reform*. New York: Simon & Schuster.

Guthrie, James W., et al. 1970. "A Survey of School Effectiveness Studies." Pp. 25–54 in *Do Teachers Make A Difference?* Washington, D.C.: U.S. Government Printing Office.

Harlem Youth Opportunities Unlimited, Inc. 1964. *Youth in the Ghetto: A Study of the Consequences of Powerlessness and a Blueprint for Change.* New York.

Hawkridge, David G., et al. 1968 a. *Foundations for Success in Educating Disadvantaged Children: Final Report.* Palo Alto: American Institute of Research in Behavioral Sciences.

———. 1968 b. *A Study of Selected Exemplary Programs for the Education of Disadvantaged Children: Final Report,* Parts I and II. Palo Alto: American Institute of Research in Behavioral Sciences.

———. 1969. *A Study of Further Selected Exemplary Programs for the Education of Disadvantaged Children: Final Report.* Palo Alto: American Institute of Research in Behavioral Sciences.

Hellmuth, Jerome (ed.). 1967. *Disadvantaged Child,* vol. 1. New York: Brunner/Mazel Publishers.

———. (ed.). 1968. *Head Start and Early Intervention.* Disadvantaged Child, vol. 2. New York: Brunner/Mazel Publishers.

———. 1970. *Compensatory Education: A National Debate.* Disadvantaged Child, vol. 3. Brunner/Mazel Publishers.

Hillson, Henry T. and Florence C. Meyers. 1963. *The Demonstration Guidance Project: 1957–1962.* New York: Board of Education of the City of New York.

Hunt, J. McV. 1961. *Intelligence and Experience.* New York: Ronald Press Company.

Hymen, Herbert H. and Paul B. Sheatsley. 1956. "Attitudes Toward Segregation." *Scientific American* 195: 35–39.

Jablonsky, Adelaide. 1971a. "Status Report on Compensatory Education." *IRCD Bulletin* 7: 1–21.

———. 1971b. "Directory of Ongoing Compensatory Education Programs." *IRCD Bulletin* 7: 1–19.

Janowitz, Morris. *Institution Building in Urban Education.* New York: Russell Sage Foundation.

Jencks, Christopher, et al. 1972. *Inequality.* New York: Basic Books.

Jensen, Arthur R. 1969. "How Much Can We Boost IQ and Scholastic Achievement?" *Harvard Educational Review* 39: 1–123.

Klineberg, Otto. 1935. *Race Differences.* New York: Harper.

———. 1944. *Characteristics of the American Negro.* New York: Harper.

Kozol, Jonathan. 1967. *Death at an Early Age*. Boston: Houghton Mifflin. flin.

Labov, William. 1968. "The Non-Standard Negro Vernacular: Some Practical Suggestions." In *Position Papers from Language Education for the Disadvantaged*. Report No. 3 of NDEA National Institute for Advanced Study in Teaching Disadvantaged Youth.

Leacock, Eleanor. 1969. *Teaching and Learning in City Schools*. New York: Basic Books.

Levine, Daniel U., and Robert J. Havighurst. 1971. *Farewell to Schools???* Worthington, Ohio: Charles A. Jones Publishing Company.

Mayer, Martin. 1961. *The Schools*. New York: Harper & Brothers.

McDill, Edward L., Mary S. McDill, and J. Timothy Sprehe. 1969. *Strategies for Success in Compensatory Education: An Appraisal of Evaluation Research*. Baltimore: Johns Hopkins University Press.

Monacel, Louis D. 1971. Statement submitted to Hearings before the Select Committee on Educational Opportunity of the United States Senate, Part 12. Pp. 5106–5644 in *Compensatory Education and Other Alternatives in Urban Schools*. Washington, D.C.: U.S. Government Printing Office.

Parsons, Talcott. 1962. "The School Class as a Social System: Some of Its Functions in American Society." Pp. 434–455 in A. H. Halsey, Jean Floud, and C. Arnold Anderson, *Education, Economy, and Society*. New York: Free Press of Glencoe.

Passow, A. Harry (ed.). 1963. *Education in Depressed Areas*. New York: Bureau of Publications, Teachers College, Columbia University.

——— (ed.). 1970. *Reaching the Disadvantaged Learner*. New York: Teachers College Press, Columbia University.

——— (ed.). 1971. *Urban Education in the 1970's*. New York: Teachers College Press, Columbia University.

Philadelphia Public Schools. 1963. *Great Cities School Improvement Program: Progress Report, September 1960–June 1962*. Philadelphia: Philadelphia Public Schools.

Piaget, Jean. 1952. *The Origins of Intelligence in Children*. New York: International Universities Press.

Riessman, Frank. 1962. *The Culturally Deprived Child*. New York: Harper and Brothers.

Rist, Ray C. 1970. "Student Social Class and Teacher Expectations: The Self-Fulfilling Prophecy in Ghetto Education." *Harvard Educational Review* 40: 411–451.

Rosenthal, Robert, and Leonore Jacobson. 1968. *Pygmalion in the Class-room*. New York: Holt, Rinehart & Winston.

Rubinstein, Annette T. (ed.). 1970. *Schools Against Children: The Case for Community Control*. New York: Monthly Review Press.

Ryan, William. 1971. *Blaming the Victim*. New York: Pantheon Books.

Schwebel, Milton. 1968. *Who Can Be Educated?* New York: Grove Press.

Silberman, Charles E. 1970. *Crisis in the Classroom*. New York: Random House.

Skeels, Harold M. 1966. *Adult Status of Children with Contrasting Early Life Experiences: A Follow-Up Study*. Chicago: University of Chicago Press.

Smilansky, Moshe. 1967. *Intellectual Achievement in Culturally Disadvantaged Children*. New York: John Wiley & Sons.

Stein, Annie. 1971. "Strategies for Failure." *Harvard Educational Review* 41: 158–204.

U.S. Senate, Select Committee on Equal Educational Opportunity. 1972. *The Report*. Washington, D.C.: U.S. Government Printing Office.

Weikart, David P. 1973. "Development of Effective Preschool Programs: A Report on the Results of the High/Scope-Ypsilanti Preschool Projects." Paper presented at the High/Scope Educational Research Foundation Conference, Ann Arbor, Michigan, May.

White, Sheldon H. 1970. "The National Impact Study of Head Start." Pp. 163–184 in J. Hellmuth (ed.), *Compensatory Education: A National Debate*, Disadvantaged Child, vol. 3. New York: Brunner/Mazel Publishers.

Wilkerson, Doxey A. 1964. "Prevailing and Needed Emphasis in Research on the Education of Disadvantaged Children and Youth." *Journal of Negro Education* 33: 346–366.

———. 1965. "Programs and Practices in Compensatory Education for Disadvantaged Children." *Review of Educational Research* 35: 426–440.

———. 1968. "Blame the Negro Child!" *Freedomways* 8: 340–346.

———. 1969a. "The Negro School Movement in Virginia: From 'Equalization' to 'Integration'." In A. Meier and E. Rudwick (eds.), *The Making of Black America*, vol. 2. New York: Atheneum Press.

———. 1969b. "Compensatory Education?" Pp. 308–318 in S. Chess and A. Thomas (eds.), *Annual Progress in Child Psychiatry and Child Development; 1969*. New York: Brunner/Mazel Publishers.

———. 1970. "Compensatory Education." Pp. 19–39 in S. Marcus and H. N. Rivlin (eds.), *Conflicts in Urban Education*. New York: Basic Books.

————. 1972. "How to Make Educational Research Relevant to the Urban Community." *Journal of Negro Education* 41: 299–302.

Wrightstone, J. Wayne, et al. 1964. *Evaluation of the Higher Horizons Program for Underprivileged Children*. New York: Board of Education of the City of New York.

Zach, Lillian. 1969. "The Effect of Verbal Labeling on Visual Motor Performance." *Journal of Learning Disabilities* 2: 218–222.

Chapter 3

EDUCATIONAL ACCOUNTABILITY

Many educators and other citizens are confused about just what account-ability means. For this reason, it is easy to get different answers from various people to the same question on accountability, which in turn confuses the original intent and the issues related to the question. Ac-countability in its most direct sense means to hold someone (or some group or agency) accountable for his behavior or action. Although ac-countability is a relatively new concept in the educational literature, the original idea dates back to the ancient Greek philosophers.

ACCOUNTABILITY IN HISTORICAL CONTEXT

As the cup of hemlock touched Socrates' lips back in 339 B.C., history recorded for the first time the act of holding a teacher accountable for what he was teaching. Four hundred years later another great teacher was to be held accountable for his teachings. In 1925, John T. Scopes was held accountable by the community for teaching about the theory of evolution which resulted in his trial and conviction. Each of us is able to recall cases, even closer to home, concerning the dismissal of a teacher on the grounds that his reading list, learning activities, or political, moral, or religious interpretations ran contrary to the values of the community. This concept of accountability (holding a teacher responsible for the views he expresses) is certainly not new.

A somewhat different view of accountability also has a history going back into time, that is, accountability for what should be taught and how it should be taught. In the medieval universities, professors and tutors were paid directly by the students. The law students at Bologna during the middle of the thirteenth century extracted this form of accountability. Writes Herr (1961), "The students who had the whip hand, kept their professors to the punctual observance of the lecture timetable, under threat of financial penalties, and revenged themselves on unpopular teachers by boycotts" (p. 244). In the United States, we can go as far back as the Old Deluder Satan Law of 1647. Enacted by the Massachusetts Bay Colony, it held each town accountable for teaching the children to read the Bible. A fine of five pounds was levied for noncompliance. On still another level, there has always been an implied form of accountability in terms of educational goals, compulsory attendance, student assessment, teacher ratings, evaluation of programs, duties of school administrators, and budget costs. As former Commissioner of Education Sidney Marland (1973) put it: "Accountability has always been with us. Until now it did not have a name" (p. 345).

In the past (as illustrated by the above examples) the teacher and/or institution was held responsible for what should or should not be taught. The responsibility for learning what was taught resided with the learner. But a concept of accountability based on the ability of the educational delivery system to assure successful student learning is a product of our times. It grows out of our recognition of the magnitude of societal problems arising in part from the failure of our schools to come to grips with the learning problems of pupils who are not succeeding. It is evident to many that our educational institutions are failing to produce the egalitarian society heralded as perhaps the prime educational goal.

To reach the goal of an egalitarian society, white liberals[1] and militant segments of minority groups raised the cry of equal educational opportunity and institutional responsibility for assuring successful learning. Both equal educational opportunity and institutional responsibility found support in the prevailing psychological theories of environmentalism and behaviorism. Americans have long put great faith in the role of the environment to shape our lives and the extent to which man and society can be improved through changes in the environment; behaviorism provided the tool for modifying behavior to suit the altered environment. The early compensatory programs of the 1960s, followed by the Elementary and Secondary Education Acts (ESEA) of 1965 served as outlets for the environmentalist's theory of intellectual development and the behaviorist's theory of changing human characteristics. By the mid-1960s the program budget for Title I of the ESEA was over a billion dollars per year.

In the name of a variety of environmental and behavioral theories, compensatory programs proliferated as educationists and social designers rushed to make claims to federal monies available, spending billions of dollars based on hunches and sometimes sloppy program designs. Glickstein (1969) summarized compensatory funding as an "ineffective free for all . . . with few federal strings attached to the expenditures" (p. 305). Perhaps the only consistent thread running through the programs was the demand that more money be spent.

To help increase the federal commitment to compensatory education, the Johnson Administration commissioned James Coleman (1966) to conduct a nationwide study on the lack of equal educational opportunity for minorities. It was the largest educational research enterprise ever conducted, consisting of about 1,300 pages, including 750 pages of statistics, to find out what was considered to be obvious: that there was a vast difference in the quality of schools attended by nonwhites and those attended by whites. "You know yourself," Coleman told an interviewer, "that the difference is going to be striking."

He was wrong. Coleman was "staggered," in the words of one of his associates. In effect, Coleman found that the effects of the home environment (to be discussed below in greater detail) on school achievement far outweighed any effects the school program had on achievement. Even worse, teacher and school characteristics could not account for the fact that blacks started about six months behind whites in reading in the first grade and ended up 3½ years behind whites in reading in the twelfth grade. The Office of Education (OE) issued a communication stating that the survey "had been carried to its logical conclusion; the Coleman Report is out of print." The findings may have been purposely obscured.

When the Westinghouse-Ohio University (1969) report was published, the Office of Education again, along with some members of the liberal-minority community tried to obscure the findings. The report evaluated Head Start programs, the best-known compensatory strategy, one of the few programs still considered a success at that time by reformers. As mentioned in the previous chapter, the report concluded that from a sample of children from 104 Head Start centers there was no significant difference in learning between Head Start children and a matched control group, and that the program failed to help disadvantaged learners catch up to their middle-class counterparts or to alleviate any of their cognitive deficiencies. Then came the summary analysis of compensatory results by Richard Fairley (1972), the Director of OE's Division of Compensatory Education: of more than 1,200 educational projects evaluated between 1970 and 1972, only ten were found successful on the basis of measurable data.

Jensen's (1969) research concerning the role of heredity over and above environment as a contributing factor in learning, and the major reason compensatory education had failed, sent further shock waves through the liberal-minority community. These findings challenged the American tenet that any individual, given an optimum learning environment, could surmount all other factors that impede learning. Jensen was denounced as a "racist," and he encountered a great deal of harassment and abuse at the hands of many members of the liberal-minority community. Many who tried to mention the genetic component and its effect on learning quickly marched into the fiercest of cross fires. Even Herrnstein (1971) was severely condemned as one of "Hitler's propagandists" for touching lightly on the racial implications of IQ, suggesting that there was some evidence of a genetic factor in the social-class differences, although environment seemed to be the most important factor.

When Jencks, et al. (1972) published their research on *Inequality*, they invited attacks from both the political left and right. They were branded as advocates of both "racism" and "mediocrity." Based on their data, they contended that the most important factor related to school success was the students' characteristics. About 45 percent of cognitive skill, as measured by test scores, could be traced to genes, 35 percent to environment, and 20 percent to a covariance factor. They concluded that as long as everyone had an equal chance there would always be inequality. Compensatory education was doomed to failure; no amount of educational spending could make a significant difference in bringing about total equality in income. Committed to egalitarianism, Jencks, et al., therefore concluded that it would require actual redistribution of income to achieve complete economic equality, regardless of ability.

In the meantime, the Brookings Institute had become a haven for the deposed liberals of the New Frontier and Great Society. The 1972 Brookings study by Schultze, et al. (1972) was a confession, topic by topic, of liberal regret. According to the authors, no person alive could say what programs in schools and communities had been successful. Chapter by chapter, we learned about the failure of one governmental program after another, including compulsory education, job training, urban renewal, and welfare, each of which cost the taxpayers billions of dollars.

The same year, the Rand Corporation, another organization staffed mainly by many liberal social scientists, published a report by Averch and associates (1972) about schools and other related programs in the educational poverty industry. The analysis suggested that, with respect to school financing, we were already spending too much in terms of what we were getting in return. In the early stages of school and related compensatory programs, input increments had a high marginal return; but they gradually diminished until the exchange of input for output was no longer equal, and finally to the point where input was wasted because there was virtually no increase in output. It was concluded that, in many areas of education, we had reached a "flat area," less output in relation to input, or worse, no return.

Representing the conservative view, Boulding (1971) presented the same input-output thesis in a report to the American Educational Research Association, noting that extra input in school programs was not yielding more output. The point of maximum return had long been passed, and the possibility of increasing school productivity seemed improbable. Private industry operating in the same manner as the school industry would have long since closed down because of the losses.

Drucker (1973a, 1973b) made a similar point about governmental spending for educational and social programs. There was little in the record to substantiate the bright beliefs of the 1960s, and the argument that the reason for the failure of these programs was that not enough money was spent. There was no evidence that extra money was the answer, as some liberal-minority groups had proclaimed, while there was sufficient data to support the claim that money already spent had no appreciable results. Implied in his analysis was the need to measure the costs versus effectiveness of these programs. He claimed the need to test our ideas before expanding them, to define our goals and priorities, to coordinate effectively the activities, to postpone making promises until the programs were evaluated and the results were in. Without ever mentioning the word "accountability," he employed the jargon of accountability and in effect advocated it.

Then Daniel Moynihan (1972a, 1972b), former advisor on domestic policies to former President Nixon, raised the issue that educational and social spending was suffused with waste and confusion, that the money spent on compensatory education and antipoverty programs went to the people running the programs and not to the poor. He also criticized extra spending on education, pointing out that close to 70 percent of the operating expenses of the public schools (estimated to be about $49 billion during the 1971–72 school year)[2] went toward salaries, and any increase in educational spending would go mainly to teachers and school administrators. Similarly, he argued there was no need to increase antipoverty spending because it was a failure and the only people who really benefited were a new class of middle-class bureaucrats who were paid to dispense the services and who claimed they were the only ones qualified because of race to dispense these services. He argued that if one-third of the $31 billion spent by the federal government alone in 1971 on social programs for the poor had gone directly to the poor, there would no longer be any poverty in the United States (as we presently define the level). Again without mentioning accountability, there was the implied assumption of the need for accountability in terms of curbing spending and obtaining intended results.

The conservative push toward accountability was vividly illustrated by former President Nixon. In his 1970 educational message, he related dollars spent to student accomplishment and stated: "From these considerations we derive another concept: *Accountability*. School administrators and school teachers alike are responsible for their performance, and it is in their interest as well as in the interest of their pupils that they be held accountable." Three years later, he defended his budget cuts in educational and social programs on the basis that many of these programs were "poorly conceived and hastily put together."

Although the political left and right started their ideological movements from opposite ends of the continuum, it was inevitable they should discover each other in the middle, or at least somewhere on the continuum. Although their ends were opposed, they found they had much in common with their quest for accountability. While the liberal-minority community advocated more money and various programs, the conservative voice felt the programs were generally unworkable because of the difficulties of changing human nature and thus sought better utilization of resources and money. For both the advocates and critics of compensatory education, it was a simple step to accountability.

The current emphasis on accountability places responsibility on teachers and schools for delivering an instructional program that assures student performance and holds school people responsible for performing according to agreed-upon terms. Compensatory education implied something was wrong with the child; under many present concepts of accountability, if the program fails, the teachers or school are at fault. For the compensatory advocates, accountability serves as a second chance to prove the value of compensatory education to the many detractors who were feeling the cost of such government spending in taxes and rising inflation. For the critics of compensatory spending, accountability is a way of enhancing educational productivity, to find out what they are getting for their educational dollar, to establish modes of proof, and to hold down taxes.

Indeed, the controversy over compensatory education led into accountability with the 1970 amendments to Title I of the ESEA, which included a form of responsibility at all levels. Although directed at compensatory spending, it moved the funded schools toward accountability by requiring expenditure and staff data on a school basis. It also required administrators of Title I money to set performance criteria, then to evaluate the programs in line with such criteria. In defending the rationale for this amendment, Fairley (1972) wrote, "Teachers will have a number of sets of data to work with in evaluating their own teaching —and the success or failure of the program they are involved in" (p. 34). Here, it is easy to see how a transfer was made in the accountability movement from evaluating the programs to evaluating the teachers.

In the same vein, both those on the left and those on the right of the political continuum generally accepted Lessinger's (1972a) statement of holding "an agent [school person, board of education, private company, and so on] answerable for performing according to agreed-upon terms, within an established time period, and with stipulated use of resources and performance standards" (p. 217). According to Lessinger (1972b), the school was a malfunctioning machine, and there was need for school systems to adopt private enterprise accountability procedures. It is only a small transition to go from Lessinger's definition of and reasons for accountability to the related demands made by the political left and right. Similarly, both the liberal-minority community and conservative voice agreed with his analysis.

With both ends of the political continuum urging some form of accountability, it was (and still is) safe for almost anyone to advocate accountability, knowing full well they will encounter much support and little criticism. With the politically active groups advocating accountability, the concept takes on a reform image, and almost everyone else falls into line and joins the marching bandwagon. At this juncture in history, accountability has come to mean many different things to many different people. The concept has become linked to many evolving educational trends: in fact it has become a unifying theme related to management by objectives, cost-effectiveness audits, system analysis, performance contracting, voucher plans, community participation and community control, consumer education, competency-based training, assessment of teacher performance, bilingual and bicultural education, program evaluation—and a host of other trends.

While it is this umbrella aspect of accountability which makes it difficult to provide a clear, agreed-upon definition of the term, it is the same broad entity that makes it acceptable to many reformers in education with various political orientations. As Lennon (1971) points out, "accountability means many things to many people, a reason, perhaps, for its easy acceptance" (p. 5). And Lieberman (1970) asserts that many groups and agencies "have a vested interest in promoting accountability" for one reason or another. What is good for one interest group, however, may not necessarily be good for education or "for the country as a whole" (p. 194). His conclusion coincides with one of our major points: "That the underlying issue is not whether to have accountability but what kind of accountability will prevail" (p. 195). Virtually everyone (except most school people) is pushing for some form of accountability; many of the major reform ideas in education are tied up with or advance accountability systems; and for one of the rare occasions, people from both ends of the political continuum agree on an educational issue: the need for introducing a specific measure of responsibility in the schools.

THE EVOLVING CONCEPT OF ACCOUNTABILITY

To date, the most comprehensive accountability models appear to have been developed by Barro (1970), Dyer (1970), and McDonald and Forehand (1973). All three models stress the complexity of the data-gathering process and analysis methods needed to assign responsibility properly to various contributing agents to the educational process. All the authors contend that it is difficult, if not impossible, to disentangle the effects of several contributions to student learning. For this reason, Dyer and McDonald and Forehand suggest that no one individual be held accountable, that instead, the school be matched with similar schools, and the entire staff of the school be held collectively responsible. Each model employs a multiple regression procedure for estimating the contributions of the various agents in the educational process. Interestingly, all the authors have serious doubts about the actual implementation of any accountability plan in the real world. They emphasize the need for caution and, in effect, inform their readers they are advancing a model mainly because the times dictate an accountability plan. While the authors stress the need for research experimentation and verification for their approaches, or for any approach to accountability, this does not seem to be the way trends are shaping up. The general demand is to implement accountability on a mass scale, to ignore pilot testing of ideas, and to worry later about the consequences. But then, this is consistent with many educational trends: a policy based on testing our ideas is often misconstrued by some groups in education as a policy against reform.

It is interesting to note the Dyer and McDonald and Forehand models are directly linked to the New York City accountability plans, which started with the now famous clause in the preamble of the 1969 teacher union contract directing the school board and union to develop an accountability system. The Educational Testing Service was eventually contracted to develop the system. Dyer was former Vice-President of ETS, having since retired, and McDonald was the ETS director who developed the package.

Briefly, Dyer advocates the concept of "joint accountability," where the entire staff is held accountable to the school board for school operations while the board in turn is held accountable for supplying appropriate resources and facilities for each school. He divides his model into four variables: (1) input (characteristics of the students); (2) educational process (activities in the school organized to bring about desirable changes); (3) surrounding conditions (school, home, and community); and (4) output (characteristics of students as they emerge from a particular phase of their schooling). These four variables contain several subvariables and are interrelated and measured to form a School Effectiveness Index (SEI) by which the staff can judge if it is producing hoped-for changes. With this profile, Dyer claims that it is possible for a school to discern in which areas of student progress it is more or less effective with regard to similar schools.

McDonald and Forehand's model also envisions each school as a unit of analysis for comparing student progress and includes provisions for community input which correspond with the school's present system of community control. The authors present a seven-page model: (1) identifying meaningful student performance, (2) identifying achievement goals and descrepancies in achievement, (3) diagnosing causes of achievement and nonachievement, (4) obtaining information about likely causes of discrepancies in achievement, (5) taking corrective action, (6) implementing the plan, and (7) evaluating the plan. The model is cyclical, and yields an on-going Student Development Index (SDI) for schools to make comparisons.

Although there are several specific problems with both models, on a general level both are using pre- and post-test student scores and controlling for differences in pre-test scores to determine which schools are more effective. The pitfalls of this approach are well known among test specialists and will be discussed below in greater detail. In comparing schools, it seems reasonable to adjust for student-teacher-school-community characteristics. But exactly what characteristics are controlled and what kind of weights are to be applied to each item are highly subjective matters. How one controls or considers the racial tensions or political factors of the schools and community is a difficult problem, as yet unresolved. If a minimum of two or three years may be required to permit the school to have an effect on student learning which is large enough to be observed, then controlling for teacher turnover and student turnover, especially in inner-city schools, are problems of concern in any accountability model. In a time when school budgets are being slashed, the accountability system for New York City (which includes about 1.2 million students, 70,000 teachers, 40,000 other professional personnel, and 965 schools), without consultants, would cost about $1 million per year for the technical staff and $600,000 per year ($50,000/100,000 students) for the computer operations. Finally, the implications of "taking corrective action" can easily lead to conflict and confrontations between the teachers and community, thus igniting the already tense racial situation in New York City.

In the meantime, the Nation's Schools (1972) reports that UFT Representative Sandra Feldman warns that accountability is turning into "a political football," with which militant minority groups are promoting conflict between the parents and teachers. Albert Shanker and Walter Degnan, presidents of the city teachers' union and city supervisory association, point out that many community representatives have already reached the conclusion that the teachers and administrators are the only ones responsible for student failure. Racial tension between the predominantly white teachers' union and supervisory association and the minority community, dating back to the 1968 ten-week teachers' strike and the Ocean Hill-Brownsville controversy, still remains in the air. According to Ornstein (1974), similar events (involving community control and accountability) seem to be occurring and subsequently polarizing other large- and medium-sized city school systems. For this reason, there is growing fear by some white teachers and administrators in city school systems that accountability may be used as a political weapon against them—not for educational reasons.

Despite the reservations and pitfalls attendant upon accountability, state legislatures and state officers of public instruction have moved forward with accountability plans of their own, apparently with little caution and less understanding of the implications of accountability. In response to the demand for accountability, state legislators have enacted numerous statutes related to accountability in the last several years. The Cooperative Accountability Project (CAP, 1973a), a 7-state respository for accountability projects,[3] reports that, as of 1972, 23 states had enacted accountability legislation and 9 others were in the process of introducing bills for 1973. CAP (1973c) predicted that approximately 45 states will pass some type of legislation on accountability by 1976. In addition, many state superintendent offices and state educational agencies are developing their own testing and evaluation programs that are in effect accountability plans. As CAP (1973a) notes, "It should not be assumed that states without legislation are not, in fact, establishing and implementing programs in these areas" (p. 4).

The majority of states have taken the position that accountability should be mandatory, leaving the specifics to the discretion of local districts. The laws range in content from definite and explicit to vague and broad guidelines. It is difficult to categorize these laws. Not only do stated sections of the law sometimes have multiple requirements, but the interpretation of the legislation is not always clear. With this in mind, it appears that 13 of the 23 states call for the assessment of students, 10 require management goals and methods of evaluation, 8 require evaluation of personnel (but in only 2 states do personnel have the right to appeal), 5 require citizen involvement, and 2 require cost analysis.

The California, Colorado, Florida, Maryland, and Michigan laws contain some of the jargon commonly found in the accountability literature. At the present, the most comprehensive accountability legislation is that enacted in California. It includes the Stull Act (Assembly Bills 293, 2999) enacted in 1971, the first in the nation that requests certified teacher competence to be partly measured in terms of student performance. Evaluation must include standards of expected student progress in each subject, assessment of personnel related to student progress, follow-up counseling and training for personnel assessed to be less than satisfactory, and dismissal procedures and revocation of certificates based on this evaluation process.[4]

Events in Florida are even more disturbing for many educators. *Phi Delta Kappan* (1973) notes that, as part of the accountability spin-off, bills have been introduced in the legislature which abolish teacher certification in lieu of local (nonuniversity) competency training and abolish all tenure rights. These measures are being advocated for purposes of facilitating accountability plans. The implications of this bill should be obvious to both professors of education and teachers alike. Professors who have been safely sitting on the sidelines and promoting accountability schemes may pay a penalty for their own ideas. As the bandwagon picks up in tempo, and the marching tune becomes louder, political fighting should intensify. And if a large number of teachers and professors find themselves driving trucks, or farmed out to Siberia, we will have learned who lacks the political clout.[5]

What do school people have to say when surveyed on the subject of accountability? According to the NEA Reasearch Division, teachers with negative views on accountability outnumber those with positive views by eleven to one. Both the NEA and AFT have expressed reservations about accountability programs. The National Commission on Teacher Education and Professional Standards (NCTEPS, 1970), one of the NEA affiliates, contends that teachers must decide "matters that relate directly to teaching . . . and by what standards teachers shall be prepared, . . . retained, dismissed, certified, and given tenure." It views the growing demands of accountability advocates as impinging on the teachers' professionalism (p. 3). The NEA maintains that the accountability movement is a "warped attempt to apply business-industrial models to learning," and that it threatens "more and more students and teachers [with] punitive, ill-conceived, and probably inoperable legislation and directives." Accountability misapplied, the organization continues, can lead "to educational fascism—compelling . . . educators and students to comply with inhumane, arbitrarily set requirements." (p. 1) And David Selden (1972), president of the AFT, feels that "accountability offers ready teacher scapegoats to amateur and professional school-haters," and that accountability advocates are approaching the idea "with all the insight of an irate viewer 'fixing' a television set: Give it a kick and see what happens." (p. 50)[6]

And Stephen Hencley (1971), writing for the Midwest Administration Center, uses the term "techno-urban-fascism" to describe accountability. The characteristics of this type of "fascism" include centralized planning, technological procedures for social purposes, and rigid, humaneless processes for behavioral manipulation. He sees accountability as implying a need to (1) centralize decision-making about teaching, (2) reduce the autonomy of teachers by viewing them as hired hands, (3) base pay on incremental gains based on standardized tests, similar to industrial piecework, (4) subvert collective bargaining by replacing contracts with accountability agreements, and (5) punish and scapegoat teachers by fixing blame for student performance inadequacies.

PROBLEMS INHERENT IN ACCOUNTABILITY

Surely most people agree that everyone, including teachers and school administrators, should be held accountable for their work. What many educators object to, even fear, is the oversimplified concept which defines accountability as the sole responsibility of the teacher or principal. Many different people have various impacts on student learning, and they should also be held accountable if we are going to employ a constructive model. The corollary to this is that behavior (learning) is never the exclusive product of one stimulus or set of stimuli provided by one person (teacher or administrator); it follows that no human being (school person) should be held totally responsible for the behavior of another person (student). Those responsible for student performance include not only teachers and administrators, but also parents, community residents, school board members, taxpayers, government officials, and, most important, the students themselves—for the learners' health and physical conditions, cognitive abilities, motivation, and self-concept, family background, and even age all affect learning.

For example, many accountability advocates tell us that we must ignore family characteristics, because they are used to alibi student failure. This ignores a wealth of research data that consistently shows that the family is the most important variable associated with student achievement scores, and all other factors are secondary. The analysis in the Coleman Report (1966), which took two years and included 600,000 children, 60,000 teachers, and 4,000 schools; the reanalysis by Mayeske and associates (1970) of the Coleman data; Jencks, et al. (1972) four-year study which included the Coleman schools; Project Talent's longitudinal study of students in more than 100 high schools, plus many smaller studies; and data from the International Studies in Evaluation (1973), commonly referred to as the Stockholm Report, a longitudinal study which took seven years to complete and is based on data concerning 260,000 students, 50,000 teachers, and 9,700 schools in 19 countries, are just samples of the noted research studies which show that home background is the most important variable linked to student achievement. Another variable that affects student learning is classmate characteristics. Only a small fraction of the independent variation in student achievement is explained by school variables, and only a small part of this variation is attributable to teachers. A series of studies by Brophy (1972), Rosenshine (1970), and Soar (1966) puts the highest correlation in the low .30's, a reliability correlation that would be considered too low to use in developing educational measurements.[7] Yet accountability implies holding the teacher responsible for student performances—connoting at best the lay public's oversimplification or ignorance of the learning process and, at worst, the rise of politics in education and the antiteacher syndrome that is spreading across the nation.

Advocates of accountability usually subscribe to the environmental theory of intellectual development. Good. But accountability advocates either have not done their homework or ignore that most environmentalists subscribe to Bloom's (1964) series of longitudinal studies as the most important piece of research in this area. Based on his research, Bloom points out that 50 percent of the child's general intelligence is developed by age four, another 30 percent by the age of eight, and the remaining 20 percent by age seventeen. His estimates are that 33 percent of general learning as based on achievement indices takes place between birth and age four, that another 17 percent takes place between the ages of four and six, and still another 17 percent takes place between the ages of six and nine. Thus, the most important growing period for intellectual development and academic learning is before the child enters school. He further points out that all subsequent learning is determined by what the child has already learned.

What this suggests is that the most important years for changing learning outcomes are the early years. Most accountability advocates not only fail to recognize that educators are therefore working against overwhelming odds to effect changes with students who show deficits in learning, but also that the change problems become increasingly more difficult as we progress through the grades and attempt to hold teachers and administrators accountable for older students. Thus a ninth-grade class with a two-year average deficit in reading provides a more difficult change problem than a sixth-grade class with a two-year deficit. Similarly, two seventh-grade classes with the same reading average but with different ranges in test scores cannot be equated, although one might assume so since the averages are similar. The class with a lower range presents a more difficult change proglem.[8] With extreme cases, we need a more powerful environment to effect positive changes.

In addition to the environmental factors impacting on learning, which presently compound the problem of assessing student learning, the testing procedures and instruments used to measure changes in learning are subject to question. Most standardized achievement and reading tests given to students contain about thirty to fifty questions. The students who score low on the tests obviously have answered few questions correctly. If a student answered only ten questions correctly on the initial test, being able to answer an extra five questions on the post-test is easier for him (because of chance variation) than someone who had almost all the items correct on the first test. In addition, being able to answer an extra five questions would place him very much higher on the relative score than would a gain score of five questions when the initial score was twenty correct answers. In this connection Tyler (1970) points out when pre/post testing slow or less able students, changes in standardized test scores for an individual student may largely be the result of chance variation or guessing, because both scores are based on a very small sample of knowledge, abilities, or skills.[9]

Another pre- and post-test problem is created by what we call "cellar" and "ceiling" effects. The first of these effects refers to a test that is so difficult that it does not measure accurately at the bottom, and the second of these effects refers to a test that fails to measure at the top end because it is too easy. In the cellar effect, less able students are penalized; and in the ceiling effect, more able students are penalized because they cannot show the real gains they have made. In both instances, the scores tend to be unreliable; moreover, whenever we are dealing in extreme scores, it is common knowledge that the coefficient of reliability is low. Obviously it would be advantageous for teachers or school administrators to use a difficult measurement for the pre-test and an easy one for the post-test, as well as to utilize cellar or ceiling effects, depending on their student population.

As a further problem, Klein (1971) and Stake (1971) point out that changes in pre- and post-test scores may illustrate "regression" effects, where the lowest original scores make the greatest gains and the higher original scores make the least. Post-test scores, relative to their corresponding pre-test scores, tend to change in the direction of the mean. These "regression" effects make the low-achieving students look better the next time tested. In contrast to the "regression" problem is the fact that Soar (1973) has found data indicating that students who initially make low scores gain little on post-tests, as do students who initially have high scores. However, students who are initially tested toward the middle tend to gain on the second test. One possible reason for this is that the change in scores may be due to the larger error of measurement of average scores. Another possibility is that the change situation may not be as much a matter of testing as of learning rate. Average students are often considered hardworking, and they will most likely take advantage of instruction—or learn more on their own than less able students. Given the "regression" effects and Soar's findings, if students are ability grouped, teachers assigned one ability group rather than another will be found to be more "effective" teachers despite the fact that the pre- and post-test results may have little bearing on the the teacher's effectiveness.

To add another problem to our list, it should be noted that raw scores on tests are transferred to grade equivalents. According to Lennon (1971), a raw score gain of not more than two or three points is sufficient to account for an improvement of one grade level placement, say from 9.0 to 10.0, as measured by most reading tests for the secondary level. And Stake (1971) reports that a range of three to eight items is sufficient to account for an improvement of one grade level placement for most of the popular batteries used in elementary schools. Indeed, test-wise students can easily guess a few items correctly on the second test. Even without coaching, this change is well within the error of measurement of an individual score. In other words, a change in one grade level may be a direct indicator of the probable extent of error in any test score, even among highly reliable measurements. Even with measures that have reliability coefficients in say the low .90 range, which is as high a level as is reached by most commonly used batteries, the reliability of gain from pre- and post-test measures comes from two fallible scores and the error variances from them summate.

Overriding the above concern is the fact that learning comes in irregular increments. As Bloom (1964), Erikson (1950), and Piaget (1959) point out, human growth including learning, does not occur in equal units of time. Furthermore, Beggs and Hieronymus (1968) and Gates and MacGinitie (1965) point out that learning comes in irregular increments, varying with the season; winter is the time of most rapid advancement and summer, the time of least. All these variations simply mean that learning does not take place at a constant rate, age, or grade level; thus the quality of instruction is not always the major factor involved in learning variation. Yet the opposite assumptions are usually made when we interpret pre- and post-test scores. We fail to recognize that some teachers may be penalized by students who are experiencing a slow rate of human growth, while other teachers may be at an advantage because they are working with students of the same grade who are developing at a faster rate. Similarly, it is possible that students in a given period of human development, slow or fast, may be ready to learn one subject more rapidly than another because different learning skills and maturation abilities are required. Randomly assigning students to teachers may reduce this problem; however, it would negate the advantages that may accrue in matching learning styles and rates with specific teaching styles.

We are further hampered by the fact that we do not have test measurements that can reliably appraise score changes over a brief period, say nine months, from September to June. Besides the variations in the rate of learning, the increments of change are small with short time intervals. Put in a different way, the effect on student learning a teacher or school has in a year is usually too small to measure with accuracy. Nevertheless, most accountability plans call for testing at the beginning and at the end of the school year, with the information thus derived being used to evaluate teacher performance or school effectiveness.

We also get into the difficulty of equating two different tests. Under most conditions, the best procedure is to use parallel or alternative forms of the same test. The trouble is, even these tests are usually not exactly uniform. The tests often fail to represent change in terms of approximate equality of units and absolute zero points. Thus changes in test scores may represent differences in units of measurement rather than actual learning. While we need truly parallel measurements to assess changes in learning, the problem is further compounded when we take into consideration the changing nature of a particular human characteristic (such as learning) and the need to make it mesh with the approximate units of the measurements of that characteristic. [10]

Then there is the temptation of teaching to the test, given a system where jobs or money are involved with some extraneous factor as test-taking skills. In fact, we already know this has occurred in the Florida teacher accountability program and with other forms of accountability, such as performance contracting. The person who is being held responsible has a choice, teaching what the students should learn or what they must know to pass a particular test. According to Klein (1971) the choice is obvious, because the benchmark against which progress is measured is based not on whether the student has been taught, but on whether his post-test scores show improvement. Grobman (1972) puts it in more diplomatic terms: "What is measured becomes important in the words of teachers and students. If memory is measured but inquiry oriented exploration is not, if rote learning is measured but building self-concept is not, it is clear where the emphasis will be" (p. 65). In fact, it is possible to conclude that the practical teacher or administrator, just to play it safe, may spend almost all of the pre/post test time interval "helping" students take the exit test to ensure they do well. Why not? Performance is going to be judged by inappropriate tests and testing procedures; the results may be published in the school or local papers, and people's jobs may depend on the results of these tests.

What does all this mean? In simple terms, scores on pre- and post-tests vary for a number of reasons which have little to do with the quality of instruction or the school program, and have more to do with a host of technical and human considerations. The above discussion is only a sample of the problems associated with pre- and post-tests, and they are mentioned only because the method of accountability now being adopted utilizes this kind of testing situation. Actually, there are hundreds of other problems dealing with test design and format, test conditions, reliability and validity—all of which have resulted in the publication of several texts.

Educators also point out that existing standardized tests, called *normative-referenced tests*, were constructed to measure the status of an individual or group at a particular time in relation to a large norm group. These tests do not accurately measure changes in learning. As soon as we attempt to infer change by comparing two measures of status, this results in low reliability and invalid change indices as compared to the satisfactory measures of status. Furthermore, Ornstein and Talmadge (1973a) have pointed out that normative measures do not contain a sufficient number of questions covering the material on which the student was working to furnish a dependable answer to the question—or to hold someone accountable.

Some accountability advocates argue that *criterion-referenced tests* can be constructed for the competencies to be learned, and thus we can include a much larger sample of appropriate questions. In theory, this is true. But most tests of this type are in the infancy stages of development, and questions concerning reliability and validity are only now being discussed in psychometric literature. In the accountability literature is expressed the misguided notion that these tests can be easily and quickly developed. As Lennon (1971) points out, "the truth is quite the opposite. The methods for development of criterion-referenced tests are less well explicated than those for the development of norm referenced tests" (p. 13). It is also unclear how to translate measurement units into units of gain or achievement.[11] Most important, the problems associated with pre- and post-testing still remain unresolved, which brings us back to the original problem of misuse of tests and abuse of accountability schemes. Suffice it to say, then, that many existing accountability systems utilize inappropriate testing procedures; thus accountability as presently being developed and implemented in many places almost borders on quackery.

Test specialists are well aware of the many problems associated with accountability schemes, and realize that simple pre- and post-tests cannot accurately evaluate the effect of treatment. We must be careful and adopt more sophisticated measures which will take several years to work out. But we are not heading in this direction; in fact, the majority of accountability advocates reject test experts as caretakers of the Establishment, and many black educators increasingly look upon those who are engaged in testing and research with suspicion and distrust, condemning them as victims of their own Anglo-Western history culture. On the other hand, the conservative community is generally looking to save money and may not be interested in spending more money on more tests. You cannot have testing both ways. First the accountability advocates want to use test procedures to validate accountability while disregarding the cautions by scholars in the field, then most of them dismiss the data forthcoming from tests when doing so serves their ideological purposes.

Accountability usually presumes that the schools know how students learn. The trouble is, we have several competing ideas about learning that introduce further difficulty in relating learning to accountability. These competing ideas range from Bereiter and Englemann's (1966) drill approach, which tends to encourage student anxiety and discourages interpersonal relations, to Skinner (1968), who breaks down learning into behavioral conditioning motivation and programmed learning, to the progressive philosophers who frown upon drill and behavioral conditioning and treat learning in terms of developing the whole child and teaching broad concepts. Also, implicit in the idea of accountability is the expectation that available tests can measure learning with sufficient precision. As illustrated above, this is not true; moreover, many of the things we are concerned with, such as conceptual thinking, creativity, and humane learning, we do not know how to measure.

There is also concern that accountability encourages instruction toward narrowly defined behaviors that are immediate target outcomes and presumably form the basis of assessment. Implied is the idea that only the things we can measure are important. This view toward education is simplistic and undesirable, and overlooks the fact that there are human transactions in the classroom that cannot easily be assessed but may be equally as important as learning how to count or read. When we deal with people in a learning environment, we are dealing with feelings, emotions, and spontaneous acts. The accountability system ignores the reality of human interaction, that much of teaching and learning has little to do with intended goals and quantified outcomes. As Adams (1972) states, "It seems . . . that nothing is more absurd than thinking that we measure all results worth achieving; what we in fact end up measuring may be trivial, insipid, and useless." The whole process of channeling learning to preconceived objectives "may very well waste the best human powers to learn" and may even destroy much of what "is creative, imaginative, and innovative" in teaching and learning (pp. 25–26). According to Dyer (1971) we may very well wind up teaching children "to pass tests at the expense of learning to hate the subject in which we test them; or to hate the whole idea of learning" (p. 4).

The accountability systems are very much tied up to the achievement of cognitive objectives at the lower end of Bloom's (1956) taxonomy of educational objectives, with emphasis on memorization of data for purposes of passing a test. Higher-order cognitive thinking or objectives in the affective domain are seldom encompassed because they are difficult to assess. And Nash and Agne (1971) write that overzealous preoccupation with behavioral and quantifiable outcomes will make teachers deaf to competencies and learning "in areas that do not lend themselves to precise assessment" (p. 148). A teacher who is found to emphasize low-level cognitive skills may well become oblivious to other areas of learning, especially to feelings, attitudes, and emotions. In this vein, Combs (1972) points out that the way the present system of accountability intends to utilize behavioral outcomes "would produce not intelligent persons but automatons." Intelligent behavior is produced by including problem solving and higher-level skills and educational experiences that extend "beyond the learning of precisely defined skills" (p. 12).

When people become obsessed with measurable outcomes, standardized tests, and short-range pre- and post-time intervals, we are bound to ignore the long-range goals that make a complete person and benefit society. We are likely to ignore imagination and creativity, civil rights and duties, loyalty and patriotism, physical, social, and ethical development, the aesthetic components of life, ability to fit harmoniously into home, family, and society. In short, the expedient procedure to assess some short-range objective while ignoring others may lead to long-term failure of the schools. We no longer serve students when learning is subordinated to precise outcomes and rigid timetables, when there is little time to think creatively or about sociopsychological development because the outcome is not being measured; it seems that we defeat the whole purpose of education when we meet the obligations under the present and narrowly defined accountability plans.

Now this does not mean that behavioral objectives, and related educational and quantifiable outcomes, have no place in education. Using behavioral objectives is only one method for evaluation; it should never become all-embracing, a sanctified idea system that rewards or penalizes school people. Teaching and learning are far too complex and are tied up with too many factors that cannot be broken down into precise and measurable units. When we combine behavioral objectives with teacher assessment and job tenure, the whole teaching process becomes at best, rigid and compulsive and, at worst, politically oriented and somewhat reminiscent of 1984 where deviations from intended goals are treated as heretical. Under the guise of making education more scientific, we may create a scientific nightmare.

Having evolved the concept of behavioral objectives, it is a simple step to go from quantifying educational outcomes to guaranteeing them. The fact is, it is impossible to guarantee the test score of an individual student, or to set a minimum standard in the same way private industry guarantees its product. The management and industrial analogy of accountability, with specific goals, quality control systems, preestablished levels of skills, minimum performance levels, time requirements, warranties, human factor engineering, cost-effectiveness analysis, and so on, overlooks the fact that teaching involves people and not nuts and bolts. The great diversity of human talent, the varying conditions of the home and peer group, and the processes in which people interact make this uniformity impossible. Human learning is too complex to break down into prescribed goals and guaranteed outcomes; furthermore, the school does not exercise control over input factors as industrial management does.

We fail to recognize that private industry makes many mistakes and has many defective products which are either absorbed as losses or passed on to the consumer as seconds under different labels, or recalled as defects. Indeed, the story of the Corvair and thalidomide are noted examples of industrial mistakes that resulted in death for many users. The private entrepreneur has clearly demonstrated that his uppermost concern is not the public interest, but profit. Big business has demonstrated that for money it will build bombs, pollute the water we drink and the air we breathe, and exploit the wealth and labor of other countries under the guise of progress. We have already witnessed what the private sector will do to capture the educational market: hand out candy bars, green stamps, radios, and money to increase student productivity and teach the test to ensure profits. Despite the so-called efficiency and guarantees of private companies, they did not improve student learning under OEO grants which cost the taxpayer $6.5 million.

If the management analogy of accountability is rejected, what can be accepted? A school can be held accountable for the scope and quality of services it provides to its students. As Lindeman (1971) contends, it can guarantee a class size, say of not more than 25 students, or that all students reading below grade level will receive special tutoring for 30 minutes each day. Regardless of the controls put on a school, however, it cannot guarantee the individual student's test performance as implied by the management analogy.

THE POLITICS OF ACCOUNTABILITY

Anyone who views accountability solely in terms of educational reform is either naïve or masking his real intentions. As is discussed in the next chapter, the process of schooling is largely political—who makes what decisions—and linked to economic considerations—not only who gets what jobs in the future, but who gets what jobs *now*. When we talk about accountability, we are also talking about who will make decisions about who will be held accountable, whether the same standards will be used to judge different teachers and administrators. If caution is not carefully exercised, racial and ethnic factors can become a major variable. We may be heading toward preferential treatment of minorities in hiring and promotion procedures throughout the job sector, where equal opportunity is turning into quotas, a practice also on the increase in city school systems, colleges, and universities (Rabb, 1972; Seabury, 1972; Seligman, 1973).

Initially a tool of the political right in response to what appeared as reckless government spending on compensatory programs and the continuous failures of such programs, accountability has become a catchword of the political left. Almost all the demands for community control are accompanied by demands to hold professionals accountable (Carmichael and Hamilton, 1967; Fantini, et al. 1970). For some proponents of reform, accountability has very little to do with good teaching and administrative abilities; it is a potential weapon which can be used by local community boards against specific groups or individuals—to hire, promote, or discharge on the basis of color or ethnicity and not merit. In fact many militant spokesmen are already claiming that, given the background and biases of whites, the latter are unable to relate to minorities and are unqualified to teach minorities (and in the same vein to dispense social and community services, conduct research in minority communities, judge minority literary works, poetry, films, and so on).

The political and economic implications of this logic should be clear to readers. Race, ethnicity, and ideology have never been recognized as elements that define good teaching or administration. Yet today they are sometimes considered as assets for minorities to capitalize on and as liabilities to exclude whites in minority communities and related educational, social, and cultural services. [12] While most school officials do not subscribe to this philosophy, recent actions in schools and colleges across the country show that many surrender to such racial and ideological demands in order to keep peace and not risk violence by militant groups or lawsuits by civil rights groups.

Today's increasing militancy of minority groups also makes it sometimes questionable whether incompetent minority teachers and administrators can or will be held accountable in the same way as whites, or if the former can be held accountable at all. Not only has it become a political liability in some cities to question the formal qualifications of minority-group members, but affirmative-action programs now urge eliminating test standards, even lowering standards for minorities. If militant ideology increases and if government goals and timetables continue to transform into quotas and reverse discrimination, heredity may become more important than competency. The net result may be that only white teachers and administrators are held accountable in some cities; at best, there may be a double standard for judging the performance of minority and white educators. [13]

When we talk about accountability, we are also talking about licensing procedures, what determines fitness to perform professional tasks competently, what power groups establish professional performance standards, and whether dual standards should be used in the name of equal opportunity for teaching and supervisory jobs. In this connection, the National Teachers Examination, English grammar qualifying tests, and even science and mathematics tests have been dispensed with in many larger school systems. Thus, for example, the NAACP has joined some educators in New York City and San Francisco in saying that such tests do not measure "merit and fitness" for the jobs involved and that the test questions are "culturally biased." In Chicago another testing procedure has evolved. The Chicago board of education has recently changed the principal's examination, eliminating most of the questions on science, mathematics, and English grammar, and has replaced them with questions on human relations and education. One could argue the latter group of questions are more relevant for the job, or one could argue that they are soft questions, geared to help minority groups pass the examination. But nowhere have the reformers proposed new licensing procedures or criteria for professional qualifications based on solid empirical evidence. The question that must be asked is: do affirmative-action programs provide a better guarantee of professional excellence than do the former testing procedures that sought to measure competence in writing, subject-matter knowledge, and job aptitude?

When we talk about accountability, then, we are also talking about which teachers and administrators get hired and fired. Are we not talking about power, as well as professional competence? Are we not talking about attenuating professional standards for one group and maintaining standards for another group, or possibly implementing different standards in the city school systems, as well as accountability?

One might raise the question that many of the demands for accountability come from white liberal educators. Many are reformers who latch onto the catchy slogans in current vogue. What propels them to ride each crest? Some are the writers of proposals, books, and articles, and consultants to and evaluators of new programs funded by governmental agencies and private foundations that have been notorious for dispensing monies on the basis of catchwords and slogans. Accountability is fashionable for the present. It's where the money is: hence, it is where many of the advocates of reform are, too. However, the performance records of innovative programs leave much to be desired. Many school systems will have to pick up the pieces when change possibly turns into conflict and chaos.

Certainly there is little evidence that accountability will reform the schools. The argument that Johnny cannot read because he was not taught is simplistic and is a distortion on the part of both the militant left and right. In addition, working-class and middle-class groups are reacting to the general inflation in costs and rise of taxes, and thus want to hold teachers accountable for salaries paid to them. While these people have little control over their federal taxes, a significant percentage of which is redistributed into educational and social programs to help poor and minority groups, they control local taxes and can vent their frustrations by voting down school bonds and budgets. In the meantime, parents of unsuccesful children are beginning to assert pressure in many big cities and wish to hold school people responsible for their children's performance. As Davies (1973) points out, a "credibility gap" exists between what the general public expects from schools and what they actually get. What Davies overlooks, and what many others fail to grasp, is that sadly the "credibility gap" is generated partly by school authorities who advertise and claim credit for student successes but try to ignore and disclaim student failures. More important, the credibility gap is enlarged by educational reformers, especially egalitarians, who tend to promise more than they can deliver. Paradoxically, the spending and reform road of the left eventually intersects the road of the right for slowing down spending and change. Where the roads intersect, there is agreement, and there is the accountability clamor.

FUTURE ISSUES

As we implement accountability programs in the schools, for better or worse, some questions will need to be answered. How do we translate generalities into specifics? How do we replace rhetoric with reason? Can we accurately measure changes in learning? Who determines who will be held accountable—and for what? How can we safeguard teachers from being scapegoated? Dare teachers and administrators state the simple truth: that the students, parents, and community must also assume responsibility?

Unless and until we answer most of these questions satisfactorily, the possibility that accountability will enhance the teaching profession may never have a chance. Too quick adoption of the concept, coupled with failure to work out inherent problems, may lead to conflict and chaos and, even worse, to a scheme to punish and to scapegoat educators by fixing total blame on them for student performance. Accountability, like so many other educational ideas, can be used by individuals who wish to attack and divide the educational system, and it can be used to advance self-serving and group interests. On the other hand, at least in theory, it can be used by educators to think more clearly about the goals of reform and methods for achieving these goals.

It must be understood that the schools, especially the public schools, have been increasingly burdened with the tasks and responsibilities that other social institutions no longer do well, or care to do. The schools have been asked to develop the child's human potential, regardless of his background or ability, to educate him as best as possible, to make him into a healthy and viable citizen. As Jennings (1972) points out, society, having directed responsibility for educating the child to the schools, now envisions school people "as ideal agents to be made accountable to the rest of society for the quality and quantity of educational results" (p. 333).

It must be constantly reemphasized that it is impossible to distinguish the multiple causes affecting student learning, and it is certainly wrong and unfair to attribute all of a child's success or failure in school to his teacher or his principal. Similarly, there is need to point out again that most student learning is associated with family characteristics, an idea that has been consistently verified by the research. No one, including teachers and school administrators, should be held accountable for something they have little control over. The most we can reasonably do is to hold school people responsible for seeing that they continually try to better the quality of education for all children in all schools, within the limits imposed by the abilities of the child and the conditions of the school.

In view of the multiple influences that affect learning and the student input and school characteristics teachers and administrators inherit, any system of accountability directed solely or mainly at school people is, at best, oversimplified and unfair and at worst, connotes a negative political and economic whip to be used against educators. Teachers do not fear evaluation; in fact, many of them welcome it and prefer that supervisors observe, evaluate, and make recommendations in a constructive manner. What teachers and administrators fear is that accountability, as it is presently being developed, will lead to an evaluation for purposes of partisan politics, ethnic favoritism, and salary restrictions.

Educational accountability often carries with it the presumption of guilt. If we listen to many of the accountability advocates, the schools are failing to do their job, and the teachers are at fault. We all know that in judging a situation, a filtering process exists. As Weiss (1973) contends, if our minds are already made up that the school people are at fault, then we know what the verdict will be before the jury passes judgment. We also know that when a committee or group empowered with the authority to pass judgment gives the verdict, it is difficult to rescind the charge and the presumption of innocence is hard to sustain. "When we investigate possible evils, we expect we will find them" (p. 22). After all, why spend all the money in evaluating school personnel and holding them accountable, unless we can then *do something*, such as get rid of some of them. As Landers (1973) points out, "The fears of teachers are both predictable and understandable if a system of accountability is to be used primarily as a device for getting rid of teachers. . . . One does not have to agree with these fears to recognize that they exist" (p. 541). A number of recent court cases in California (which reaffirmed that schools are not responsible for student performance) and in Iowa (which reaffirmed that a teacher cannot be fired because her students fail to perform well on tests) underscores this fact.

Getting rid of incompetents may be a worthwhile enterprise; but for many groups, evaluating school people may have more political and ideological than educational implications. In a well-run school system, professional people can be trusted to render opinions about employees. Most administrators know how to make judgments without being vindictive. In the context of today's political and social trends, it is doubtful if most outside groups, especially from the extreme ends of the political continuum, will act dispassionately for the good of education.

All groups must protect their vital interests, and school people are no different. In view of present trends, it makes sense for the teaching profession to consider that individuals or groups who make decisions regarding who is accountable for what are not always acting out of good will or in the interests of the majority, much less those of the group being held accountable.

Few people would disagree with the theory of accountability. What we find fault with is the present implementation of the theory. Present accountability systems tend to carry with them a presumption of guilt and negative reasons for their implementation. In addition, many of the systems border on narrow and misguided practices. But we recognize the fact that accountability is here to stay, at least for the foreseeable future. With this in mind we end with the following summary statements and recommendations to help safeguard professional integrity:

1. Each school system must take a hard look at the accountability plans being developed. Responsible officials, both lay and professional, must be prepared to impose restraints and regulations so as not to scapegoat educators or to promote educational malpractice.

2. It is important for school people to take the initiative in working with parents and community members in defining accountability, and, at the same time, to help parents and citizens understand the input factors and school conditions and learn what they can reasonably expect from the schools. Any accountability plan must deal with the public view and understanding of accountability. Any acceptance of a new plan, including accountability, depends to a large extent on the knowledge of lay people and their existing relationship with educators.

3. School people should share in determining accountability systems. Against the backdrop of educational trends, this may not happen. Teachers and school administrators must be involved in all stages of development and coordination of accountability plans. The less they are involved, the more vulnerable they are and the greater the likelihood that the profession will be weakened.

4. It is insufficient for local districts to duplicate similar efforts or establish individual accountability tests and evaluation processes. Assuming a viable accountability system could be developed in practice, it would be more realistic and less costly if all activities were coordinated at the state level. Without trying to create

bureaucratic overload, one central office would do a more efficient job and could more easily hire the technical staff required. Centralization would also reduce overlap and waste and guard against local ideological impediments.

5. Accountability plans should not be implemented on a mass scale without careful pilot testing and verification of intended results. Procedures will need to be refined and modified as problems arise. Full implementation without carefully testing ideas, the direction in which many school districts now seem to be headed, may result in many technical problems, professional dangers, and political hazards.

6. Judgment of quality of instruction and the school program should be made by school people themselves, under the assumption —perhaps somewhat idealistic—that they are capable of and willing to do an honest job. Just as professional organizations are in charge of accreditation and self-study procedures, educators should be in charge of evaluating accountability systems. However, each school should be visited annually by at least one public committee that would make a public report—thus possibly reducing problems and tensions that may otherwise arise and snowball.

7. To help safeguard against unfair and invalid evaluations of individuals, the best procedure is to compare similar schools and to use the information for purposes of self-evaluation and for improving the entire school program, that is, to ask what the more successful schools are doing that is different from what the less successful schools are doing and to try to implement appropriate program changes.

8. If individual teachers and administrators are to be evaluated, grievance and appeal committees must be established with adequate professional representation. Anyone evaluated as less than satisfactory may be required to attend in-service training. But rulings that involve loss of job or certification are, at present, overzealous, considering how little we know about what a good teacher or administrator is, and about the subjective factors related to assessment.

9. It is safe to assume that teachers, regardless of their ethnic backgrounds, are drawn from a similar manpower pool and have similar abilities. There should be little difference in percentage of the average performance among different ethnic groups of teachers in similar schools. If one ethnic group appears to be rated unsatisfactory in a given school or school district considerably more often than another group, an investigation may be war-

ranted to protect against intimidation of, or favoritism toward, one group.

10. We will have to guard against the possible danger of pitting human beings against each other, especially if jobs and certification are at stake. If we are not careful, we may unnecessarily unleash aggressive tendencies. We may find present tensions over test scores being stretched to the breaking point, where a ruthless battle is waged over scores in conjunction with a new style of technical and bureaucratic competition. The whole idea of competition, performance standards, test skills, profits, and penalties may reduce some school staffs to warring camps with multiple scapegoats.

11. Ideally the school districts or state agencies should provide guides or data for professionals and lay people alike about test problems and errors of measurement scores. Two separate reports may be necessary. These would be similar in content, but the one intended for parents and citizens would be written without the technical jargon.

12. The pre- and post-test accountability model that fixates on time periods of one- or two-grade intervals needs to be modified. It is important to recognize that a host of problems arise in interpreting score changes and that we lack sophisticated tests that accurately measure changes in learning over short periods. Until appropriate tests are available, the measurement of change will remain largely fortuitous, and implementation of accountability will tend to be defective.

13. Norms for changes in learning will have to be established for students of different ages, abilities, socioeconomic backgrounds, and so on to fit specific learning objectives. If the major student input variables (such as the above), as well as major school characteristics (such as classroom size, amount of materials, and staff characteristics), are considered, we will need large categories and advanced statistical procedures. The trouble is, there are not enough students in most school districts (except perhaps New York City, Los Angeles, and Chicago), even in some states, for appropriate categories. Unless we operate on a state and, in some instances, regional basis, we will wind up with nonexistent change norms.

14. At the present, most accountability systems center on a narrow range of abilities and learning outcomes. One would hope that other skills and domains of human development would be considered. Rather than dealing in short-term outcomes, there is need to consider long-term goals. We need to keep in mind just what

kind of human beings we want our children to become; this means a long-term and future orientation.

15. Finally, accountability should be a process by which we can evaluate ourselves: how to teach better, how to improve the school program, how to turn out a better student.

CONCLUSION

The concept of accountability is spreading throughout the country. This is happening regardless of the fact that there are several problems inherent in the models, not least of which is a lack of understanding that different models of accountability make different sets of demands on different groups. In addition, accountability is plagued by difficulties in measuring learning, by lack of research evidence to show that it benefits students, and by lack of arrangements for formally evaluating these models on a pilot basis before plunging ahead. Mass implementation without verification is senseless, reflecting little more than political ideology and educational bandwagonism.

What we need is a common language and some comparisons which permit self-examination and openness on all sides of the philosophical, racial, and political dividing lines. We need to put away our political and economic motives, to talk to one another as persons concerned for the welfare of all students. We need to advocate the importance of research, not rhetoric. We must provide a forum that permits us to understand fully issues such as the concept of accountability before advocating any idea as one certain cure-all.

NOTES

1. The term liberal often connotes different meanings to different people. In the next two chapters, it is used to refer to a group that leans toward the left center, and sometimes further left, on the political continuum. With regard to the War on Poverty and civil rights movement, compounded by various groups who claim the privileges of "minority" status, the liberal tends to romanticize these groups and deny objective criticism of them. He tends to reject the 1960 coalition politics of labor and minority groups of the old Democratic party as being outmoded and irrelevant. Similarly, the liberal tends to ignore the interests and now rights of the working class and middle class; his contempt for them is sometimes very obvious, ranging from spiteful intellectual bigotry in terms of his prose to overlooking their existence because he feels they are not newsworthy and do not threaten the system.

2. See *Digest of Educational Statistics* (1972), tables 1, 6-8, 23, 25. The school industry is the largest industry in the country. During the 1971–72 school year, there were some 45.9 million students in public elementary and secondary schools (K-12), 2.1 million teachers, 133,000 school administrators, and 17,955 school districts—all costing taxpayers $48.8 billion. Not only does public education directly involve almost 25 percent of the populace either in a learner or job capacity, the percentage soars to approximately 75 percent when we include higher education, job training, and adult education. The portion of the GNP for education doubled from calendar year 1955 to 1971, and the actual costs quadrupled from $16.8 billion to $85.1 billion. With the increasing scope of education and public outlay of money, the school industry eventually had to come under close scrutiny of the public domain.

3. Colorado, Florida, Maryland, Michigan, Minnesota, Oregon, and Wisconsin.

4. Also see CAP (1973 *b*) and Redfern (1973).

5. The reader must understand that policy makers, whether on the city, state, or federal level, rarely read the professional literature concerning the policy they are deciding. What they often read are the newspapers and a few popular magazines; by accident they may come across an item that is policy related and make a mental note. For the greater part, governmental officials spend their time in caucus and committee meetings, citizen meetings, and social parties. The rest of their professional time is mainly devoted to getting reelected or elected to a new post. Policy makers react to the demands of their constituents and the general climate of change. For this reason, public policy is not always based on what is sound and rational but on what is expedient and practical.

Legislative bodies depend on social scientists and consultants to keep them abreast and to advise them on subjects related to their policy domain. These researchers or change agents, because they are human, are limited by their own values and biases and often present a view that coincides with their own version of the "truth." They write their documents and present their arguments in the way they view the world. Often these people are promoting their own political and economic self-interests and group interests; rarely do they represent the teaching profession. There is no absolute way for policy makers, assuming they have good intentions, to discern always just what is subjective or objective, what is misleading or accurate, what data is being purposely omitted or included in the reports or discussions. Because of the aura of expertise, and because these consultants are being paid for their services, legislative bodies are sometimes influenced by them. With so many people advocating accountability for various reasons, the consultants are bound to do the same. With almost everyone playing the same popular tune, we are bound to have some overzealous ideas about the form and substance of accountability.

6. For a further analysis of the views teachers have toward accountability, see Ornstein and Talmage (1973*a*, 1973*b*).

7. One might contend that this correlation coefficient of .30 can be used as an argument for accountability, especially since teachers are being paid for their work. The trouble is, we are leaving out at least 70 percent of the variation of learning, most of which is attributable to the influence of parents, who should also

be held responsible in some way. This fact does not mean that we should transfer blame to (students or) parents. Rather, we should be realistic in our assessment of the teaching-learning process.

8. For further analysis of this problem see Cronbach (1970) and Grobman (1972).

9. Although Tyler does not mention it, there are some highly sophisticated tests that do assign differential weights to pre/post gain scores based on the probability of obtaining a higher score on a post-test if one has X additional chances. The trouble is, this is a very sophisticated testing measure and it is questionable if school systems will employ this procedure.

10. Pre- and post-test scores may vary for still other reasons. Guilford (1954) and Lennon (1971) point out that, even with like-named tests, the variation scores from one test to another may have less to do with instruction than with different (1) norms, (2) times at which they were standardized, (3) content, (4) reliability coefficients, (5) item-difficulty indices, (6) item-discrimination correlations, and (7) grade-equivalent levels.

11. Similarly Ebel (1971) and Hamelton and Novick (1973) point out that we lack a well-developed theory for constructing criterion-referenced tests, and the difficulties and limitations of these tests could lead us to abandon them.

12. On another level this trend may reflect the political rise of one ethnic group and the political decline of another group—the rise of black or Chicano power and the fall of white ethnic power in many cities across the country.

13. Racial quotas have been publicly announced in at least two of the thirty-two New York City Community Districts and three of the eight Detroit Regions, and it is common knowledge that many of the other decentralized units are employing quotas without publicly acknowledging the fact. In San Francisco, the superintendent of schools publicly announced a policy of quotas from 20 to 37.5 percent over the next five years for hiring and promoting administrators. In a landmark court decision, U.S. District Judge Sammuel B. Conti ruled against the school board policy. The superintendent then pointed out in an interview that the word "quota" would be omitted from the new school board resolution, and he would continue to pursue an affirmative-action program.

Concerning New York City, see Bard (1972), Moseley (1972) and the Shanker column in the *New York Times* August 15, November 28, 1971; February 20, March 26, May 14, July 30, and August 20, 1972. Concerning Detroit, see *Detroit Free Press*, March 26, 1972; *Detroit News*, March 3, 10, 14, 23, 28, 29, April 4, 19, 1972. *Summaries of Regional Board Meeting Minutes* (1971–1972). Concerning San Francisco, see Rabb (1972) and *San Francisco Chronicle*, November 2, 1972.

REFERENCES

Adams, Dennis M. 1972. "Some Questions Concerning Behavioral Objectives." *Journal of Teacher Education* 23: 25–26.

Averch, Harvey A., et al. 1972. *How Effective is Schooling? A Critical Review and Synthesis of Research Findings*. Santa Monica, Calif.: Rand Corporation.

Bard, Bernard. 1972. "The Battle for School Jobs: New York's Newest Agony." *Phi Delta Kappan* 53: 553–558.

Barro, Stephen M. 1970. "An Approach to Developing Accountability Measures for the Public Schools." *Phi Delta Kappan* 52: 196–205.

Beggs, Donald L. and Albert N. Hieronymus. 1968. "Uniformity of Growth in the Basic Skills Throughout the School Year and During the Summer." *Journal of Educational Measurement* 5: 91–98.

Bereiter, Carl and Siegfried Englemann. 1966. *Teaching Disadvantaged Children in the Preschool.* Englewood Cliffs, N.J.: Prentice-Hall.

Bloom, Benjamin. 1964. *Stability and Change in Human Characteristics.* New York: Wiley & Sons.

Bloom, Benjamin, et al. 1956. *Taxonomy of Educational Objectives, Handbook I: Cognitive Domain.* New York: McKay.

Boulding, Kenneth. 1971. "The School Industry as a Possible Pathological Economy." Paper presented at the Annual AERA Conference. New York, February.

Brophy, J. E. 1972. "Stability in Teacher Effectiveness." R & D Report, Series 77. Research and Development Center for Teacher Education, University of Texas at Austin, July.

Carmichael, Stokely and Charles V. Hamilton. 1967. *Black Power: The Politics of Liberation in America.* Vintage ed. New York: Random House.

Coleman, James S., et al. 1966. *Equality of Educational Opportunity.* Washington D.C.: U.S. Government Printing Office.

Combs, Arthur W. 1972. *Educational Accountability: Beyond Behavioral Objectives.* Washington, D.C.: Association for Supervision and Curriculum Development.

Cooperative Accountability Project. 1973 a. *Characteristics of and Proposed Models for State Accountability Legislation.* Denver, Colo.: The Author.

—— 1973b. *Legislation by the States: Accountability and Assessment in Education.* Denver, Colo.: The Author.

—— 1973c. "Status of Accountability Legislation." Mimeographed. March.

Cronbach, Lee J. 1970. *Essentials of Psychological Testing.* 3d ed. New York: Harper & Row.

Davies, Don. 1973. "Toward a New Consumerism." Pp. 129–135 in A.C. Ornstein (ed.), *Accountability for Teachers and School Administrations.* Belmont, Calif.: Fearon.

Detroit Free Press. March 26, 1972.

Detroit News. March 3, 10, 14, 23, 28, 29, April 4, 19, 1972.

Digest of Educational Statistics, 1971. 1972. Washington, D.C.: U.S. Government Printing Office.

Drucker, Peter F. 1973 *a.* "Can the Businessmen Meet Our Social Needs." *Saturday Review* (March 13): 41–44.

———— 1973*b*. "Rejoinders." *Saturday Review* (March 13): 48, 53.

Dyer, Henry S. 1970. "Toward Objective Criteria of Professional Accountability in the Schools of New York City." *Phi Delta Kappan* 52: 206–211.

————. 1971. "The Role of Evaluation in Accountability." Paper presented at the Conference on Educational Accountability sponsored by the Educational Testing Service. Chicago, June.

Ebel, Robert. 1971. "Criterion-Referenced Measurements Limitations." *School Review* 79: 282–285.

Erikson, Erik H. 1950. *Childhood and Society.* New York: Norton.

Fairley, Richard L. 1972. "Accountability's New Test." *American Education* 8: 33–35.

Fantini, Mario D., et al. 1970. *Community Control and the Urban School.* New York: Praeger.

Gates, Arthur I. and Walter H. MacGinitie, 1965. *Technical Manual for the Gates-MacGinitie Reading Tests.* New York: Teachers College Press, Columbia University Press.

Glickstein, Howard A. 1969. "Federal Educational Programs and Minority Groups." *Journal of Negro Education* 38: 303–314.

Gordon, Edmund W. and Doxey A. Wilkerson. 1966. *Compensatory Education for the Disadvantaged.* New York: College Entrance Examination Board.

Grobman, Hulda. 1972. "Accountability for What?" *Nation's Schools* 89: 65–68.

Guilford, J. P. 1954. *Psychometric Methods.* 2d ed. New York: McGraw-Hill.

Hamleton, Ronald K. and Melvin R. Novick. 1973. "Toward an Integration of Theory and Method for Criterion-Referenced Tests." Paper presented at the Annual AERA Conference. New Orleans, February.

Hencley, Stephen P. 1971. "Impediments to Accountability." *Administrators Notebook* 20: 1–4.

Herr, Fredrich. 1961. *The Medieval World.* New York: New American Library.

Herrnstein, Richard J. 1971. "IQ." *Atlantic* (September): 43–64.

International Studies in Evaluation. 1973. *Reading Comprehension Education in Fifteen Countries*, vol. 3. Stockholm, Sweden: Almquist & Wiksell.

Jencks, Christopher, et al. 1972. *Inequality: A Reassessment of the Effect of Family and Schooling in America.* New York: Basic Books.

Jennings, Frank G. 1972. "For the Record." *Teachers College Record* 73: 333–337.

Jensen, Arthur R. 1969. "How Much Can We Boost IQ. and Scholastic Achievement." *Harvard Educational Review* 39: 1–123.

Klein, Stephen M. 1971. "The Uses and Illustrations of Standardized Tests in Meeting the Demands for Accountability." *UCLA Evaluation Comment* 4: 1–7.

Landers, Jacob. 1973. "Accountability and Progress by Nomenclature: Old Ideas in New Bottles." *Phi Delta Kappan* 54: 539–541.

Lessinger, Leon M. 1970 a. "Engineering Accountability for Results in Public Education." *Phi Delta Kappan* 52: 217–225.

—— 1970b. *Every Kid a Winner: Accountability in Education.* New York: Simon & Schuster.

Lennon, Roger T. 1971. "To Perform and to Account." *Journal of Research and Development in Education* 5: 3–14.

Lieberman, Myron. 1970. "An Overview of Accountability." *Phi Delta Kappan* 52: 194–195.

Lindeman, Erick L. 1971. "The Means and Ends of Accountability." Paper presented at the Conference on Educational Accountability sponsored by the Educational Testing Service. Chicago, June.

Marland, Sidney P. 1973. "Accountability in Education." *Teachers College Record* 73: 339–346.

Mayeske, George W., et al. 1970. *A Study of Our Nation's Schools.* Washington, D.C.: U.S. Government Printing Office.

McDonald, Frederick J. and Garlie A. Forehand. 1973. "A Design for Accountability in Education." *New York University Education Quarterly* 4: 7–16.

Moseley, Francis S. 1972. "The Urban Secondary School: Too Late for Mere Change." *Phi Delta Kappan* 53: 559–564.

Moynihan, Daniel P. 1972 a. "Equalizing Education: In Whose Benefit?" *Public Interest* (Fall): 69–89.

——1972b. "The Schism in Black America." *Public Interest* (Spring): 3–24.

Nash, Robert J. and Russell M. Agne. 1971. "Competency in Teacher Education: A Prop for the Status Quo." *Journal of Teacher Education* 22: 147–156.

Nation's Schools. 1972. "Trying to Fix the Blame in New York for Poor Performance." 89: 66–67.

NCTEPS of NEA. 1970. "The Meaning of Accountability: A Working Paper." Mimeographed. November.

NEA Press release, January 4, 1973.

Ornstein, Allan C. 1974. *Metropolitan Schools: Administrative Decentralization vs. Community Control.* Metuchen, N.J.: Scarecrow Press.

Ornstein, Allan C. and Harriet Talmage. 1973 a. "A Dissenting View on Accountability." *Urban Education* 8: 133–151.

―――. 1973b. "The Rhetoric and the Realities of Accountability." *Today's Education: NEA Journal* 62: 70–80.

Phi Delta Kappan. 1973. "Tenure, Certification Battles are Shaping Up in Florida." 54: 561.

Piaget, Jean. 1959. *The Language and Thought of the Child.* 3d ed. New York: Humanities Press.

Rabb, Earl. 1972. "Quotas by Another Name." *Commentary* (January): 41–45.

Redfern, George B. 1973. "Legally Mandated Evaluation." *National Elementary Principal* 52: 45–60.

Rosenshine, Barak. 1970. "The Stability of Teacher Effects Upon Student Achievement." *Review of Educational Research* 40: 647–662.

San Francisco Chronicle. November 2, 1972.

Seabury, Paul. 1972. "HEW and the Universities." *Commentary* (February): 38–44.

Schultze, Charles L., et al. 1972. *Settling National Priorities: the 1973 Budget.* Washington, D.C.: Brookings Institute.

Selden, David. 1972. "Productivity, Yes. Accountability, No." *Nation's Schools* 89: 50–51, 56.

Seligman, Daniel. 1973. "How Equal Opportunity Turned into Employment Quotas." *Fortune* (March): 160–66.

Shanker, Albert. Column in the *New York Times,* August 15, November 28, 1971, February 20, March 26, May 14, July 30, and August 20, 1972.

Skinner, B. F. 1968. *Technology of Teaching.* New York: Appleton-Century Crofts.

Soar, Robert S. 1966. "An Integrative Approach to Classroom Learning." NIMH Project Nos. 5-RIII, MH 01096 and 7-RII, MH 02045. University of South Carolina and Temple University.

———. 1973. "Accountability: Problems and Possibilities." Paper presented at the Annual AERA Conference. New Orleans, February.

Stake, Robert E. 1971. "Testing Hazards in Performance Contracting." *Phi Delta Kappan* 52: 583–589.

Summaries of Regional Board Meeting Minutes. 1971–1972. Detroit Office of School Decentralization, Board of Education of the City of Detroit.

Tyler, Ralph W. 1970. "Testing for Accountability." *Nation's Schools* 86: 37–39.

Weiss, Edmund. 1973. "Educational Accountability and the Presumption of Guilt." *Educational Digest* 38: 21–24.

Westinghouse Learning Corporation and Ohio University. 1969. *The Impact of Headstart.* Preliminary Draft: An Evaluation of the Effects of Headstart on Children's Cognitive and Affective Development. Washington, D.C.: U.S. Government Printing Office.

Chapter 4

ADMINISTRATIVE DECENTRALIZATION AND COMMUNITY CONTROL

As characteristics of metropolitan populations have changed, the problems confronting the schools, and especially the inner-city schools, have increased. Nonwhites, many of them from lower-income groups, have become the majority student population in many city school systems, particularly in the elementary schools. At the same time an out-migration of blacks to the suburbs has begun, and some suburban and county school systems are experiencing the problems once considered only characteristic of city schools.

Education critics have focused on the city schools, however, contending (1) that the nonwhite students bring a culture and set of values different from those of the white middle-class students upon which the school systems have been built and (2) that the schools still reflect the old culture. In the few school systems that have exhibited change and a sensitivity to pluralistic social values, the critics contend alterations have mainly resulted from political pressure and community organization, especially from black politics and black organizations. Where changes have occurred, however, there has been concurrent concern that black power is duplicating the errors of white racism and ethnocentrism. There is also apprehension among whites that a growing number of blacks are no longer committed to educational change within the existing educational structure, that they question the structure's legitimacy.

ADMINISTRATIVE-COMMUNITY ANALYSIS

Evolving partly out of frustration in the effort to desegregate schools and society and partly from the concept of black power, demands have emerged for community control of the schools, that is, policy making in education by parents and community representatives. In their influential book titled *Black Power*, Carmichael and Hamilton (1967) rejected a black-white partnership on the ground that it was a myth. They urged blacks to organize on their own terms and to use "the black community as a base of organization to control institutions in that community." This included taking "control of the ghetto schools" away from the professional and white educators, because it was alleged that they "bring with them middle-class biases, unsuitable techniques and materials, [which] are at best dysfunctional and at worst destructive" to black children (p. 166). More recently, Sizemore (1972) has argued that blacks are powerless and oppressed and need to liberate themselves from whites by establishing "organizations and institutions which permit [them] to carry on the 'critical and liberating dialog which presupposes action.' " Arguing that education is not a neutral institution, she advocates that blacks gain complete control of black schools, not only for direct educational purposes (as is commonly argued in the literature), but also to maintain "solidarity against oppression, enhance the myths, rites, and rituals which preserve this solidarity . . . and produce ideologies that make liberation possible" (p. 283).

This increasing pressure, compounded by criticism of the Establishment from many liberal educators, has played a part in forcing school authorities in many city school systems to decentralize and increase community involvement in the schools. This black-minority demand for change—whether legitimate or not, whether education or ideology—seems to have its counterpart (mostly arising for other reasons) in some suburban and county schools, and many of these school systems also have decentralized and increased community involvement. What have emerged, then, are the following (not mutually exclusive) administrative-community alternatives for governing metropolitan schools: (1) administrative decentralization, (2) community participation, and (3) community control, with either alternative 2 (participation) or alternative 3 (control) usually accompanying alternative 1 (decentralization). A brief definition of each of these three school organizational trends is presented below.

1. *Administrative Decentralization*. Administrative decentralization is a common occurrence in metropolitan school systems comprising 50,000 or more students. A particular school system may decentralize and stop at this point, or it may (and usually does) then proceed to increase commun-

ity participation. In only two systems, New York City and Detroit, have the state legislatures enacted some form of community control.

With administrative decentralization alone, the locus of political power remains with a single, central administration and board of education. The bureaucracy is broken into field or administrative units, and sometimes these units are further divided. In still another form of decentralization, frequently more traditional in nature (although it is sometimes found in current organizational plans), the school system is divided into attendance units, which include one or more high schools with their feeding elementary and middle or junior high schools. In both forms of decentralization, there is usually a field administrator (such as an area or district superintendent) responsible for the schools within his boundaries.

By breaking down the bureaucracy, the administration is in principle brought closer to the schools and community, and there is closer communication between the schools and central office. There is also a shift of influence from the central office to the field administration. That is, some of the services and departments transfer from the central office to the field level. In theory, the field administrators and school principals attain power to make some decisions which were formerly made at the central office. Accountability is still directed upward, not toward the community, although the field administrators presumably are sensitized to the community residents within their boundaries. Because the professionals and school board members retain power, most school people prefer this kind of organization.

2. *Community Participation.* Although decentralization need not lead to increased community participation, it often does. With this policy, the decision-making authority and power still remain with the professionals, especially at the apex of the administrative hierarchy. Community participation usually results in the formation of advisory committees and groups beyond the usual parent-teacher associations and other voluntary groups. As the name suggests, these committees are only advisory in nature, and may include representatives of parents of school children, community residents without children attending the public schools, teachers, administrators, students, and local business, political, religious, and social agencies.

The committees that are formed may operate at the various levels of the school system—the local school, decentralized field or unit level (if the schools have been decentralized), and central office—making recommendations and serving as a liaison between the schools and the community. Committee members are usually appointed by the school principal if the committee is operating on the individual school level, or by the field administrator and/or central office administrator if the committee is operating on a field or central level; however, a few school systems encourage local elections for membership on these advisory committees. Community participation is usually accepted and supported by teachers, administrators, and school board members, as well as by many minority parents and community leaders; it is, however, rejected by some critics of the teachers and schools and some militant groups because it does not transfer authority and power to the community.

(3) *Community Control.* Demands for community control often are made by individuals in the black community (not only with regard to the schools but also with respect to other social institutions as well). It is argued that the schools have been unresponsive to the needs and interests of black children. Because the professionals have "failed" to educate these children, liberals, black militants, and a growing number of black moderates argue for the chance for the community to succeed, or at least to fail, and on its own terms. The general procedure is usually to advocate the decentralization of the schools within the existing framework, which in turn facilitates community control, or at least serves as a catalyst for greater community input. But while community control can be created through some form of decentralization, the decentralization process does not necessarily lead to community control.

Community control connotes a legal provision for an elected local school board functioning under specific guidelines and in conjunction with the central board of education. It means a sharing of decision-making authority and power between the local and central school boards. Community control of the schools carried to the fullest extent implies total governance by the community, or by so-called representatives of the community, over (1) school personnel, including hiring, firing, and promoting; (2) curriculum, including course electives, ordering textbooks, and evaluation; (3) student policy, including student-teacher relationships, discipline, and testing; and (4) financing, including federal funding, allocation of money, and determination of the budget. In short, the powers of the professionals and central school board members are abridged, actually transferred to the community. This kind of change is rejected by most teachers and administrators, especially many whites in big-city schools who fear reverse discrimination and increasing quotas in hiring and promotion policies and even loss of their jobs.

We can collapse the three alternative models into two options: administrative decentralization and community participation versus administrative decentralization and community control. Most professionals advocate the first option because their authority and power remain less subject to scrutiny. Many liberal educators, black militants, and an increasing number of other minority groups prefer the second option; this connotes a shifting of political control to a few members of the "community."

In reality, there is little controversy over decentralization per se, because most people, including teachers and administrators, the critics of these educators, and minority groups, tend to favor, or at least to accept, this organizational model. The professional educators see a need for it and accept it because they still retain power; the critics accept it because they view it as the first step toward community control. The controversy concerns community control: which group—the professional educators or community groups—will have the power and authority to run the schools. The main concern, then, is not limited to education, which is commonly emphasized in the literature on community control, but extends to politics and related issues of self-interest and group ideology. We will ignore administrative decentralization, for the time being, because there is relatively little controversy over it, and focus on the reasons for and against community control.

Reasons for and Against Community Control

The reasons for and against community control have been examined in depth by Fantini, et al. (1970), Levin (1970), Lyke (1970), and Ornstein (1972b, 1974b). Here, we will summarize and extend the data of the aforementioned authors. In addition, we will present a different approach for examining the underlying issues: by establishing two groups (proponents and critics) who set forth their reasons for and against community control. Table 2 is divided into two parts and each part has two columns. In the first part, first column, the critics list reasons against community control: in the opposite column the proponents of the concept respond. The procedure is then reversed: in the second part, proponents of community control outline their reasons, and the critics respond in the opposite column. Each group, then, is given the opportunity to advocate and defend its position. The idea is for the reader to review the major arguments for and against community control and possibly to analyze these arguments in the context of a school with which he is familiar.

RESEARCH ON ADMINISTRATIVE-COMMUNITY ORGANIZATION

Before the mid-sixties, there was little interest in school decentralization or community control. The research on school reorganization during this period was largely concerned with rural consolidation and centralization and community participation. For example, Dawson (1955) noted that the

TABLE 2
A DEBATE BETWEEN THE CRITICS AND PROPONENTS OF COMMUNITY CONTROL
Part I

Arguments Against by Critics	Responses by Proponents
1. Community control will impede integration.	a. Integration connotes white assimilation. b. The schools in most cities are more segregated now than prior to the Supreme Court's *Brown* decision in 1954. c. Most whites and now many blacks do not want to integrate.
2. Community control will balkanize the cities.	a. Most cities are already balkanized.
3. Community control is a scheme for alleviating pressure from the black community.	a. The parents are motivated to action because their children are failing in school. b. They will be motivated to seek high quality education for their children.
4. Parents and community residents (especially from low-income areas) are inexperienced and inept in dealing with complex educational issues.	a. As for inexperience, train the incoming local school board members. b. As for ineptness, this is insulting. How do we know this, if these people have not had the opportunity to run the schools?
5. Community control will destroy the merit system.	a. Competitive examinations are white-oriented. b. There is no proof that those who pass the examinations are "fit and qualified" for their jobs. c. Maintain the list of eligibles and permit the local school boards to select personnel from the list.
6. Community control will weaken the teacher's union.	a. It is already splintered by political and racial issues in most cities. b. The union is already weakened, not by community control but by depleted school budgets, the citizens' revolt against higher taxes, and the surplus of teachers.

7. Community control is a distraction from the greater need for money to educate children, especially ghetto children.

   a. This is only one method of reform.
   b. We can implement community control and still seek increased finances.

8. Community control will enhance black racism.

   a. What about 400 years of white racism?
   b. Black children need an education that will help them cope with white discrimination.

9. Community control will lead to rejection of white participation.

   a. White personnel who are sensitive to the needs and interests of black children will be encouraged to remain in their schools.

Part II

Arguments *For* by Proponents	Responses by Critics
1. Community control will make teachers and administrators accountable to the people.	a. It will lead to vigilante groups (as in New York City and Detroit).
	b. It is questionable if anyone can objectively assess the performance and even the output of teachers and administrators, much less parents and community representatives, since the experts in the field of testing and evaluation find it difficult if not impossible to evaluate teachers and administrators with reliability and validity.
	c. Many community representatives have already reached the conclusion that professional educators are the only ones responsible for student failure; other variables such as the home, community, and the students themselves must be taken into consideration.
2. Community control will lead to educational innovation.	a. The local school boards will concentrate their interests on politics and issues of self-interest and ideology.
	b. Innovation is based on pilot testing and evaluating programs; community control has not been sufficiently pilot-tested or evaluated.

TABLE 2 (continued)
A DEBATE BETWEEN THE CRITICS AND PROPONENTS OF COMMUNITY CONTROL

Arguments Against by Critics	Responses by Proponents
3. Community control will lead to greater parental and public participation.	a. The majority of the people, including parents, are indifferent to educational issues—or at least do not participate in school meetings or vote on educational issues. b. Politically oriented groups, ranging from black militants to white segregationists, will gain control of the schools for their own purposes (as in New York City and Detroit).
4. Community control will enable local school boards to hire qualified principals and superintendents (on the basis that they can relate to ghetto children and serve as models to emulate).	a. This will lead to increased ethnic and racial favoritism in appointing and promoting administrators (a pattern already evident in city school systems).
5. Community control will enhance flexible hiring and promotion practices and attract teachers and administrators with more initiative and innovative capacity.	a. "Flexibility" connotes that competitive performance, experience, and objective tests can be replaced by patronage, nepotism, and pork-barrel practices. b. Initiative and innovation are difficult to define; they mean different things to different people. For some they are euphemisms for reverse discrimination.
6. Community control will raise student achievement.	a. There is no proof that this will happen. We should pilot-test this assumption before mass changes are implemented. What happens if achievement is the same or even declines with community control? b. There is no evidence that black teachers and administrators can do a better job in raising achievement among black students. Check the record in school systems where there is a majority of black teachers and administrators (e.g., southern black schools; Washington, D.C.; Philadelphia; St. Louis; Baltimore; Gary; Newark; etc.).

118

7. Community control will promote self-government for blacks, as well as for other minorities.

   a. It is a return to the myth of "separate but equal."
   b. It will foster white ethnicity and backlash.
   c. Inherent in this concept is the surrender of the suburbs to white domination while blacks obtain control of the ghetto—a ghetto depleted in finances and saddled with decay, drug addiction, violence, crime, traffic congestion, pollution, overpopulation, etc.

8. Community control will lead to educational reform.

   a. It thwarts future possibilities for school desegregation, which should be the immediate goal of educational reform.
   b. Despite the present retrenchment in federal government, it is recognized as the only institution with the strength, expertise, and financial resources to reform school and society. (In the past, virtually all major social reforms—education, welfare, housing, health services—have been initiated by the federal government.)

Source: Allan C. Ornstein, "The Politics of School Decentralization and Community Control," a report to Dan Walker, governor of the state of Illinois, August, 1972, pp. 6–8. © 1972.

number of school districts decreased from 119,000 in 1938 to 48,700 in 1954. Dawson and Ellena (1954) pointed out that a total of 1,088 centralization proposals were made during the 1952–53 school year, and only 93 were defeated. Similarly, there was little demand for community control; this did not fully emerge until the concept of black power crystallized and became a mounting force in the late sixties.

Prior to this period, there was a recognized need for greater community participation (not control) in school affairs, and for developing cooperative school-community relations. Thus in the fifties, three influential school administration groups, the National Conference of Professors of Educational Administration (NCPEA), the eight regional centers of the Cooperative Program in Educational Administration (CPEA), and the association of the 34 leading universities of the University Council for Educational Administration (UCEA) outlined clinical and research programs in administration to identify the role of the school in community improvement projects, to seek ways for enhancing school-community relations, and to find types of administrative leadership that would foster desirable school-community relations and parental participation. In this connection, Rothchild (1951) showed that only 15 percent of the administrators surveyed were satisfied with the amount of parent participation in school policy. Reflecting this desire to enhance school-parental-community relations, much of the literature in the 1950s and early 1960s was concerned with criteria and methods for improving interaction between the professional staff and lay public.

By the mid-1960s, the racial climate in the large city schools and the quickened pace of change related to administrative decentralization and demands for community control made it difficult for social scientists to conduct valid research on these twin concepts. The problem was aggravated by a general lack of communication between the research community and the practitioner, as well as by the growing militancy of blacks who were becoming suspicious of and often rejecting the social scientist because he was white and viewing him as irrelevant, culturally biased, and antagonistic toward the black community. Needless to say, very little empirical data are available on decentralization or community control. There is, however, a wealth of expository literature on these two organizational models, but the content is highly intuitive, subjective, and reflective of the authors' personal biases and political ideologies.

Most of the research that evolved, then, is "quasi" or "soft" in nature, actually descriptions and reports based on sentiment and nonempirical data. Two types of quasi research resulted, the first of which described the pathologies of the school bureaucracy and boards of education through personal recollections, observations, anecdotal data, interviews, and case descriptions. The books by Rogers (1969) about New York City, Pois (1964) about Chicago, Resnik (1970) about Philadelphia, and Schrag (1967) about Boston fall into this category. The second type of quasi research was made up of policy reports which included recommendations for change and were prepared by management firms, in-house school committees, or legislative commissions. The methods employed in this type of quasi research included observations and questionnaires in the schools; interviews with consultants, school personnel, and community residents; and ideas gleaned from various committees, commissions, task force meetings, public hearings, community forums, and write-in suggestions. Almost all of the large and medium-sized school systems have at least one recent policy report and, in many instances, several reports on administrative-community organization. These reports often received wide coverage in local newspapers; and the Bundy Report, issued by the New York City Mayor's Advisory Panel (1967), received national attention.[1]

While most of the current data on administrative-community school plans are based on soft research, a few empirical studies can be cited which show that involving parents (not community groups) with their children's learning correlates with increased student development in academic and attitudinal areas. For example, Schiff (1963) found that parental participation and cooperation in school affairs led to increased student achievement and school attendance and fewer discipline problems. In Hess and Shipman's (1966) study of middle-class and lower-class mothers' attitudes toward their children in school, the investigators concluded that involving parents in school activities might help low-income children improve their self-concepts and images of the teachers and school, as well as help their mothers acquire teaching skills which could be used at home. Brookover and his associates (1965) showed that low-income junior high school students whose parents were involved in school matters had acquired improved self-concepts and made significant academic gains in comparison to students whose parents were uninvolved in school matters.

Rempson (1972) evaluated an experimental program for increasing parental participation of blacks and Puerto Ricans in twenty-seven elementary schools in New York City. Based on self-reports, he found that participants expressed gains in improving their ability to guide their children's growth, a strengthened self-image, and increase of their knowledge of the school functions. It was also found that significantly (the levels of significance were not reported) more Puerto Rican than black fathers participated in school activities but that more black parents than Puerto Rican parents participated in these school activities (suggesting in part to this reader that English-speaking ability influences parental participation in American schools).

From personal observations of compensatory programs across the nation, Fusco (1966), Gordon and Wilkerson (1966), and Jablonsky (1968) concluded that the schools which included the participation of parents seemed to have greater success in educating lower-income students than those which did not. However, most of the recent evaluation reports on compensatory education indicate that increases made by students in the initial years have not been maintained, thus suggesting among other reasons the influence of the "Hawthorne effect" which links changes in the subjects' performance with knowledge of the experimental situation itself rather than the treatment variables introduced by the programs. In fact, because there was no follow-up study for the other four successful research studies mentioned above, it is possible that the Hawthorne effect was also operating.

Improved achievement among preschool children from low-income families as the result of parent participation has been reported by Deutsch (1964, 1971). Similarly, Cloward and Jones (1963) reported that parents of all socioeconomic classes who were involved with school activities were more likely to exhibit interest in the academic achievement of their children. Coleman and his associates (1966) concluded that the student's sense of control over his environment is a factor that strongly affects his achievement; perhaps greater parental involvement increases the student's sense of control. A similar hypothesis is also stated by Lopate and her associates (1970): that "active participation of parents in school affairs . . . may enhance cultural identity and self-concept, and in turn raise achievement" (p. 143).

It is important to note that the above data should not be equated with the effects of community control or even with community participation as it is presently evolving. It would be incorrect to conclude that since parental participation in assisting children with school learning seems to enhance student achievement and attitudinal development, the same result necessarily follows from community control or even from the current advisory form of community participation.

Empirical investigations of the effects of community control are limited because it is a recent development operating on a system-wide basis in only two major cities (New York and Detroit) and being tentatively tried in a few pilot projects.[2] Adequate research on community control has not yet been developed. Two studies that have some bearing on community control are examined below.

Ravitch (1972) summarized the literature which endorsed the Ocean Hill-Brownsville experiment in New York City and which claimed that students in the district had achieved academic success. These success stories were based on personal observations from social and literary critics (including I. F. Stone, Alfred Kazin, Dwight MacDonald, and Nat Hentoff), liberal organizations (such as the New York Civil Liberties Union and the New York Urban Coalition), the district's self-evaluation reports, Queens College Institute for Community Studies (which funded more than $1 million in Ford Foundation grants to the demonstration district) and the Ford Foundation which also initiated the Bundy Report.

Ravitch points out that, while the demonstration district lasted from the fall of 1967 to June 1970, throughout 1968 and 1969 Rhody McCoy, the unit administrator of the district, refused to administer reading tests to the students, but "nevertheless continued to release figures attesting to the rapid improvement of reading scores" (p. 72). She asserts that there was no control group to gauge the district's effectiveness, that there was no systematic or reliable method of record keeping, "and that any other district which handled its internal affairs so inefficiently would have been dissolved by state authorities" (p. 72).

In the spring of 1971, one year after the district had been dissolved, standardized reading tests (Metropolitan Reading Achievement Tests) were administered to the students of the eight schools in the district in conjunction with the city-wide testing program. According to the results of the reading scores, the Ocean Hill-Brownsville experiment was a failure. Writes Ravitch (1972), "Every school in the [experimental] district reported poor reading scores—as compared with other schools in the city . . . [and] even with other ghetto schools generally" (p. 72). The school with the highest score had 24.5 percent of its students reading on or above grade level, with the other seven schools reporting lower scores than they had in 1967. For example, seventh graders at J.H.S. 271 had mean scores of 5.4 in 1967 (the normal reading score should have been 7.7) and 4.7 in 1971; the same pattern appeared in the other grades in the other schools of the experimental district.

One must consider that the district was heavily funded by supplementary Ford Foundation and state money; it had a ratio of one staff member to every eight to ten students, was supplied with the latest educational "hardware," presumably had the support of the staff since the community school board allocated jobs (in fact, this latter situation caused the 1968 New York City teacher strike), and yet it was a failure in terms of teaching students to read, probably the most important aspect of the curriculum in terms of school success. On the other hand, one must remember that the district was plagued with a series of conflicts and controversies, and even though the schools remained open during the 1968 teacher strike, the school atmosphere was not conducive to academic learning. The atmosphere was perhaps more political than educational. To be sure, the Ocean Hill experience cannot be viewed as a "test" of community control, rather as only one example—perhaps the most noted one.

Talmage and Ornstein (1973) developed a thirty-item instrument and used a five-point scale ranging from "strongly agree" to "strongly disagree" to measure perceptions toward accountability and community control.[3] As many as 305 teachers from Chicago were surveyed and divided into three groups—preservice, student teachers, and inservice—then categorized by sex, teaching level, ethnicity, and school location. Items administered fell into three major areas: curriculum and instruction, personnel matters, and student performance.[4]

Minority teachers had significantly higher scores (.001) than white teachers on the desirability of the "local community members [refering to adults who did not necessarily have children enrolled in schools], having much to add to the school academic program." The mean score was significantly higher (.01) for those who preferred to teach in the outer city and suburban schools than for those who identified with inner-city schools for the following items: "Parents [adults who had children enrolled in the local school] should have a role in hiring the school personnel"; "the local community should be consulted on decisions concerning transferring a teacher"; and "parents should be members of the school's curriculum committees." This suggested that teachers in the inner city (most of whom were white) were threatened by current demands of parents and local community members, or were less likely to look positively on parent and community participation in matters concerning personnel and curriculum.

Comparing preservice and in-service teachers, the latter were significantly less positive about three items related to being held accountable to community members for their instructional performance and to perceiving relations with the community as a factor that would improve the behavior of the students. This suggests that preservice teachers are more likely to favor a greater amount of community participation. With more exposure to educational reality and conditions in local schools and communities, attitudes of teacher groups tended to become less positive toward community involvement. The authors concluded that future studies should probe perceptions of student, parent, and community groups in the same areas. Comparison of perceptions could give leaders a basis for working out accountability-school community relations.

In summary, research on community control is limited, partly because ideological and racial conflicts have prevented rigorous research and partly because so few school systems have implemented plans which approach community control. Much of the data on community control, therefore, has been formulated in terms of a debate or a specific position (for or against). Research is expensive, but lack of research on community control may be more expensive in the long run to the students and society in general. As La Noue (1972) suggests, "Given existing racial hostilities and other problems in our cities, decentralization [also implying community control] will not be easily reversible. If it fails, the human social costs will be great" (p. 25). Until the research clearly shows the effects of administrative decentralization and community control, we should proceed with caution.

ADMINISTRATIVE DECENTRALIZATION OF THE SCHOOL SYSTEMS

Most of the large and medium-sized school sytems in city and suburban settings report some type of administrative decentralization or are considering it. Table 3 is based on three sources of data; the Anne Arundel survey (1970) and studies by Ornstein (1974 *a*, 1974 *b*). In all, 69 school systems with 50,000 or more students are considered. This represents 90 percent of all school systems enrolling at least 50,000 students. The school systems are listed in descending order according to student enrollment with the largest one first. The enrollment figures are based on actual student enrollment for 1972 and 1973. In three cases, however, the figures are estimated, as indicated in the table notes.

Of the 69 school systems listed in table 3, 42 had been decentralized and 8 were considering it. In addition, one school system (Clark County, Nev.) moved from centralization to decentralization, then back to centralization. Large school systems tend to have decentralized more than the smaller ones. For example, 19 out of 23 (83 percent) of the school systems enrolling 100,000 or more students had decentralized or were considering it. Thirty-one of 46 (68 percent) school systems enrolling between 50,000 and 100,000 students had decentralized or were considering it.

The overwhelming majority of the school systems started the decentralization process in or after 1967. Even the larger school systems that had decentralized in previous stages recently implemented a major decentralization plan. Eight school systems (Philadelphia, Memphis, Milwaukee, Boston, Denver, Jefferson County, [Colo.], Minneapolis, and Austin) reported decentralization based on senior high schools and their feeding elementary or junior high schools.

Two school systems (Indianapolis and San Francisco) had decentralized only the elementary schools, and one school system (Minneapolis) had decentralized only the inner-city schools. In addition, the Cincinnati schools decentralized into separate elementary school districts and secondary school districts. The decentralized unit names varied and included such terms as "districts," "areas," "zones," "regions," "complexes," "clusters," "units," and "pyramids," with the first two terms combined used in 80 percent of the decentralized school systems. In four cases (Chicago, St. Louis, Seattle, and Minneapolis), the decentralized unit was subdivided into smaller units. The number of decentralized units varied from as little as one area and two pyramids in Minneapolis to as many as 32 community districts in New York City. Although not indicated by the table, the most frequent number of students per decentralized unit was between 15,000 and 25,000 students, with a range from 2,500 to 8,500 in Milwaukee to 154,000 to 216,000 in Chicago (Ornstein, 1974*b*).

TABLE 3
ADMINISTRATIVE DECENTRALIZATION PLANS OF SCHOOL SYSTEMS
ENROLLING 50,000 OR MORE STUDENTS

School System	Enrollment	Status of Decentralization	Date	Units
New York, N.Y.	1,200,000	Decentralized	1969[a]	32 community districts
Los Angeles, Calif.	621,000	Decentralized	1971[a]	12 areas
Chicago, Ill.	558,000	Decentralized	1968[a]	3 areas; 27 districts
Philadelphia, Pa.	290,000	Decentralized	1968[a]	8 districts[b]
Detroit, Mich.	277,500	Decentralized	1971[a]	8 regions
Dade County, Fla.	240,000	Decentralized	1965[a]	6 areas
Houston, Tex.	225,000	Decentralized	1971	6 areas
Baltimore, Md.	190,500	Considering decentralization[c]		
Hawaii, State	181,500	No plans		
Prince George's County, Md.	162,500	Decentralized	n.d.	3 areas
Dallas, Tex.	155,000	Considering decentralization[c]		
District of Columbia	140,000	Considering decentralization[c]		
Memphis, Tenn.	139,000	Decentralized	1971	4 areas[b]
Fairfax County, Va.	136,000	Decentralized	1967	4 areas
Baltimore County, Md.	132,000	Decentralized	1965	5 areas
Milwaukee, Wis.	129,000	Decentralized	1967	14 clusters[b]
Broward County, Fla.	129,000	Decentralized	1968	5 areas and 1 complex
Montgomery County, Md.	126,500	Decentralized	1971	6 areas
San Diego, Calif.	125,000	No plans		
Duval County, Fla.	109,500	No plans		
New Orlanes, La.	110,000*	Decentralized	1968	4 districts
Hillsborough County, Fla.	105,000*	No plans		
St. Louis, Mo.	104,000	Decentralized	1970[a]	5 districts; 10 units

126

School System	Enrollment	Status of Decentralization	Date	Units
Indianapolis, Ind.	97,500	Decentralized	1969	3 regions; 10 areas[d]
Boston, Mass.	97,000	Decentralized	1966	6 areas[b]
Jefferson County, Ky.	96,500	No plans		
Atlanta, Ga.	96,000	Decentralized	1956	5 areas
Denver, Colo.	95,000	Decentralized	n.d.	9 areas[b]
Pinnellas County, Fla.	88,000	Considering decentralization[c]		
Fort Worth, Tex.	86,000	No plans		
Orange County, Fla.	86,000	Considering decentralization[c]		
Nashville-Davidson County, Tenn.	85,000	Decentralized	1966	3 districts
Albuquerque, N.M.	85,000	Decentralized	1969	3 areas
San Francisco, Calif.	80,500	Decentralized	1971	7 zones[d]
Charlotte-Mecklenburg, N.C.	80,000	Considering decentralization[c]		
Cincinnati, Ohio	79,000	Decentralized	1973	4 elementary districts; 2 secondary districts
Anne Arundel Cty., Md.	77,000	Decentralized	1973	4 areas
Clark County, Nev.	76,000	No plans[e]		
Seattle, Wash.	74,000	Decentralized	1970	2 regions; 12 areas
Jefferson County, Colo.	74,000	Decentralized	1971	9 areas[b]
San Antonio, Tex.	73,500	Decentralized	1969	3 areas
Newark, N.J.	73,000*	No plans		
Pittsburgh, Pa.	70,000	Decentralized	1970	3 areas
Tulsa, Okla.	70,000	No plans		
Portland, Oreg.	69,000	Decentralized	1970	3 areas
Buffalo, N.Y.	68,000	Considering decentralization[c]		
Palm Beach County, Fla.	68,000	Decentralized	1969	4 areas
Kansas City, Mo.	68,000	Considering decentralization[c]		
East Baton Rouge, La.	67,500	No plans		
Mobile, Ala.	66,000	No plans		

TABLE 3 *(continued)*

School System	Enrollment	Status of Decentralization	Date	Units
Brevard County, Fla.	63,000	Decentralized	1969	3 areas
Omaha, Nebr.	62,500	No plans		
El Paso, Tex.	62,500	Decentralized	1972	3 areas
Granite, Utah	62,000	Decentralized	1971	3 complexes
Minneapolis, Minn.	61,500	Decentralized	1967	1 area; 2 pyramids [b,f]
Oklahoma City, Okla.	60,500	No plans		
Oakland, Calif.	60,000	Decentralized	1971	3 regions
Greenville County, S.C.	57,500	Decentralized	1972	4 areas and 1 experimental area
Wichita, Kans.	57,000	No plans		
Jefferson County, Ala.	57,000	No plans		
Austin, Tex.	56,000	Decentralized	n.d.	11 clusters[b]
Fresno, Calif.	56,000	Decentralized	1973	6 areas
Polk County, Fla.	55,000	Decentralized	n.d.	4 areas
San Juan, Calif.	54,000	No plans		
Akron, Ohio	54,000	No plans		
Dayton, Ohio	53,000	Decentralized	1971	3 units
Kanawha County, W.Va.	52,000	No plans		
Garden Grove, Calif.	51,500	Decentralized	1970	3 areas
Norfolk, Va.	51,000	No plans		

[a] The school system has decentralized in stages with the specific year representing the latest major administrative-community changes.

[b] Based on feeder schools to a high school.

[c] Considering decentralization: Baltimore considering 6-9 areas; Dallas, undetermined; District of Columbia, undetermined; Pinnellas County considering 3-4 areas; Orange County, undetermined; Charlotte-Mecklenburg, undetermined; Buffalo considering 5 districts; Kansas City, Mo., undetermined.

[d] Decentralization is limited to elementary schools.

[e] Moved from centralization to decentralization and returned to centralization.

[f] Decentralization is mainly limited to inner-city schools.

[*] Denotes those student enrollment figures that are based on Anne Arundel survey, 1972-73, and are estimates.

Based on results from the above surveys, the major purposes for administrative decentralization were:

1. To reduce the administrative span of control.
2. To provide greater staff sensitivity to local populations.
3. To enhance school-community relations.
4. To provide greater articulation and continuity in the K-12 programs.
5. To provide more efficient maintenance and supply support of the school unit.
6. To reduce bureaucratic overlap and waste.

Oddly enough sufficient evidence was not found to support the generalizations about administrative decentralization and any concurrent plans for community involvement. The reasons tended to be based on intuition and logic, on polemics from the literature, and possibly on unstated reasons such as the pressure to reform the system. Very few of the school systems indicated that an evaluative procedure for their new organizational models had been implemented, and very few pointed out the need for pilot testing some of the related assumptions, goals, and recommendations.

Of the 69 school systems listed in table 3, only two report any type of community control with legal provisions for an elected local board of education functioning in conjunction with the central school board; they are New York City and Detroit. A far more frequent arrangement beyond the usual P.T.A. and school voluntary groups is the appointment of advisory committees at either the school or systems levels. These committees are usually appointed by the school administration; only in a few cases are these advisory groups elected by the community. Nevertheless, all these committees are advisory, as their names suggest; and whenever guidelines are established, the school boards usually reaffirm their own power and expectations that the advisory committees abide by the rules and regulations. It would seem, then, that school systems are usually willing to adopt or consider plans for administrative decentralization and community participation. As for community control, except for the above two city school systems (that is, New York and Detroit), it has not been implemented. For the most part, the officials running the schools have managed to maintain control. Many organizational policy reports of large school systems, such as those of Los Angeles and Philadelphia, and medium-sized school systems, such as those of Anne Arundel and Portland, have clearly concluded that community control has the potential for more harm than good; and nearly every report on administrative-community guidelines has clearly stated that policy making should remain in the hands of the central school board.

ADMINISTRATIVE-COMMUNITY ORGANIZATION PLANS
OF TWELVE SELECTED SCHOOL SYSTEMS

For purposes of this section, we will discuss the decentralization and community plans of New York City and Detroit, as of now the only two school systems enrolling 50,000 or more students which have combined administrative decentralization with community control. Then we will examine ten medium-sized school systems that are representative of various parts of the country; these school systems have combined administrative decentralization with community participation and thus represent the norm.

New York City, New York

The New York City school system is the largest in the country, consisting of approximately 965 schools, 110,000 professional personnel and 69,000 teachers, and 1.2 million students. The student racial composition is about 36 percent black, 35 percent white, 24 percent Puerto Rican, and 5 percent other. The city board of education consists of five appointed members.

Since the turn of the century, the New York City schools have been decentralized into attendance districts, each headed by a district superintendent who was responsible to the deputy superintendent. Local district boards also existed but on an appointed and advisory basis. In November 1967, the Mayor's Advisory Panel submitted its report, *Reconnection for Learning*, commonly referred to as the Bundy Report, after the chairman of the panel McGeorge Bundy. The report is perhaps the most important document in promoting the concept of community control. Among its 16 recommendations were suggestions that the schools in New York City be decentralized from the 30 attendance districts at that time into 30 to 60 community school districts, ranging in size from 12,000 to 40,000 students and that elected community boards be organized and have broad powers over personnel, curriculum, student policy, and finances. The city school board would have only limited powers in the area of student transfers, contract negotiations with the teachers, and school integration.

In March 1968, the school board issued a decentralization proposal, *A Plan for Educational Policy and Administrative Units (Further Decentralization of the Public Schools)*. The proposal reaffirmed the concept of decentralization and local district boards, but rejected the concept of community control as destructive to the cohesiveness of the school system. The school board expanded the advisory role of the local district boards but concluded "that a massive [reorganization] in the largest school system in the world in one swoop . . . would cause unnecessary and harmful disorganization" (p. 4).

Eventually interest groups lined up for and against community control. On one side of the issue were liberal and radical groups such as the mayor's office, the antipoverty agencies, the Ford Foundation, and the Urban Coalition, as well as militant segments of the minority community, who saw the need for community control of the schools. On the other side of the issue were the teachers' union and supervisory association, the board of education, the League for Industrial Democracy, and some moderate segments of the minority community such as the A. Phillip Randolph Institute, the black trade unionists, and the NAACP—all of whom still envisioned civil rights and integration in terms of the early 1960 coalitions and rejected community control as a form of separatism. Eventually, the battle over control of the schools divided a large portion of the city along racial lines and led to the Ocean Hill-Brownsville controversy and the ten-week 1968 teachers' strike.

In the end, a compromise bill was worked out which has satisfied few interest groups. In April 1969, the New York State Legislature amended the education law (Senate Bill 5690 and Assembly Bill 7175) and directed the city board of education to establish 30 to 33 community districts, each with a minimum of 20,000 students in average daily attendance, and each to be governed by an elected community board that would select its own community district superintendent; hire, discharge, and promote its personnel; share powers with the central board in matters concerning curriculum and student policy; and allocate budget items. At present, there are 32 community districts, comprising between 14 and 33 elementary and junior high schools and 20,000 to 38,000 students. The high schools remain under the jurisdiction of the city school board, because the attendance boundaries cut across several communities.

Detroit, Michigan

The Detroit school system is the fifth largest in the country, consisting of approximately 325 schools, 17,000 professional personnel and 12,000 teachers, and 277,500 students. The racial composition of the schools is about 65 percent black and 35 percent white. The seven-member central board of education was increased to thirteen members as a result of the 1971 decentralization plan. Five board members are elected in city-wide elections, and one member is elected from each of the eight decentralized regions.

Like New York City, the Detroit schools were decentralized for several years along attendance boundaries. In April 1970, the Michigan State Legislature passed Public Act 244, later revised to Public Act 48, which legally decentralized the Detroit schools into seven to eleven regions and created an elected board for each region, with the precise guidelines to be worked out by the Detroit school board. In Detroit, the concepts of decentralization and community control were vehemently advocated by black militants and white segregationists. Both groups envisioned community control as a means for gaining control of "their" schools, partly because both were uninterested in integration. The extent of their combined voting influence was reflected in the August 1970 referendum. A. L. Zwerdling, the president of the city's board of education, as well as the board majority, who viewed integration as a primary goal in any decentralization plan, were recalled by almost a 2-1 margin. This set the stage for decentralization and separatism.

In accordance with the decentralization law, the Detroit school board and its Office of School Decentralization published two in-house reports. The first report was the *Working Draft of Possible Guidelines for Implementation of Public Act 244*, a two-part report which was released in April and May 1970. About 100 issues were identified that involved decisions which could be made by the central school board separately, regional school boards separately, or both school boards. For each issue, the choices were defined within the limits of the law. In a few instances, there was only one choice permitted by law. After several workshops and public meetings, the board of education in August 1970 issued the *Public Reaction Draft of Decentralization Guidelines*. The *Guidelines* recommended that the school system be divided into eight regions, each governed by an elected regional board and each headed by a regional superintendent who would be responsible to the local board. The regional school boards would be granted broad powers over curriculum, staff organization, and in-service training, and would share powers with the central school board in such areas as personnel, student policy, testing and evaluation, and contract federal and state funds. As stated earlier, the central school board was expanded to 13 members. In October 1970, the Detroit board of education made some minor revisions and issued the guidelines under which the system now operates. At the present, the eight regions comprise between 24 and 56 schools and 20,000 to 35,000 students.

Dade County, Florida

The Dade County school system consists of approximately 235 schools, 12,000 licensed personnel and 10,000 teachers, and 240,000 students, making it the sixth largest school system in the country. The student racial composition is approximately 51 percent white, 27 percent black and 22 percent Spanish surnamed (mostly Cuban). The school board consists of seven elected members. The school system encompasses the government of Miami, along with 26 local municipal governments; it covers the entire county which is approximately 50 miles long and 40 miles wide. Only 27 percent of the 1.3 million people live in the urban center of Miami, while about 33 percent live in suburban areas and over 40 percent live in unincorporated and rural areas.

As a result of former superintendent Joseph Hall's recommendations in his July 1963 report, *Administrative Reorganization in the Dade County Schools,* the school system was divided into four districts. At that time, the four districts comprised between 48 and 60 schools and from 42,800 to 49,200 students. The move was based on bringing the instructional and administrative services closer to the schools. Each district was provided with a small number of appropriate personnel, including a district superintendent who was in charge of the schools within his unit and responsible to the school superintendent.

In August 1964, the school superintendent recommended in his report, *Reorganization of Dade County School System into Six Districts,* that the boundaries be changed to create six districts, which became effective in July 1965. The main criterion for the new boundaries was to cope with the growing student populations. The result was that the four districts with the greatest growth potential contained 30 to 33 schools, and the two central districts with the least growth potential comprised 36 and 47 schools, respectively. Each district contained from 25,000 to 40,000 students. By 1973, there were 33 to 38 schools in the four districts with the greatest growth potential and between 31,500 and 44,000 students; the two central districts comprised 44 and 46 schools, respectively, and approximately 45,000 students. Community participation was limited.

Houston, Texas

The Houston school system is the seventh largest one in the country. It consists of approximately 230 schools, 17,000 employees and 10,000 teachers, and 225,000 students. The school system is approximately 46 percent white, 39 percent black and 15 percent Mexican American. The school board is elected by the voters and consists of seven members.

Under the superintendency of George C. Garver, the Houston schools were decentralized in February 1971. The move was based on the 1970 recommendations of the Peat, Marvick, Mitchell & Co. report, *Houston Independent School District Management Review and Analysis.* The school system has been divided into six areas, each headed by an area instructional superintendent who is in charge of the schools within his boundaries and is responsible to the chief instructional superintendent at the central office. The six areas comprise between 33 and 45 schools and from 34,000 to 40,000 students.

Although the main purpose of the decentralization was to streamline the administrative organization and to consolidate the K-12 program, court order pressure to desegregate influenced the student racial composition of the six areas. Community participation has been enhanced by the administrative reorganization. Advisory groups from the community work with the principals and are either appointed by each principal or, in some instances, elected by community residents. The procedure varies according to the six areas and the specific advisory group, but they act only in an advisory capacity.

Memphis, Tennessee

The Memphis school system consists of approximately 165 schools, 10,000 professional employees and 6,200 teachers, and 139,000 students. Fifty-five percent of the students enrolled are black, and 45 percent are white. The board of education is composed of nine members, seven elected by political districts and two elected at large by popular vote.

In October 1969, Superintendent E. C. Stimbert and the board of education appointed a committee of professional education and management specialists to study the organization and administration of the Memphis schools. The committee submitted its report—commonly called the Haynes report, after Dr. Ford Haynes, the chairman of the Department of Secondary Education at Memphis State University and chairman of the committee, but entitled *A Staff Reorganization Study of the Memphis, Tennessee, School System*—in April 1970. Among its many recommendations was that the system be divided into four areas, each comprising an equal number of schools and students within what was geographically feasible. Each of the four areas would be headed by an area assistant superintendent, along with an appropriate staff, who would be in charge of the schools within his area and would be responsible to the newly created deputy superintendent. The purpose of the plan was to streamline the central administration, reduce the administrative span of control, and to enhance school-community relations.

The plan went into effect in July 1971. Each area consists of seven to eight pyramids established around a high school and its feeding junior high and elementary schools. Each area comprises between 33 and 44 schools and between 33,000 and 39,000 students. Area advisory councils have also been established for purposes of involving students, teachers, administrators, parents, and community residents. No standard model was suggested; instead, the rules have been drawn up by the area assistant superintendent with approval from the deputy superintendent. Council members are chosen by the area assistant superintendent with approval from the deputy superintendent. In their advisory capacity, the councils assist in the development of educational programs and consult with the chief area administrator.

St. Louis, Missouri

The St. Louis school system consists of approximately 180 schools, 7,400 professional personnel and 4,100 teachers, and 104,000 students with an approximate 65 to 35 black/white student ratio. The school board consists of 13 elected members.

In 1962, the school system was divided into five elementary districts, and an additional district was established in 1964, each headed by an assistant superintendent. The purposes of decentralizing were to reduce the administrative span of control and to improve local school-community relations. Each assistant superintendent was responsible for administering the elementary schools and also met on a regular basis with the newly formed parent congress in his district.

Moves to extend the assistant superintendent's responsibilities to the high schools began in 1966 with a pilot program in one of the districts. The following year a second pilot program was established in another district, and in the 1968–69 school year this administrative structure was implemented on a school-system basis.

In January 1969, the Office of Superintendent's statement, *Recommendations for Greater Local Participation in the Total Operation of the Schools*, reaffirmed the advisory role of the parent congresses; they were to be elected by the community, and the number of representatives from each school could not exceed four. It was further recommended that the titles of the six assistant superintendents be changed to district superintendent. Further steps to decentralize the schools were taken in June 1970, as a result of the Office of Superintendent's report, *St. Louis Public Schools Reorganization Plan*. The school system was divided into ten administrative units, each with its own administrative assistant and parent congress. Two units were paired (mainly on a geographical basis) to form a district, resulting in a total of five districts. In each district there are two high schools, between 20 and 28 elementary schools, and from 19,000 to 23,000 students.

Each district superintendent is responsible for coordinating the parent congresses in his district in conjunction with local needs and city-wide policies. The district superintendent is responsible to the central office and meets regularly with the board of education to interpret district needs and recommendations made by the parent congress.

Anne Arundel County, Maryland

The school system consists of approximately 99 schools, 3,500 professionals and 3,000 teachers, and 77,000 students. About 88 percent of the student population is white; the remainder is black. The school board is appointed by the governor and consists of seven members. The county is mainly suburban, including the small city of Annapolis and lying between the cities of Baltimore and Washington, D.C.

Plans for decentralization were submitted to the board of education in April 1970 in a report entitled, *Recommendations Concerning Administrative Decentralization of the Anne Arundel County School System*. The purpose of the plan was to provide greater continuity of the K-12 school program and administrative services to the schools, as well as to enhance community involvement through citizen advisory committees.

In 1973, the school system was decentralized into four areas. Each area comprises between four and seven secondary schools, eighteen to nineteen elementary schools, and 16,000 to 23,000 students. The area directors are in charge of the schools within their boundaries and are accountable to the deputy superintendent of instruction. In addition, several instructional positions and resource teachers of different subjects have been added to each area, in line with coordinating the elementary and secondary program.

The Anne Arundel Citizens Advisory Committees and Operating Procedures (1973), a report based on the 1970 amendments to the school law, outlines the extent of community involvement. A local citizen advisory group for each school meets regularly with the school principal to advise him on the school program. There is an area citizen advisory committee for each of the four areas, consisting of one representative from each local committee, which meets regularly with the area director. In addition, a school-wide citizen advisory committee, consisting of representatives from each area, meets with the board of education. In all cases, the committees only make recommendations and are not permitted to act in a decision-making capacity.

Pittsburgh, Pennsylvania

The Pittsburgh school system consists of approximately 115 schools, 3,350 teachers, and 70,000 students. The white enrollment is about 60 percent, and the black enrollment is about 40 percent. The board of education consists of 15 members, appointed for a six-year term by the judges of the Court of the Common Pleas of Allegheny County.

In 1970, the schools were decentralized for purposes of reducing the administrative bureaucracy and coordinating the curriculum. Each of the three areas is headed by a superintendent who is accountable to the school superintendent. The duties previously performed by the associate superintendents for the elementary schools and secondary schools have been transferred to the three area superintendents, thus illustrating the goal of continuity for the K-12 program. Each area consists of between 29 and 47 schools and about 23,000 students.

Although there are several local advisory committees, the most interesting one is the Reorganization Advisory Committee which advises the board of education on policies pertaining to school organization, overcrowding, and desegregation. Members are selected by the school superintendent, and they are divided into three subgroups based on the three decentralized areas (Pittsburgh Information Officer, 1972).

Portland, Oregon

The Portland school system consists of approximately 114 schools, 7,400 personnel and 3,600 teachers, and 69,000 students. The white/black student population ratio is 91 to 9. The board of education consists of seven elected members.

In its March 1970 resolution on the *Portland Schools for the Seventies,* the school board adopted six objectives, among them the need to provide administrative autonomy to the schools and greater citizen participation. To help achieve these objectives, three administrative areas were formed comprising between 38 and 45 schools and from 22,000 to 29,000 students. Each area was headed by an area superintendent responsible to the deputy superintendent. An advisory committee was organized for each area.

In July 1971, the board of education detailed selection methods, rules of procedures, and duties for advisory committees. Based on the *Rules of Procedures for Area Advisory Committees* (1971), the school board selects nine members, including seven community members and two high school students, from each area. Each area superintendent meets with this committee on a regular basis and listens to recommendations concerning educational matters.

El Paso, Texas

The El Paso school system consists of 63 schools, 3,125 certified personnel including 2,800 teachers, and 62,500 students. The official student enrollment is approximately 53 percent Mexican-American, 43 percent Anglo, 3 percent black, and 1 percent other. The board of education consists of seven members elected by the registered voters. Although the city was annexed to Ysleta several years ago, the two school districts remain independent, and the Ysleta district is about two-thirds the size of the El Paso district.

After studying various decentralization guidelines for two years, a plan was implemented in September 1972. According to the *Administrative Communication of El Paso Public Schools* (1972) and the *El Paso Times* (July 21, 1972), the school system has been divided into three areas, each with about 21 schools and 21,000 students. Each area superintendent is in charge of the schools in his area and reports directly to Superintendent H. E. Charles. Curriculum specialists from the central office have been reassigned to the area offices to improve curriculum services at the school level.

Since 1970 several community advisory groups have been formed to improve school-community-city relations. These groups include (among others, not mentioned): a student advisory committee, consisting of students from each of the nine high schools, which meets twice each month with the school superintendent to discuss school affairs; an advisory committee on Mexican-American educational needs, a group of twelve Mexican-American school employees appointed by the school superintendent which meets weekly to enhance communication between the Mexican-American community and school administration; an ad hoc committee on technical and vocational education, consisting of 14 El Paso businessmen who meet with and inform the board of education on business trends in the metropolitan area; a planning task force committee, a group of 35 citizens who study all aspects of education for the school system. In addition, as a result of decentralization, each area superintendent meets regularly with a newly elected parent advisory council to discuss school curriculum and services.

Minneapolis, Minnesota

The Minneapolis schools consist of 94 schools and 3,200 teachers that serve approximately 61,500 students. The student population is about 87 percent white and 13 percent minority—including 9 percent black, 3 percent Indian, and .5 percent each of Oriental and Spanish-speaking children. The board of education consists of seven members, each elected for six years on a 2-2-3 staggered basis.

Upon assuming the superintendency in January 1967, John B. Davis, Jr., stated in his first policy address the need for decentralization to improve administrative facilities and school-community relations. Based on his report, *Decentralization of Schools in Minneapolis*, the first pyramid was established in August 1967. It was based on one high school and its eleven feeding schools and served approximately 10,000 students. Two years later, the board of education established a second pyramid, based on two high schools and serving thirteen feeder schools also with approximately 10,000 students. Both pyramids are located in or near the inner city.

The two pyramids have been unified into one area and are headed by an area assistant superintendent. Accountability is directed upward at the central office to the two associate superintendents for elementary education and secondary education. An advisory council has been formed, which includes one parent representative from each school, in both pyramids. The advisory council meets with the area assistant superintendent. In addition, there is an elected sixty-member advisory group called the community council, composed of parents, professional staff, and students, which meets regularly to evaluate programs within the area. Curriculum and instructional services have been consolidated for both pyramids.

Oakland, California

The school system consists of approximately 91 schools, 2,700 teachers, and 60,000 students. The student population is 60 percent black, 25 percent white, 9 percent Spanish-surnamed, 5 percent Oriental, and 1 percent other. The board of education consists of seven elected members.

Upon assuming responsibility as superintendent in January 1970, Marcus A. Foster (now deceased) received permission from the board of education to hire Price-Waterhouse to study the school system and recommend administrative changes. The consulting firm submitted its report, *Recommendation for Improving the Management Effectiveness of the Oakland Unified Schools,* in September 1970. Among its recommendations was to create three regions, each headed by a regional associate superintendent who would be in charge of the schools. The purpose was to facilitate the management of the schools and to increase the level of citizen participation.

Implementation of the plan started in January 1971. Each region comprises approximately 30 schools and 19,000 to 22,000 students. In the spirit of the Price-Waterhouse report, a Master Plan Citizen's Committee was formed in April 1971 to study six major aspects of the school system's policies and future programs: curriculum and instruction, school plant, community resources, decentralization, school finances, and school desegregation. The committee consists of approximately 370 members from public and private agencies, as well as community and student representatives from each of the schools.

Each of the 91 schools also has its own school site planning committee for purposes of focusing on local issues and problems. According to the *Master Plan Citizens Committee Guidelines* (1971), every interested citizen, teacher, and student may attend these local meetings. These local school committees send representatives to the Master Plan Citizens Committee, thus enhancing communication between the local and city-wide committees. The Master Plan Citizens Committee is divided into the six aforementioned study groups which in turn are subdivided into smaller resource groups to permit intensive study of problems. The board of education has final authority over all the committees and subcommittees; however, the local school committees have authority to select three candidates for the position of principal when there is a vacancy, with final selection made by the school superintendent.

In summary, the twelve school systems have decentralized or have continued the decentralization process since 1967. In New York City and Detroit, decentralization has accompanied community control; the process has solidified neighborhood school boundaries and solidified school segregation. In these two school systems, the principal and decentralized field administrator are now accountable to an elected local school board.[5] In the remaining ten school systems, the principal remains accountable to an administrator on a vertical hierarchy. Instead of being theoretically accountable to someone at the central office, the principal is now presumably accountable to the decentralized field administrator, who in turn is supposed to be accountable to someone at the central office—usually the deputy superintendent or school superintendent.

Typically, advisory groups were formed prior to and concurrent with the decentralization move. In most instances, the decentralization moves resulted in additional formal advisory groups. There usually was an expressed desire on the part of the school system to ensure a representative racial mix from the community on local and system-wide advisory committees. In all instances, the rules and guidelines of these advisory committees clearly reaffirmed that the decision-making authority remained with the board of education. Rules often stated that the committees could not disturb the operation of the schools or could not act as a pressure group. In many instances, it was specified that the rules of procedure could be amended at any time by the board of education. The most aggressive form of community participation was in Oakland, where the various advisory committees served as vehicles for interested students, parents, and community and city residents to educate themselves on school matters, voice their opinions, and participate in school planning. The nature of the input was still advisory.

RESEARCH SUGGESTIONS FOR THE FUTURE

A few years ago, Fantini (1970), one of the major proponents of administrative decentralization and community control, criticized those who urged caution because there was a lack of empirical evidence. He wrote:

> The first question [of the skeptic] usually is: What evidence is there
> that neighborhood control of urban schools improves student

achievement? The answer is that if there is no evidence it is because there really are no community-controlled urban public schools. . . . However, what we do have ample evidence of is the massive failure that the standard, centrally controlled urban school has produced. It is ironic, therefore, that those in control of a failing system should ask others offering alternatives to demand results before there has been any chance for full implementation. (p. 52)

That same year, T. Clark (1970) reviewed the current books on administrative decentralization, using the term interchangeably with community control. He concluded:

What a considerable portion of the literature on decentralization to date amounts to is special pleading for a particular solution. . . . Very little attempt is made to develop ideas coherent enough to warrant the term "theory," and the casual use of favorable examples seldom justifies the label of empirical research. Where knowledge is incomplete but problems immediate . . . one can still expect generalizing intellectuals and amateur politicians to come forth with solutions. (p. 509)

[D]ecentralization . . . may ameliorate some pressing problems. Such efforts can serve as useful vehicles for social as well as social-scientific experimentation. But unless there is more systematic social-scientific analysis of these efforts than we have generally had to date, we may never understand their many consequences. (p. 514)

These two statements clearly reflect the position differences between the role of the reformer and that of the social scientist (researcher). The former often may seek change for the sake of change, often without much support from research. In contrast, the social scientist often opposes mass change without evidence. According to Robinson (1972), "This confrontation is by no means new; in fact, its very existence may be deemed a necessary requirement for a vital society." But like so many other differences today, it appears much sharper, and it seems that "there is heightened respect for change per se, quite apart from any presumption . . . of improvement" (p. 587). Similarly, there appears to be a decline of respect for the value of research and a concurrent claim by those who do not understand research (including many community activists, teachers, administrators, and even professors) that the researchers are elitists.

The central fallacy of many reform educators is that their ideas are often based on "bandwagon wisdom," with little research evidence. A good number of these educators are unscientific and antiresearch; they sometimes plunge into implementation without knowledge that what they are doing really works.[6] They may use fashionable terms and clichés and expect others to accept their "wisdom" on faith. In many cases, reformers like to think up new programs and ideas rather than try to implement them; in fact, they sometimes run from their programs and ideas just before the roof caves in.

Not only does the pace of school reform make one pessimistic, now it becomes increasingly questionable whether the schools can do much to help solve any of the major problems of society. Certainly there is demonstrated failure of ghetto schooling, but there is also no empirical evidence that administrative decentralization or community control will reform the schools. Without quality research, we base our claims at best on bandwagon wisdom, at worst on political ideology.

Without research, claims based on unsupported evidence, intuition, and logic can continue to be voiced, and testimonials from the advocates of change and ideology can always be found. So long as there is no adequate research related to decentralization and community control, the bite of the opponents' criticism is reduced. Moreover, opponents are put on the defensive, criticized for resisting change, branded as caretakers of the Establishment and status quo.

This, indeed, is exactly what happened to Ocean Hill-Brownsville, as mentioned earlier Ravitch (1972). The advocates of community control claimed favorable changes: "that Ocean Hill had already achieved academic success"; innovative methods had "succeeded in raising the reading levels of many children in the districts in a remarkably short time"; by February 1, 1970, "every youngster in the school system [would] be classified as a reader." The opponents could only claim that there was no available statistical data, since "it [Ocean Hill-Brownsville] was the only district in the city which had not participated in the standardized city-wide reading tests" (pp. 71–72). The eventual comparison of reading scores showed the experiment to be a failure; nevertheless, the New York City school system was pressured into a city-wide policy which provided for a strong measure of community control.

If a school system initiates an across-the-board-change, such as community control or almost any other "reform" measure, without evidence that the change has positive effects on learning, the change may be not only educationally unsound and irresponsible but may also indicate that education is not the real issue. As Bard (1972, concerning New York City), Aberbach and Walker (1971, concerning Detroit), and La Noue (1972, concerning both cities) suggest, much of the issue of community control was political and economic, and the pressures behind the changes were racial and ideological. If the changes in New York and Detroit have a negative impact on student learning, return to the former unitary school system will be difficult—actually, with the present racial situation, nearly impossible.

According to K. Clark (1972*a*), one of the original advocates of decentralization and community control, "the evidence does not now add up to any indication" that these changes are making "for a better break for our children in schools." Those involved in decentralization and community control "have forgotten what the purpose was. The purpose was not a struggle for power or control" (p. 1). He claims that if we find we are "wasting our time and people are going to squabble and fight and . . . neglect the children," then we [should] try to find other ways in which the children will be given priority" (p. 26). The point is, it is too late; community control in New York City is a fact, and it is not going to go away, regardless of how guilty or sorrowful a few of the original advocates now feel. They should have realized the potential for conflict; they should not have been so naïve. Elsewhere K. Clark (1972*b*) reports that "school decentralization has been a 'disastrous' experience in which the basic issue, teaching children, has been substituted by selfish forces . . . These forces include the radical politics of small local groups" (p. 7). How could anyone argue for decentralization and community control without taking into account the political implications? Once a group gains power, it is usually unwilling to surrender it, despite the general harm it may perpetuate. (Only in a school system where racial tension is minimal or nonexistent can there be change from centralization to decentralization, then an easy return to centralization.) Indeed, the process of schooling is largely political—who makes what decisions—and linked to economic considerations—not only who gets what jobs in the future but who gets what jobs *now*. As Goodlad (1971) says, "Schooling is conducted within a framework of power and struggle for power. It is no more protected from abuse of power than are other political enterprises" (p. 16).

When we talk about community control, especially in the large cities, we are also talking about who will make decisions, about who will be hired, discharged, and promoted, whether those in power or those vying for power will use it as a means of advancing their own causes and self-interests, and whether the same standards will be used to judge different teachers and administrators. If caution is not carefully exercised, racial and ethnic factors can become major variables. Or as Billings (1972) asserts, the "conflict over community control . . . of school represents nothing more or less than a struggle of power between blacks and whites" (p. 277). When we talk about community control, then, we may be, according to Ornstein and Talmage (1973), talking about

> . . . *which teachers and administrators should be hired, promoted, fired, or go unemployed in a period when teaching jobs are difficult to come by and where in urban areas there is an upsurge of racial patterns in the appointment of "acting principals" in ghetto schools and increasing competition among whites for administrative slots in white enclaves.* (p. 144)

Where community control exists in New York City and Detroit, local power groups and militant leaders have fought over procedures for selecting and discharging administrators, sometimes with little regard for legality or due process. As we have already reported, racial quotas have been publicly announced in a few of the community-controlled areas in both school systems.[7] And in each of the school systems there are candidates who have recently obtained their teaching licenses and have been placed on waiting lists while unqualified people from off the streets have been hired to staff the classrooms. Militant groups are not only forcing the resignation of many elected community board members in both school systems, but there are allegations in the New York and Detroit newspapers of black militants fighting with and threatening the lives of black moderates. There is also testimony that elected school board members in both school systems direct questions to supervisory candidates to find out their political and ideological views (Bard, 1972; K. Clark, 1972 *a*, 1972 *b*; Lyke, 1970; Ornstein, 1973).

When we talk about community control, we may also be talking about a spoils system. According to Bard (1972) and Moseley (1972), we are referring to who gets jobs with salaries ranging up to $25,000 and $40,000, where race and ideology become important criteria—perhaps more important than merit. The stakes are high, of course, especially for the proponents and for those who stand to gain (or lose) their jobs. Aware of the usual discrepancies between rhetoric and reason, not to mention promise versus reality, many advocates of community control would prefer to limit evaluation, or at least control it so that the "findings" are known before the report is written.

Lack of comparable data and of concrete evidence tends to work in favor of those who advocate change without evidence. This is especially true for those who end up controlling the new policies and making decisions on who is held accountable and what criteria are used to determine accountability. As Campbell (1972) writes, "Given the inherent difficulty of making significant improvements . . . and given the discrepancy between promise and possibility . . . there is safety under the cloak of ignorance . . . if [a group] has committed itself in advance to the correctness and efficacy of its reforms, it cannot tolerate learning of failure" (p. 188). Similarly, Rossi (1972) points out that those who advocate new policies are often against research and evaluation because they "might find that effects are negligible or nonexistent" (p. 227). In fact, it seems likely that community control may have little or no effects on student achievement because there are so many other variables associated with school learning that schools themselves have little control over. As Guba (1969) writes, "over and over comparative studies of alternatives in education have ended in a finding of 'no significant difference.' " It would appear that "the educationalists are incapable of desiring any approaches that are better than those things that they are already using" (p. 31).

One might argue, then, that community control need only to show no difference in student achievement to be considered worthwhile. This is debatable. When advocating change, new programs should demonstrate a positive effect; this is especially true when the promises and potential are claimed to be so great. Before going overboard on any scheme, we need evidence that it works, especially when we are dealing with serious matters that threaten job security of teachers and administrators.

What kind of research in urban schools is feasible and potentially useful? The need is to implement pilot programs, with randomized and controlled comparisons. Data would be forthcoming which should tentatively validate or invalidate our hypotheses. The findings should be replicated in similar settings. However, it is misleading to take the results of one or a few experiments as conclusive evidence. There are no totally typical cities, no entirely typical communities, no typical decentralization plans, no typical community control plans. Longitudinal studies for 5 to 10 years would supply a wealth of data, but because of politics and pressure we cannot wait that long to obtain data; this type of study might be conducted in conjunction with the case study approach, with tentative findings being disseminated every year. Not only ought we to conduct rigorous testing in the initial pilot program, but once it has been decided that reform is to be adopted as standardized practice throughout the system, we still need to evaluate it experimentally in each of its stages.

Future research in the area of school decentralization and community control might also focus on the survey questions listed in table 4 below. The first set of questions provides school-community background information. The second set of questions is specifically related to both concepts. Both differences within a group and those between groups should be measured.

The questions in table 4 are related to conflicting demands at different levels of intensity by various interest groups. To date, the issues related to administrative decentralization and community control have not been satisfactorily resolved by the various interest groups. Indeed, there is continuing need for research to fill in the unresolved issues and unknown consequences of these two organizational models. One must deal with the question of whether the students and society really benefit and clarify the roles of the various interest groups in both sets of changes in the school system. We have little research evidence that administrative decentralization and community control improve education. A systematic response to these issues is, of course, crucial for the proponents of the various decentralization and community control schemes; otherwise, what we have are unsupported assertions quoted as statements of facts.

TABLE 4

SURVEY QUESTIONS RELATED TO ADMINISTRATIVE DECENTRALIZATION AND COMMUNITY CONTROL

Part I

School-Community Questions to Provide Background Information

School	Community
1. How does the school provide opportunity for the community to learn about the school?	1. How does the community provide opportunity for the school to learn about the community?
2. How do school personnel feel about the community? Why?	2. How does the community feel about the school personnel? Why?
3. How does the school support the community?	3. How does the community support the school?
4. How does the school use community resources and leadership?	4. How does the community use the school resources and leadership?
5. How does the school provide opportunity for the community to participate in the educational program?	5. How does the community provide opportunity for the school to participate in the community program?
6. What can be done to improve the situation?	6. What can be done to improve the situation?

Part II

Questions Related to Decentralization and Community Control

Administrative Decentralization	Community Control
1. Who are the advocates?[a]	1. Who are the advocates?
2. What are the motivations of the people involved?[a]	2. What are the motivations of the people involved?
3. How seriously does the public want to decentralize? (Is it just a small, well-organized minority of educators or residents?)	3. How seriously does the public want community control? (Is it just a small, well-organized minority of educators or residents?)
4. What are the various roles of the students, parents, community leaders, professional staff, etc.?	4. What are the various roles of the students, parents, community leaders, professional staff, etc.?
5. Do students, parents, community residents, teachers, etc. have a greater voice under decentralization?	5. Do students, parents, community residents, teachers, etc. have a greater voice under community control?
6. What role problems develop among the various interest groups?	6. What role problems develop among the various interest groups?
7. How do various interest groups feel before and after decentralization is implemented? (What are the differences when race and class are controlled?)	7. How do the various interest groups feel before and after community control is implemented? (What are the differences when race and class are controlled?)
8. How do the various interest groups want to be represented? (What are the differences when race and class are controlled?)	8. How do the various interest groups want to be represented? (What are the differences when race and class are controlled?)

[a] Questions 1 and 2 under Administrative Decentralization are derived from La Noue (1972).

TABLE 4 (*continued*)

Part II (*continued*)

Questions Related to Decentralization and Community Control

Administrative Decentralization	Community Control
9. How do labor unions, political groups, and municipal and community agencies effect decentralization?	9. How do labor unions, political groups, and municipal and community agencies effect community control?
10. How does the current racial and job situation affect decentralization? (What impact has it made on the racial and ethnic distribution of teaching jobs and administrative positions?)	10. How does the current racial and job situation affect community control? (What impact has it made on the racial and ethnic distribution of teaching jobs and administrative positions?)
11. How does decentralization affect the student's learning?	11. How does community control affect the student's learning?
12. What decentralized unit size (in terms of geographical or metropolitan location, area size, number of students and racial composition of schools) is most effective?	12. What type of community control (in terms of geographical or metropolitan location, area size, number of students, and racial composition) is most effective?
13. What administrative levels (central office, district or field office, individual schools) should be decentralized?	13. What administrative functions (curriculum, personnel, student policy, budget) should be controlled by whom?
14. When does bigness lead to inflexibility?	14. When does community control lead to racial discrimination or political chaos?
15. When does smallness lead to reduced range of educational services?	15. When does professional control lead to reverse discrimination or status quo education?
16. What is the cost of decentralization?	16. What is the cost of community control?

17. What support (internal and external) does a community school board require to function successfully?

18. What changes in educational policy and approaches have community school boards been able to implement that were not possible under the central school board?

19. How does community control affect school integration? (Can they be implemented together?)

20. What is the impact of community control on metropolitan development and cooperation? (Can we have community control and still promote metropolitan cooperation?)

21. What is the impact of community control and federal reform? (Can they be implemented together?)

22. How can conflicts be reduced so basic education issues take priority over power?

17. What support (internal and external) does a decentralized unit require to function successfully?

18. What changes in educational policy and approaches have decentralized units been able to implement that were not possible under the centralized administration?

19. How does decentralization affect school integration? (Can they be implemented together?)

20. What is the impact of school decentralization on metropolitan development and cooperation? (Can we decentralize and still promote metropolitan cooperation?)

21. What is the impact of school decentralization on federal reform? (Can they be implemented together?)

22. How can conflicts be reduced so basic educational issues take priority over power?

Thus T. Clark (1970) points out that many of the proponents of decentralization and community control, "including some of Athenian stature,
operate from a number of questionable assumptions" (p. 513). Similarly,
La Noue (1972) comments that many of the conclusions about decentralization and community control, either stated or implied, seem unjustified
in terms of available evidence.

The point is, the so-called "solutions" (administrative decentralization, community control, even community participation) are mainly
slogans rather than closely worked out concepts with consequences understood and accounted for in the rhetoric. We assume that the "community" voice is the most vocal and articulated, and we have yet to hear
from the majority of silent parents who have their own aspirations for
their children's lives and their own ideas about how the school should
fulfill them. Once these plans are adopted on a system-wide basis, they
would be very difficult to reverse in many large school systems, especially
where ideology and racial conflict are apparent. What we need, then, is
research that will test the worth of unsupported statements and claims.
We have to test our hypotheses and use caution against drawing unwarranted conclusions. The aim is to develop experimental designs to obtain
data, and to see whether our findings can be replicated in different
settings. We need a partnership between practitioners and researchers,
among the various interest groups, and especially between blacks and
whites, if a breakthrough is to be made to a higher level of mutual
understanding and quality education for children and youth.

CONCLUSION

It must be realized that most of the so-called experts, whether they are
from Harvard University, teachers' organizations, or the black community, are as flummoxed as the rest of us when it comes to defining precisely
and then solving the ills of metropolitan America and its schools. To a
large extent educational reformers from both sides of the political continuum draw on a shared vocabulary: social justice, racial equality, equal
opportunity, and all the rest. The difficulties come—and the splits
appear—when rhetoric must be translated into action. One who is familiar with the literature grows no less weary of the critics who offer few
constructive and realistic solutions than of the current administrators
who tirelessly excuse the status quo. One begins to feel that their imagination has outstripped reality.

What is even more disturbing is the increasing inability of all sides in
the great debate about improving the schools to find a common language
that can bridge their various concerns. We certainly have the money and
resources to improve our schools, and to improve the education of all

children and youth. What we still need is to find this common language; we need to put aside our self-interests and ideologies, to reduce the irrationalism and emotional exchanges, and finally, to depolarize.

NOTES

1. A lengthy analysis of research on administrative decentralization and community organization is found in Ornstein (1974*a*, 1974*b*).

2. In addition, Louisville is in the process of going beyond community participation but as of 1973 there were no specific guidelines for community control.

3. Most of the items pertained to accountability. For our purposes, only those items related to community control are examined.

4. Internal consistency reliability and pre- and post-test reliabilities were satisfactory (Hoyt's ANOVA reliability = .700; preservice teachers, Pearson Product Moment Correlation, r = .893; in-service teachers, Pearson Product Moment Correlation, r = .744).

5. During the first school board elections in 1970 in New York City, only 15 percent of the eligible voters turned out; most of them were from organized groups affiliated with churches, political clubs, antipoverty agencies, and the like. The second school board elections in 1973 produced a smaller percentage, 11 percent of the eligible voters, despite wide publicity. It can be stated that the advocates of community control grossly exaggerated the demand for "participatory democracy," and it is also questionable whether the local school board members really represent the community, and especially the parents of the school children, or only a few partisan or political groups.

6. For example, compensatory education cost us billions of dollars before we found out it does not work. By late 1972 there were more than 250 performance contracts, although there was little evidence that such contracts achieved what they purported to achieve. Across the country reformers now advocate the use of behavioral objectives and performance criteria. Institutions of higher learning often find they cannot get federal funds unless behavioral objectives and performance criteria are written into their teacher training programs; yet there is very scanty evidence that these ideas work, improve teacher training, or can be successfully implemented.

7. See chapter 3, footnote 13.

REFERENCES

Aberbach, Joel D. and Jack L. Walker. 1971. "Citizen Desires, Policy Outcomes, and Community Control." Paper presented at the Annual American Political Science Association Conference. Chicago, September.

Administrative Communication of El Paso Public Schools. 1972. El Paso, Texas: Board of Education of El Paso, August.

Administrative Reorganization in the Dade County Schools. 1963. Submitted by Joseph Hall, Superintendent of Schools, to the Members of the Board of Public Instruction. Miami, Fl.: Board of Public Instruction of Dade County, June 12.

Anne Arundel County Public Schools. 1970. *Decentralization Plans Followed by Public School Systems with Student Enrollments of 50,000 or More*. Anne Arundel, Md.: The Author, March.

Bard, Bernard. 1972. "The Battle for School Jobs: New York's Newest Agony." *Phi Delta Kappan* 53: 553–558.

Billings, Charles E. 1972. "Community Control of the School and the Quest for Power." *Phi Delta Kappan* 53: 277–278.

Brookover, Wilbur, et al. 1965. *Self Concept of Ability and School Achievement*. Vol. 2. East Lansing, Mich.: Bureau of Educational Research Services, Michigan State University.

Campbell, Donald T. 1972. "Reforms as Experiments." Pp. 187–223 in C. H. Weiss (ed.) *Evaluating Action Programs*. Boston: Allyn & Bacon.

Carmichael, Stokely and Charles V. Hamilton. 1967. *Black Power: The Politics of Liberation in America*. Vintage ed. New York: Random House.

Citizens Advisory Committees Guidelines and Operating Procedures. 1973. Annapolis, Md.: Board of Education of Anne Arundel County, Maryland.

Clark, Kenneth B. 1972*a*. News article in the *New York Times*, May 8, pp. 1, 26.

———. 1972*b*. News article in the *New York Times*, December 3, p. 7.

Clark, Terry. 1970. "On Decentralization." *Polity* 2: 508–514.

Cloward, Richard A. and James A. Jones. 1963. "Social Class: Educational Attitudes and Participation." Pp. 190–216 in A. H. Passow (ed.) *Education in Depressed Areas*. New York: Teachers College Press, Columbia University.

Coleman, James S., et al. 1966. *Equality of Educational Opportunity*. Washington, D.C.: U.S. Government Printing Office.

Dawson, Howard A. 1955. "District Reorganization." *School Executive* 74: 86–87.

Dawson, Howard A. and William J. Ellena. 1954. "School District Reorganization." *School Executive* 73: 39–42.

Decentralization of Schools in Minneapolis. 1967. Submitted by John B. Davis, Jr., Superintendent of the Schools, to the Members of the Board of Education. Minneapolis, Minn.: Board of Education of Minneapolis.

Deutsch, Martin. 1964. "Facilitating Development in the Preschool Child: Social and Psychological Perspectives." *Merrill Palmer Quarterly* 10: 249–263.

———. 1971. "Perspectives on the Education of the Urban Child." Pp. 103–119 in A. H. Passow (ed.) *Urban Education in the 1970s.* New York: Teachers College Press, Columbia University.

District Boundary Lines Under the Community School District System. 1969. Special Committee on Decentralization (Committee of the Whole). New York: Board of Education of the City of New York, December.

El Paso Times, July 21, 1972.

Fantini, Mario D. 1970. *The Reform of Urban Schools.* Washington, D.C.: National Educational Association. Reprinted by permission of *Today's Education.*

Fantini, et al. 1970. *Community Control and the Urban School.* New York: Praeger.

Fusco, Gene C. 1966. "Reaching the Parents." Pp. 145–161 in R. D. Strom (ed.) *The Inner-City Classroom.* Columbus, Ohio: Merrill.

Goodlad, John I. 1971. "What Educational Decisions by Whom?" *Science Teacher* 38: 16–19 ff.

Gordon, Edmund W. and Doxey A. Wilkerson. 1966. *Compensatory Education for the Disadvantaged.* New York: College Entrance Examination Board.

Guba, Egon G. 1969. "The Failure of Educational Evaluation." *Educational Technology* 31: 29–38.

Hess, Robert D. and Virginia C. Shipman. 1966. "Maternal Attitude Toward the School and the Role of Pupils: Some Social Class Comparisons." Paper presented for the Fifth Work Conference on Curriculum and Teaching in Depressed Areas. New York: Teachers College Press, Columbia University.

Houston Independent School District Management Review and Analysis. 1970. Vol. 1. Submitted by Peat, Marvick, Mitchell & Company to the Superintendent of the Schools. Houston, Tex.: The Author, November.

Jablonsky, Adelaide. 1968. "Some Trends in Education of the Disadvantaged." *IRCD Bulletin* 4: 1–11.

La Noue, George R. 1972. "The Politics of School Decentralization: Methodological Considerations." Paper presented at the Annual AERA Conference. Chicago, April.

Levin, Henry M. (ed.) 1970. *Community Control of Schools*. Washington, D.C.: Brookings Institution.

Lopate, Carol, et al. 1970. "Decentralization and Community Participation in Public Education." *Review of Educational Research* 40: 135–150.

Lyke, Robert F. 1970. "Political Issues in School Decentralization." Pp. 111–132 in M. Kirst (ed.) *The Politics of Education at the Local, State and Federal Levels*. Berkeley, Calif.: McCutchan.

Master Plan Citizens Committee Guidelines. 1971. Adopted by the Oakland Board of Education on January 19, 1971. Oakland, Calif.: Board of Education of Oakland, 1971.

Mayor's Advisory Panel on Decentralization of the New York City Schools. 1967. *Reconnection for Learning: A Community School System for New York City*. New York: Ford Foundation.

Moseley, Francis S. 1972. "The Urban Secondary School: Too Late for Mere Change." *Phi Delta Kappan* 53: 559–564.

Ornstein, Allan C. 1972*a*. "The Politics of School Decentralization and Community Control." A report to Dan Walker, governor of the state of Illinois. Chicago, August.

———. 1972*b*. *Urban Education: Student Unrest, Teacher Behaviors, and Black Power*. Columbus, Ohio: Merrill.

———. 1973. "Administrative/Community Organization of Metropolitan Schools." *Phi Delta Kappan* 54: 668–674.

———. 1974*a*. *Metropolitan Schools: Administrative Decentralization vs. Community Control*. Metuchen, N.J.: Scarecrow Press.

———. 1974*b*. *Race and Politics in School/Community Organizations*. Pacific Palisades, Calif.: Goodyear.

Ornstein, Allan C. and Harriet Talmage. 1973. "A Dissenting View on Accountability." *Urban Education* 8: 133–151.

Pittsburgh Information Officer. 1972. Letters to Allan C. Ornstein, March 13, June 28.

A Plan for Educational Policy and Administrative Units (Further Decentralization of the Public Schools). 1968. New York: Board of Education of the City of New York, March.

Pois, Joseph. 1964. *The School Board Crisis: A Chicago Case Study*. Chicago: Educational Methods.

Portland Schools for the Seventies. 1970. From the Board of Education, Resolution No. 3553. Portland, Ore.: Board of Education of Portland, March.

Public Reaction Draft of School Decentralization Guidelines. 1970. Detroit: Office of School Decentralization, Board of Education of the City of Detroit, August.

Ravitch, Diane. 1972. "Community Control Revisited." *Commentary* (February): 70–74.

Recommendations Concerning Administrative Decentralization of the Anne Arundel County School System. 1970. Submitted by the Superintendent's Committee on Decentralization. Annapolis, Md.: Board of Education of Anne Arundel County, April.

Recommendations for Greater Local Participation in the Total Operation of the St. Louis Public Schools. 1969. From the Office of the Superintendent of the Schools. St. Louis, Mo.: Board of Education of St. Louis, January.

Recommendation for Improving the Management Effectiveness of the Oakland Unified Schools. 1970. Submitted by Price-Waterhouse Co. to the Superintendent of the Schools. Oakland, Calif.: The Company, September.

Rempson, Joe L. 1972. "The Participation of Minority-Group Parents in School Activities: A Study and Case Study with Guidelines." Paper presented at the Annual AERA Conference. Chicago, April.

Reorganization of Dade County School System into Six Districts. 1964. Submitted by Joseph Hall, Superintendent of the Schools, to Members of the Board of Public Instruction. Miami, Fl.: Board of Public Instruction of Dade County, August.

Resnik, Henry S. 1970. *Turning on the System: War in the Philadelphia Public Schools.* New York: Pantheon.

Robinson, Donald W. 1972. "Change for its Own Sake." *Phi Delta Kappan* 53: 587.

Rogers, David. 1969. *110 Livingston Street.* Vintage ed. New York: Random House.

Rossi, Peter. 1972. "Boobytraps and Pitfalls in the Evaluation of Social Action Programs." Pp. 224–235 in C. H. Weiss (ed.) *Evaluating Action Programs.* Boston: Allyn & Bacon.

Rothchild, Bob K. 1951. "High School Teacher-Community Relations in Northeast Missouri." Ph.D. dissertation, Teachers College, Columbia University.

Rules of Procedures for Area Advisory Committees. 1971. From the Board of Education, Resolutions No. 5292 and 5332. Portland, Ore.: Board of Education of Portland, June 28, July 12.

Schiff, Herbert J. 1963. "The Effect of Personal Contractual Relationships on Parents' Attitudes Toward Participation in Local School Affairs." Ph.D. dissertation, Northwestern University.

Schrag, Peter. 1967. *Village School Downtown*. Boston: Beacon Press.

Sizemore, Barbara A. 1972. "Is There a Case for Separate Schools?" *Phi Delta Kappan* 53: 281–284.

A Staff Reorganization Study of the Memphis, Tennessee School System. 1970. Submitted by the Committee for the Study of the Organizational Structure of the Memphis, Tennessee, Public Schools to the Board of Education. Memphis, Tenn.: Board of Education of the City of Memphis, April.

St. Louis Public Schools Reorganization Plan. 1970. From the Office of the Superintendent of the Schools. St. Louis, Mo.: Board of Education of St. Louis, June.

Talmage, Harriet and Allan C. Ornstein. 1973. "Teachers' Perceptions of Decision-Making Roles and Responsibilities in Defining Accountability." *Journal of Negro Education* 42: 212–221.

Working Draft of Possible Guidelines for Implementation of Public Act 244. 1970. Detroit: Office of School Decentralization, Board of Education of the City of Detroit, April. 2 vols.

Chapter 5

SCHOOL DESEGREGATION[1]

The month was April 1971. The issue was racial segregation in the nation's schools. During U.S. Senate consideration of the administration's proposed Emergency School Assistance Act, Senator Ribicoff of Connecticut introduced a much more extensive amendment to encourage desegregation of metropolitan schools and society. The debate produced some of the most dramatic moments in the recent history of the Senate:

> Mr. Javits: . . . *with the greatest respect for what the Senator is trying to do . . . I feel that it [the Ribicoff amendment]would only result in our getting mired rather than providing for a momumental achievement on the road to an infinitely better educational system for the country.*
>
> *I find, most regretfully—and, as I say, with the greatest of respect —that I will have to support the motion to table.*
>
> Mr. Ribicoff: . . . *I must confess a deep disappointment in the statement just made by the Senator from New York. . . .*
>
> *I want to say to my distinguished northern colleagues that if this motion to table carries, you will be painting yourselves into a corner. I do not see how you can ever point your fingers at a southern*

*Senator or a southern school district and tell them that they are
discriminating against black children when you are unwilling to
desegregate schools in your own cities. . . . I cannot understand
how any Senator can refuse to stand up for what is right and can
advocate double standards. If we continue to do this we are
hypocrites. . . .*

*. . . our problem is that time is running out. This country is on its
way to total apartheid . . . . One of the reasons why we are sent
here is to study the problems that bedevil our country and come
to a decision concerning them . . . . We have reached a state
in America where ambassadors will soon have to be sent across
the lines dividing the blacks and the whites. . . .*

*Mr. Javits: The reason . . . that personal attacks are so dis-
heartening, is that they tend to obscure the issue. We are here to
serve the people, not to challenge each other's motives and not to
insult each other . . .*

*. . . So . . . and I say what I do only because I would be less than a
man if I did not say it, and for no other reason . . . the statement of
the Senator from Connecticut is not going to unmake me as an
advocate of civil rights in the eyes of the country, my constituents,
or the world. If it did, it would hardly be a world worth fighting for
or living for.* (U.S. Congress, Senate, Congressional Record,
April 20, 1971, S5203, S5205, S5207.)

The issues at hand were complex and confused. As often happens in
such circumstances, they made for strange bedfellows, with conservative
southern Senators such as Allen and Eastland joining northern liberals
such as Mondale and Stevenson in support of Ribicoff's proposal. The
amendment (about which, more later) failed of passage, and in the inter-
vening years the issues have become, if anything, still more complicated
and uncertain. A few ambiguities have been reduced somewhat by subsequent court decisions; but even so, confusion and doubt still exist, and
the underlying problem is not about to disappear.

On a topic so highly characterized by conflicting evidence and view-
points, it is fundamentally important to be as clear as possible in disting-
uishing what we know from what we do not. Only by identifying and
holding on to a core of firm knowledge can we hope to find a way toward
answers that are defensible because the problem—in objective terms
—allows for no others. Accordingly, the next sections summarize what
we believe can be said with a good deal of confidence concerning the

segregation of metropolitan schools and society in the United States. Because no attempt can be made in a chapter of this length to document fully or to discuss all the evidence bearing on the topics considered below, readers are urged to pursue them further by reading the sources cited and other related materials.

INTERGROUP ATTITUDES AND CONTACT

It frequently is argued that integrated education is necessary if students of differing racial and social background are to develop positive attitudes toward one another. Interracial contact, it is contended, contributes to interracial understanding and cooperation; conversely, the absence of contact generates and/or perpetuates hatred and misunderstanding.

Given the complexity of social phenomena, neither generalization can be considered totally valid or invalid. Obviously, there will be some times when they are true and some when they are not. The best one can hope to do is determine whether they are more nearly true or false at a particular period of time in a given society.

As regards the first generalization, appreciable evidence does suggest that interracial contact *can* improve interracial attitudes in our own and other societies, provided that the conditions of contact are such as to favor this result. These conditions, as identified in a review of research on the topic (Amir, 1969), include:

> . . . when there is equal status contact between the members of the various ethnic groups . . . when an 'authority' and/or the social climate are in favor of and promote the intergroup contact . . . when the contact is of an intimate rather than a casual nature . . . when the ethnic intergroup contact is pleasant or rewarding . . . when the members of both groups in the particular contact situation interact in functionally important activities or develop common goals or superordinate goals that are higher ranking in importance than the individual goals of each of the groups. (p. 338)

On the second generalization, it is impossible to prove that lack of contact increases interracial hatred and conflict. (There is no way to "prove" that conflict would be greater were there less contact than now exists.) However, it is known that personal contact is potentially much more effective than information or rhetoric in overcoming interracial stereotypes;[2] in the absence of contact, it is hard to see from whence there might arise a reduction of interracial stereotypes and conflicts in societies in which they already exist in abundance.[3] Because our own society unquestionably is still plagued by such stereotypes and conflicts, it is legitimate to predict that they will not be moderated very substantially in the absence of positive interracial contact.

ACADEMIC ACHIEVEMENT AND INTEGRATED EDUCATION

It is more difficult to specify what we know and what we do not with respect to achievement and integrated education, because the volumi- nous research literature bearing on this topic is not always internally consistent. Despite this difficulty, there is adequate evidence to support the conclusions that: (1) integrated education can be academically benefi- cial for students from economically disadvantaged minority groups;[4] and (2) socioeconomic integration is much more important than racial integra- tion per se in improving the academic performance of disadvantaged students.[5] As stated in the final report of the U.S. Senate Select Commit- tee on Equal Educational Opportunity (1972):

> *It seems clear from the available research that increased academic performance for disadvantaged children cannot be expected to flow from racial or ethnic desegregation alone. The key element in increasing academic performance of low-income children, whether or not they are from minority groups, appears to be socioeconomic integration . . . . It is one of the greatest tragedies of the last 8 years that the importance of assuring that school integration takes place along economic, as well as racial and ethnic lines, has re- ceived little attention from local school officials implementing in- tegration plans and the Office of Education in rendering technical assistance. (p. 30)*

These, of course, are the conclusions advanced by James S. Coleman (1966) and his associates who carried out the landmark study on *Equality of Educational Opportunity*. The Coleman Report has been extensively reanalyzed and reassessed in a variety of ways. Most of these reanalyses support nearly all the basic conclusions (for example, Mayeske 1970), but others challenge some of them. For example, Smith (1972) has shown that the report probably underestimated the relationship between student- body social class (that is, the socioeconomic background of one's class- mates) and academic achievement. To provide a summary of this body of research, a Rand Corporation report (Averch, et al., 1971) reexamined a number of studies on this issue and concluded that "there is no strong evidence that student-body effects exist. . . . There is no strong evidence to the contrary" (pp. 43-44).

The conclusion probably is justified if it is taken (as intended) to summarize what we know with complete certainty; however, the criteria used to assess possible student-body effects in the Rand study were extremely restrictive (again, as intended), and fairly large differences according to social class of the school would have had to be present to "warrant" detection. Less impressive differences taking place from year to year easily could have escaped "significance." Thus, other researchers such as Spady (1973) have reviewed the pertinent literature and, while paying particular attention to methodological adequacy, concluded that student-body socioeconomic composition is associated with achievement. In view of the many studies that indicate some improvement in the achievement of low-status students transferred from low- to higher-status schools, the most accurate conclusion possible at the present time is that social class integration can make some difference.[6] (While most of these studies have one or more technical shortcomings, they cannot be entirely dismissed as a body of evidence on this basis.) Thus, overall there is a good deal of justification[7] for the conclusions of observers such as Pettigrew, et al. (1973) and Coleman (*Report on Education Research,* 1970), whose respective assessments are that:

> . . . [*it is*]*unrealistic to expect any type of educational innovation to close most of the racial differential in achievement while gross racial disparities, especially economic, remain in American society. Furthermore, we know of no social scientists who ever claimed school desegregation alone could close most of the differential. We are pleased to note the many instances where effective desegregation has apparently benefited the achievement of both black and white children, and where over a period of years it appears to close approximately a fourth of the differential. (p. 99)*

> . . . [*research results*]*don't say that the average Negro child will begin to perform at the same level as the average white child if he attends the same school . . . [but] the gap between the average Negro and the average white will be narrowed . . . by about 20 to 25 percent by the Negro's increased achievement due to school integration. (p. 5)*

Several additional points should be made before proceeding:

1. Research on student-body (socioeconomic integration) effects generally deals with a number of diverse classrooms and schools. In some, integration is implemented effectively; in others, integration is handled rather poorly, and often it is nothing more than "mixing of the bodies." This makes it difficult to estimate what would happen if integration were implemented more competently in most schools and classrooms.

2. There is no reason to believe that socioeconomic integration is academically harmful for middle-status students as long as they are not placed in predominantly low-status schools.

3. Achievement gains associated with socioeconomic integration probably are due, among other things, to a more manageable institutional climate (for teachers and students alike), a reduction in the sense of "powerlessness" on the part of minority students, and greater insistence on more meaningful standards of performance for low-status students (even though the latter phenomenon also is associated with a decreased sense of positive self-concept as a learner).

4. The (realistic) aspirations for future educational and social attainment of low-status students also apparently are increased as a result of socioeconomic integration, although the dynamics of the process are different in that reference-group considerations are more directly important than is true with respect to achievement. (Improved aspirations are intimately related, of course, to the achievement syndrome, and in practice can scarcely be separated from it.)

5. The generalizations described above are still justified when account is taken of the probability that low-status students who attend socioeconomically integrated schools because they live in mixed neighborhoods or volunteer to participate in integration plans are less educationally disadvantaged than their counterparts in predominantly low-income schools.

6. More needs to be learned concerning the types of students who may benefit most from integration and the implications such findings have for providing options in desegregation plans. For example, one might argue that the lowest achieving students either would stand to gain the most by being placed in a better learning environment (Weinberg, 1972) or would tend to gain little or nothing because they start from too far back (St. John, 1972). Actual research evidence on this point is contradictory.

7. If minority students other than black students are in a limited number of schools in which they constitute most of the enrollment, court orders may require their desegregation along with black students. For example, court orders have required the desegregation of Mexican-American students in Denver and Chinese-American students in San Francisco. From the viewpoint of increasing intergroup contact, this policy makes a good deal of sense, but from the viewpoint of equal educational opportunity (achievement), it may not. It is not at all clear, for example, that the majority of Chinese-American students in predominantly Chinese neighborhoods in San Francisco are economically or educationally disadvantaged or that neighborhood schools there provide a poor environment for learning. Conversely, there certainly are low-income white neighborhoods in Chicago, New York, and other big cities in which

Polish, Italian, or other white ethnic students are segregated in unproductive, low-status schools serving one or two ethnic groups. (This situation is likely to continue as long as parents in these neighborhoods do not demand an end to socioeconomic segregation.) To our knowledge, issues specifically involving segregated education for nonblack minorities have not been thoroughly considered in any U.S. court of law.

LOW-INCOME SCHOOLS

The rationale for integration does not depend solely on evidence that low-status students achieve better when they are placed in middle-status schools. Turning the argument around, one may inquire about the possibilities of improving achievement if they remain in predominantly low-status schools.

Here we can speak with more certainty than is possible with respect to integration. Probably the only really firm knowledge we now have on which to develop policy is that low-status schools are not good places in which to learn. If you do not believe it, you have only to look at the statistics on achievement in big-city schools, or, better yet, go and spend three or four days in a school in the slums.

Furthermore, the possibilities of changing low-status schools into productive learning environments must be viewed with some skepticism, judging by the paucity of examples in which this has been accomplished (above the third or fourth grade) despite much effort to do so. It is true that a few apparently successful low-status elementary schools can be found in various cities,[8] and extensive national search has identified the characteristics of programs that seem to be comparatively successful in improving the academic performance of disadvantaged students (Hawkridge, et al. 1968; Vargo, et al.1971). Nevertheless, the fact remains that such schools and programs are dishearteningly few and far between at the elementary level and virtually nonexistent at the secondary level. Familiarity with such schools in big cities forces us to conclude that substantial reform in most inner-city schools (particularly at the secondary level) is not going to occur in the foreseeable future. Realistically, performance levels in most inner-city schools are likely to remain unacceptably low for as long as we continue to tolerate socioeconomic segregation in metropolitan schools and society.

Several additional points about compensatory education should be made before proceeding:

1. As suggested above, compensatory education has been somewhat effective up to the third or fourth grade in a few schools and school districts in the sense that well-implemented programs have succeeded in raising achievement levels to a point at or near the national average. It is

not completely clear whether the rapid fall-off in achievement after the primary grades in such schools is the result of increasing influence of the peer group and the neighborhood, an inadequate foundation for concep-tualization as abstract thinking becomes more central in school work, an increase in alienation among students, lack of knowledge concerning effective curriculum and instruction in the middle grades, and/or other related causes which become more important as students proceed through the grades.

2. This phenomenon may have implications for the design of inte-gration plans. It may suggest that integration is most important after the primary grades, when the negative forces in a segregated, low-income environment become stronger and more obvious. Such an approach would have the additional advantage of avoiding significant traveling distances for very young children, whose parents rightfully are particu-larly concerned to minimize the time it takes to go to and from school. On the other hand, it also can be argued that integration is especially impor-tant in the early years when attitudes and basic skills are most rapidly formulated and established.

Some educators argue that community participation in decision mak-ing for low-status schools might help make them into more effective educational institutions. Others say that, in low-status minority schools, emphasis on pride in blackness, brownness, and redness could make a substantial contribution toward establishing a more positive learning environment. Still others say that if teachers had more respect and higher expectations for low-status students and/or if inner-city schools— particularly high schools—were much smaller and less bureaucratic, det-rimental influences (on learning) in such schools and their neighbor-hoods could be readily overcome. Unfortunately, there is little solid empirical evidence to indicate that these changes ultimately can make a significant difference.

And so, we are left with socioeconomic integration—currently the most viable alternative which, if well implemented, offers hope that the achievement gap between advantaged and disadvantaged students may perhaps be reduced by as much as one fourth on a substantial scale without much compensatory programming and possibly more than that if properly combined with compensatory services. [9]

This amount of achievement gain could be extremely important, because for many students it would mean the difference between literacy and illiteracy, between possessing the academic skills to succeed in the labor force and consignment to the nether realm of urban slums. Equally important, successful socioeconomic integration on a large scale also may serve to improve interracial attitudes among children and youth if it results in substantial racial integration at the same time. But, is it possible to implement integration successfully on this scale, and at what cost?

FEASIBILITY OF DESEGREGATING URBAN AND METROPOLITAN SCHOOLS

Because no extensive surveys have been conducted to determine how many low-status students actually attend low-status schools, it is not possible to obtain very precise estimates of the proportion of students whose school assignment would have to be changed to end socio-economic segregation in public schools in the nation's metropolitan areas. Data we have collected for other purposes in Kansas City suggest that approximately 15 to 20 percent of the city and suburban public school students in the metropolitan area attend predominantly working-class schools. Because Kansas City demographic data tend to closely parallel national data, we would guess that the comparable national percentage would be similar.

However, data are available on racial integration. They indicate that minority students in big cities generally attend racially and/or ethnically segregated schools and that only a slight amount of progress has been made in recent years toward desegregated education. Table 5 for example, (p. 167) highlights the extent of segregation in 1971 in thirty-four big-city school districts which had a black population of 30 percent or higher. In twenty-three of these districts, two-thirds or more of the black students were attending schools that were 80 percent or more black. The percentage of black students attending predominantly black schools by this definition fell by 10 percent or more in only eight of these districts between 1968 and 1971, usually as a result of court-ordered desegregation in the South. Because most minority students are in big-city rather than suburban school districts, this means that metropolitan area school systems as a whole also tend to be segregated along racial lines: white students attend predominantly white schools, and black students attend predominantly black schools.

At the same time, however, available data also suggest that in physical terms the diffculties of providing socially and/or racially desegregated education for most disadvantaged students frequently are greatly exaggerated. That is, the great majority of disadvantaged students could be assigned to middle-status schools without incurring impossible costs in terms of time and money for travel, particularly if schools in the metropolitan area are treated as part of a single system for this purpose.

For example, an analysis of central-city school districts in 29 urban areas was carried out by the Lambda Corporation in 1971. The results indicated that relatively little *additional* busing beyond that normally provided anyway would be necessary in order to assign most minority students to nonsegregated schools while maintaining a 35-minute limit on the transit time for each student. The study concluded that current residential isolation of urban minority groups is not:

> *. . . as serious a barrier to school desegregation as has usually been assumed. Even in the largest cities analyzed, almost complete elimination in the schools seems possible without exceeding . . . economically reasonable limits on the number of students bused. . . . Very substantial decreases in racial isolation can be accomplished without transporting any students who could otherwise walk to school. . . . The key to realizing such reductions in racial isolation lies in the definition of local attendance zones, and in the effective use of existing levels of busing. . . . The results . . . suggest that requirements to provide almost complete desegregation can be as little as one third to one fourth of the amount estimated by conventional rule-of-thumb techniques. (pp. 4–7)*

In some respects the Lambda Corporation's report is too sanguine about the theoretical possibilities of integrating schools in our metropolitan areas. The report deals with race rather than social class, and socioeconomic integration probably would require more busing and reassignment than racial integration. No consideration is given to the important question of "tipping points," though actual desegregation plans definitely should place high priority on ensuring that no additional schools become largely low-status in either socioeconomic composition or scholastic climate. Maximum desegregation is defined in terms of equivalence between each school's racial composition and the composition of the district in which it is located, thus minimizing the extent of the problem in cities like St. Louis and Washington, D.C., in which black students and/or low-status students already constitute a majority. The 29 areas in the sample include several very large cities, but the omission of others such as Chicago with its large and segregated black population and Los Angeles with its long travel distances suggests that somewhat more pessimism might be in order concerning our largest city school districts.

On the other hand, for most of the 29 cases, the conclusions apparently do not depend on the assumption that busing or reassignment would take place across school district boundaries in the metropolitan areas studied. (The report states that comparisons on this basis were calculated but does not state the degree to which they influenced the overall conclusions or the results for each city.) Nor does the report (attempt to) take into account the possibility that appreciable desegregation could be achieved through magnet schools, metropolitan exchange programs, part-time learning centers, or other possibilities which incidentally already are fundable in part under the Emergency School Aid Act of 1972.[10] In sum, it is legitimate to conclude that the report is not too far off in its fundamental thesis concerning the physical feasibility of

TABLE 5

PERCENT OF BLACK STUDENTS ATTENDING SCHOOLS 80 PERCENT OR MORE BLACK IN THIRTY-FOUR BIG CITY SCHOOL DISTRICTS WITH ONE-THIRD OR MORE BLACK ENROLLMENT IN 1968 AND 1971 [a]

District	1968	1971
Washington, D.C.	96.5	97.6
Compton, Calif.		97.8
Atlanta, Ga.	91.8	85.9
Newark, N.J.	88.4	91.3
Orleans Parish, La.	83.3	80.8
Richmond, Va.	88.6	36.5
Baltimore, Md.	83.8	84.1
St. Louis, Mo.	89.0	89.8
Gary, Ind.	90.7	95.7
Detroit, Mich.	79.1	78.6
Philadelphia, Pa.	76.9	80.2[b]
Oakland, Calif.	77.1	73.1
Cleveland, Ohio	90.8	91.3
Birmingham, Ala.	92.7	74.7
Chicago, Ill.	90.3	91.6
Memphis, Tenn.	95.4	89.2
Kansas City, Mo.	78.1	86.4
Caddo Parish, La.	97.4	66.6
Louisville, Ky.	64.9	82.3
Chatham County, Ga.	86.5	7.6
Charleston County, S.C.	84.2	62.4
Norfolk, Va.	82.3	1.2
Cincinnati, Ohio	50.9	54.9
Mobile County, Ala.	87.5	44.2
Dayton, Ohio	82.7	78.1
Pittsburgh, Pa.	60.0	61.6
Flint, Mich.	42.4	46.6
Buffalo, N.Y.	65.1	59.0
Baton Rouge Parish, La.	94.2	72.0
Houston, Tex.	90.9	86.0
Indianapolis, Ind.	62.5	60.1
Dallas, Tex.	93.0	83.4
Rochester, N.Y.	34.4	33.7
New York, N.Y.	60.5	69.2

Source: U.S. Senate Select Committee on Equal Educational Opportunity (1972), pp. 116–117.

[a]Ranked according to 1971 black percentage in enrollment.

[b]1970 figure.

167

achieving substantial desegregation without greatly exceeding existing levels of busing.

Like the physical practicality of busing, the financial costs also are frequently greatly exaggerated. Foster (1972) has summarized the situation in this respect as follows:

> The total cost of busing, including expenses for operation and capital outlay expressed in dollars per-pupil-bused, generally falls within a range of $40 to $60 annually. In any event, transportation costs . . . seldom exceed 4 percent of the total and generally range from 1.5 to 3.0 percent. (p. 16)

Even if Foster's estimates are considered too low for very large metropolitan areas with relatively high costs and travel distances, they still suggest that all but the most gradiose (and poorly designed) busing plans would not add more than 5 or 6 percent to existing school district budgets. Given the achievement and other gains that may be expected if integration is well implemented, and in view of the demonstrated failure of most compensatory education programs, this order of increased or reallocated outlay may be defensible purely on the basis of cost-benefit trade-offs between expenditures and public school outputs.[11]

The evidence cited above indicates that social class and racial desegregation are desirable and theoretically could be accomplished for most pupils in the public schools in many metropolitan areas. Whether it is likely to be provided and how well it is likely to be implemented are, of course, quite different matters.

Obviously, the political difficulties are immense. Integration highlights and sometimes magnifies a number of very real and visible problems ranging from the imperative to individualize instruction effectively in the classroom all the way to overt racial conflict in the school and the community. Unless it is well implemented, integration frequently not only may fail to achieve its original goals, but also may increase group conflict and place students and teachers in physically dangerous situations. Even when implementation is satisfactory, some overt racial and social conflict should be expected, and achievement gains may not be evident for several years, if at all. With plenty of political and community "leaders" poised to encourage and orchestrate both imaginary and justified public fears, the cause of integration is poorly served when integration is mandated without sophisticated attention to the real issues (discussed above) or adequate preparation and determination to ensure effective implementation with minimum disruption in school and community.

However, it is important not to exaggerate the problems associated with major school desegregation programs. The U.S. Commission on

Civil Rights (1972*a*, 1972*b*) issued two reports on the progress of integration in fourteen communities with large-scale programs (including several "hot spots" that made news headlines because of racial eruptions) and concluded that:

> *In some, the fears that were anticipated—lower quality education, violence and crime, lengthy bus rides—have been proven to be groundless. In others, the fears, at least in part, have been substantiated . . . . Of all these, the least serious problem has been the students themselves. In most cases they have adjusted quickly and smoothly to the new school environment, often despite fears and anxieties of their parents. (1972a, p. 2)*

The first report dealt with developments in Pasadena (California), Tampa-Hillsborough (Florida), Charlotte-Mecklenburg (North Carolina), Winston-Salem/Forsyth (North Carolina), and Pontiac (Michigan). Based on interviews and material gathered by staff members from January through March 1972, the commission found that:

> *Reports of racial incidents among students . . . were generally exaggerated. In all five cities, such incidents occurred primarily at the inception of desegregation and declined sharply after the first few days. Often, as in Pontiac, tensions generated by protests outside of the schools contributed to problems within the schools.*

> *Most bus trips, except in Winston-Salem, took less than 30 minutes. In none of the cities did the Commission staff learn of any bus accidents in which a student was injured— a pattern that is consistent with the excellent safety record of school busing throughout this country. No teacher complained that busing interfered with the education of children. Students did not appear to mind their ride to school, and often said they enjoyed it. Busing for integration did, however, create inconveniences for many families. (1972b, p. 2)*

The second report dealt with desegregation efforts in nine additional school districts, including communities in both the North and South, in both urban and rural areas. As part of the introduction, the commission noted that:

> *The integration of some school systems was accompanied by a great public outcry. Stories were heard of fights on buses and in the schools, of upset parents, disrupted schools, curtailed learning, and of other damages to the communities' school life. The actual*

*situation in most districts stood in strong contrast to the news-
paper headlines and television newscasts. Most parents did not
block school entrances, most teachers did not resign in droves, and
few students engaged in disorders. (1972a, p. 1)*

Discussing "fears" which had been partly substantiated, however,
the commission particularly noted that

*in some communities a number of white parents withdrew their
children from the public schools and either moved to a different
school district or enrolled them in newly created private academies.
Although the situation has tended to become stabilized, the problem of 'white flight' has by no means been entirely resolved.
(1972a, p. 2)*

In reaching conclusions similar to those of the Civil Rights Commission, the Resource Management Corporation (U.S. Senate Select Committee, 1972) studied 879 schools receiving federal desegregation assistance in 1970–71 and found that:

*—41 percent of students attending desegregated schools for the
first time reported changes for the better on "going to school with
students of another race," while only 5 percent reported changes
for the worse.*

*—80 percent of students interviewed agreed that "students are
cooperating more and more as the year goes on."*

*—While 33 percent of black students and 23 percent of white
students said they would rather go to another school if they could,
only 6 percent reported they did "not like it here" and 80 percent
reported learning more in school than the previous year.*

*—A substantial majority of teachers and principals reported im-
provements in interracial relationships among students, and only
2 percent reported worsening relationships. (p. 229)*

REQUIREMENTS FOR EFFECTIVE IMPLEMENTATION
OF INTEGRATION

As mentioned above, integration is associated with educational as well as
political problems. We should not view a school as truly "integrated" (as

opposed to "desegregated") unless pupils with differing backgrounds actually learn together at the classroom level and all or most of them receive good instruction and have positive interracial contact. But to put it mildly, schools in general hardly can be considered noteworthy for their success in implementing existing instructional programs. Much less can we realistically expect them to implement integration effectively without large-scale programs for improving the quality of education in racially and socially mixed classrooms.

The most important thing to keep in mind about a plan for integrated education is that its underlying goals—providing more equal educational opportunity and improving interracial understanding—are unlikely to be achieved if it is implemented mostly on the basis of "business as usual." In the absence of definite action to avoid the following problems, they —among others—frequently become prominent when a previously white or middle-status school is desegregated:

Lack of Contact in the Classroom

Because middle-status students generally are working at a more advanced level, homogeneous grouping in schools organized on a grade-level basis often will result in segregation within the school and/or the classroom. That is, low-status students will be placed in separate groups from middle-status students, and the purpose of integration will be defeated immediately because students will have little interracial contact in the classroom and low-status students still will be in an unproductive learning environment.

Because teachers in the great majority of schools have too little experience, knowledge, or resources to individualize instruction and thus avoid the alternatives of homogeneous grouping on the one hand and "common denominator" instruction on the other, a substantial amount of training and resources will be required to provide effective education in desegregated schools. The degree to which retraining and additional resources may be required should not be underestimated. Keeping in mind that most teachers already have had several years of training and that existing materials—except the new, expensive "multi-media" systems—have not been strikingly successful in advancing individualization, it is clear tha major programs of in-service education must be combined with substantial instructional improvement efforts if integration is to achieve its basic goals. This is particularly difficult because many "experts" and "consultants" on instructional methods often have limited success in conducting school district in-service training programs.

Even if students are not, for all practical purposes, resegregated within the school or classroom, interracial instruction still may not contribute to achieving the goals of integrated education. Some students may not participate meaningfully in instructional activities because they are inhibited by the presence of students or adults from another racial group; minority students may withdraw or become disruptive if they perceive their own or their group's achievement as inferior to that of middle-status white classmates; and students with differing racial and social background may become more prejudiced toward each other if their experience in the classroom reinforces or fits in with existing negative stereotypes of one or another group.

Earlier in this chapter we quoted Amir's (1969) enumeration of some of the conditions that tend to make interracial contact positive rather than negative. These conditions included *equal-status contact, functional interaction in pursuit of common superordinate goals,* and a *favorable social climate.* Clearly, it is not easy to ensure equal-status contact in the classroom if one group is much more advanced educationally than another, and the school can only slightly influence the general social climate. Moreover, as shown in a series of studies by Cohen and Roper (1972), extraordinary efforts sometimes are necessary to increase the participation of low-status individuals in social interaction situations even when they are objectively as competent in terms of a given task or activity as are the high-status participants in the group.

Nevertheless, there is much teachers *can* do to ensure that interracial contact will be positive. For example, teachers can identify each student's strengths and weaknesses and then structure classroom experiences so that most of their pupils have opportunities to participate and whenever possible excel in activities most suited to their talents and interests. Through careful selection of small-group membership and assignments, teachers can increase opportunities for interracial cooperation on common goals. By assigning students to interracial teams engaged in subject matter learning games, they can increase the frequency of cross-race cooperation and friendship, provided that competition in the games is between teams rather than individuals (Devries and Edwards, 1972). And teachers also can do a great deal to establish a general classroom atmosphere that encourages interracial friendship and understanding.

Segregated Relationships Outside the Classrooms

Outside the classroom, students of differing racial groups often have little or no contact with one another. Ten years ago this would not have been true so frequently as it is now, but today in-group pressures among both whites and blacks sometimes work strongly against any informal, interracial contact, particularly at the secondary level.

Educators cannot force students of differing groups to develop friendly relationships, but there is much that can be done to make this more likely without coercion or compulsion. For example, when there is positive contact in an informal and friendly atmosphere within the classroom, it is more likely to develop outside the classroom as well. When students of differing groups discuss and study race-related problems as part of the curriculum, a better basis may exist for bridging interracial barriers outside the classroom and the school. Educators need not sit back and assume nothing can be done to encourage the development of positive social contact among differing groups of students.

Social and Racial Differences in Perceptions and Attitudes

When a substantial number of low-status students enter a largely middle-status school, conflicts and disagreements associated with differences in social class values and behaviors are likely to become apparent. Two of the most important of these conflicts arise from teachers' difficulties in providing equal treatment and in respecting individual differences among students in situations of this type.

Reviewing her study of integrated schools in Riverside, California, Mercer (Moss, 1970) pointed out that

> . . . even-handed justice, for the minority child may mean more punishments than rewards because his behavior is significantly different. And if the system becomes too punitive, he may reach the point where he simply doesn't care. . . .

> If the teacher chooses the alternative value—respect for individual differences—she finds herself gradually using two standards: the traditional standard for the majority group children and a different, less demanding one for the new arrivals to the system.

> One of the first consequences of dual standards is that the entire system begins to disintegrate. Children cannot understand why one child is punished for an act and another is not punished for the same act. . . . Discipline standards for all children begin to crumble. . . . Significantly, the only elementary school in the entire district that was threatened by a serious, planned racial incident—a gang fight on the last day of school—was the one school in which the dual standard was attempted. (pp. 79–80)

Essentially the same dilemma exists with respect to academic standards. If low-status students are achieving at a less advanced level, the teacher may grade by a single standard and thereby make them appear inferior and incompetent. Use of a double standard, on the other hand, tends to reduce the motivation of both low- and middle-status students by making it seem that work and effort count for nothing. "The eventual outcome of the double standard," Mercer points out, is to defeat "the purpose of integrated schooling" by depriving disadvantaged students of the opportunity to learn how to meet standards and expectations higher than those characteristic of most low-status schools.

Is it impossible to solve the dilemma posed by equal treatment versus respect for individual differences in socially and racially integrated schools? It may be impossible to overcome it entirely, but there is much that can be done to minimize or avoid its potentially deleterious consequences. As in any successful effort to respond to a difficult dilemma, the only true solution is to dispose of much of the problem by changing the fundamental situation so that entirely new outcomes can be pursued and achieved.

For example, through individualization and "continuous progress" instruction, much of the dilemma involving academic standards can be avoided because a student's achievements are evaluated according to his own past performance and capabilities rather than against other individuals and groups. By providing opportunities to participate in rule-setting and disciplinary decisions, teachers can help students learn to meet acceptable standards of conduct both inside and outside the classroom. And the most attractive aspect of such approaches is that they are educationally sound and desirable in the first place, and not just gimmicks to smooth conflict in socially mixed schools.

On the other hand, we do not want to be glib or simpleminded about the possibilities of encouraging positive interracial contact, individualizing instruction, or teaching students to behave independently. Rules and regulations need to be enforced while also improving the quality of education in socially mixed schools or any other type of school. The task is far from easy or it would have been widely accomplished long ago. Nevertheless, the goal is not unattainable, and examples as well as suggestions are available to help in the process of working to attain it. [12]

CRUCIAL ELEMENTS FOR HIGH-QUALITY
INTEGRATED EDUCATION

Before turning to other issues, it is desirable to review some of the elements that are crucial to the success or failure of a plan for providing high-quality education in integrated schools. These elements include:

Sizeable In-Service Training Programs for Teachers and Other Staff Members

As noted above, the teacher's job takes on additional dimensions in schools and classrooms with a racially and socially mixed group of students. Besides dealing with greater diversity in the achievement level of his students, the teacher in an integrated setting also must be effective in handling value conflicts and in facilitating positive intergroup contact. Because very few teachers have had adequate training to discharge these responsibilities successfully, most need a great deal of assistance as part of a larger program to improve all aspects of the operation of the school. (Of course, teachers in relatively homogeneous segregated schools also could benefit from such assistance and training, but the need is not so critical because problems generally are not so overt and explosive there.) Staff and instructional development programs at integrated schools should include at least the following priorities: understanding of and sensitivity to problems involving differences and the causes of conflict between racial groups; skills for individualizing instruction; ability to utilize new instructional materials and media; competence in working with different-sized instructional groups; knowledge of how to encourage positive interracial contact inside and outside the classroom; motivation and skill to work more closely with parents and community groups; and competence in working with colleagues to improve instruction throughout the school.

Outstanding Administrative Leadership

Schools seldom function satisfactorily unless administrators—particularly the building principals—provide outstanding leadership, and this is doubly true of racially or socially mixed schools. Although one cannot assume that even the most outstanding administrator necessarily will be able to lead the way toward solutions of all major problems in a conflict-ridden school or community, on the other hand these problems frequently are so severe that average administrators are unable to cope with them.

In particular, successful administration of integrated schools requires a great deal of initiative and skill in establishing mechanisms and policies to mitigate and eliminate potential problems before they arise or become serious, especially at the secondary level. Chesler, Jorgensen, and Erenberg (1970) have provided an excellent checklist which illustrates some of the questions principals should ask themselves in working systematically to furnish such leadership in integrated schools:

Do I as a principal

—often solicit the views and reactions of different student groups?
—know how to find out about and influence the behavior of teachers who practice overt or subtle forms of racial or ethnic discrimination?
—tell my superiors how I feel when their plans do not meet my educational goals?
—become annoyed and angry when confronted with inadequacies in the school and say or do things which I later regret?
—deal openly with the possibility of racial tension among staff members?
—feel prepared to terminate the contracts of teachers who are intellectually or emotionally brutal to children of any race or subgroup?
—implement needed programs and changes before or after pressure groups confront me? (p. 5)

The role of the principal in the critically important task of maintaining discipline in a desegregated school has been underlined by Bash and Long (n.d.) as follows:

> . . . *misbehavior traditionally has not been condoned in a segregated Negro school. In the typical segregated Negro school one of the primary concerns of the principal was to keep "order" in his school. . . . In the typical segregated white school, the principal did not feel the threat that the Negro principal perceived. White teachers and students experienced a more relaxed atmosphere. . . . Upon entering the desegregated school the Negro student may be puzzled by the relaxed atmosphere . . . [and] "over step" the bounds. . . . The "penalty" may not be severe or out of the ordinary, but it likely is perceived to be so . . .*

> *In the desegregated school the principal, white or Negro, must orient teachers to the problems that can arise . . . [including] the different styles of in-school life to which the Negro and white (teachers and) children are accustomed, to the potential conflicts which may emerge, and to a procedure to follow in the event there is intergroup conflict. . . .*

> *The principal should be careful to avoid overcompensation because of race. Too much emphasis upon race as a factor related to discipline problems produces negative feelings among all students. (pp. 32–34)*

Day-to-Day Assistance in Diagnosing Problems and Implementing Solutions to Problems Associated with Desegregation

Even given substantial training and excellent administrative leadership, teachers in many desegregated schools still will require and can benefit greatly from various supporting services designed to ensure effective implementation of educational programs in school and classroom. One of the best ways to provide this type of support is through a team of consultants assigned at least temporarily to assist the staff of a desegregated school in achieving a variety of goals inside and outside the classroom. The function of such a team has been described by Beker (1967) as follows:

> As consultants, *the specialists tried to help personnel see incoming youngsters as individuals by. . . providing special information about them. They handled integration-related crises, freeing other personnel for regular duties. . . . They made referrals to the school nurse, mental health workers, or other specialists as needed . . . .*

> *In their* supportive *roles, the specialists attempted, through working with youngsters individually and in groups, to help both newcomers and old-timers to handle their anxieties and fears. . . . They attempted to promote the academic orientation and achievement level of newcomers performing less well than their "hosts" by establishing tutoring groups, by seeing that bussed children were able to get public library cards like their classmates did, and by other means . . .*

> *In working with* parents, *integration specialists encountered two disparate communities—that of the parents of the "host" children and that of the newcomers. In the case of the former, it was often necessary to interpret the changes . . . and to reassure them that the quality of the children's education need not suffer. The parents of the incoming youngsters often had to be encouraged to become part of the new school and to see it as their own. (pp. 189-191)*

METROPOLITAN BASIS FOR INTEGRATION

Are the possible benefits worth the possibility of widespread political conflict and enormous difficulties certain to be encountered in devising and carrying out potentially effective large-scale plans for socioeconomic and racial integration? Each educator must answer this question for himself. About all an observer can do at this time is reiterate the one point about which we can be most certain: To allow students to attend predominantly low-status schools is to condemn most of them to a cycle of inadequate school achievement and extreme disadvantage in terms of entering the labor force and obtaining economic advancement and security once in it.

Instead of carefully developed desegregation plans which are as politically and educationally sound as can be devised by responsible government officials and educators, what do we have today? From every side, we are surfeited with misleading clichés that purport to be meaningful judgments about integrated education. "It demeans black children to say they can't learn unless sitting next to white children" and "I'm all in favor of spending for education but not for buses" are but a few of the simplistic statements put forth by black and white separatists seeking to advance their own interests and ideologies.

Meanwhile, the burden of furthering equal educational opportunity has been mostly abandoned by the executive and legislative branches of the federal government and consequently has fallen largely on the judiciary. Unfortunately, the judicial branch of government is not very well equipped to prescribe solutions for complex issues highly dependent on incomplete research, much less to implement solutions in local communities. As often happens when courts are confronted with this kind of task, the result in recent years has been rather a mindless development and application of precedents dating back to the 1954 Brown decision. For example, court-ordered integration plans have dealt almost exclusively with racial and minority status, even though social class integration is a prime consideration that should receive prior emphasis when considering achievement effects.

Perhaps, however, we should not be so harsh in speaking about the courts. School boards generally have been equally negligent in failing to provide sensible leadership to desegregate the public schools; either they have mostly ignored the critical issue of social class balance, or they have proposed only token plans that have little potential for improving the educational environment of a significant number of students.

To our knowledge, the only major school-district integration proposal that gave direct, primary, and adequate attention to the issue of social class balance was that proposed by the Norfolk, Virginia, Board of Education in 1970.[13] Based on testimony by James S. Coleman and other expert consultants, the board's plan called for placing 40 percent of the district's 25,000 black pupils in predominantly white schools and assuring every black child at least three years of "optimally" integrated education. Explicit goals of the plan were to avoid reassigning middle-class students to predominantly low-status schools and to ensure that additional schools did not become predominantly low-status in student composition.

However, because three-quarters of black elementary students would have remained in nearly all-black schools, on June 22, 1970, the Fourth Circuit Court of Appeals disallowed the proposal with the comment that, "Creation of predominantly middle-class schools in a district where all pupils would be assigned to them may be unobjectionable. But here many of the schools will not be middle class and, by the board's own standards, they will be inferior" (*Integrated Education*, 1970, pp. 22–23).

Because the Norfolk plan also placed considerable emphasis on keeping busing to a bare minimum, it is possible that a more adequate plan could have been prepared to reduce substantially the number of low-status and predominantly black schools. But even then, the court might have thrown it out on the grounds that school officials cannot recognize the inherent inferiority of low-status schools without at the same time eliminating *all* such schools.

This dilemma immediately draws attention to the underlying reasons integration must be implemented on an area-wide basis in many metropolitan areas if it is to be socially and educationally beneficial to the health of the metropolitan community over the long run. In many metropolitan areas, particularly the larger ones with a substantial proportion of minority residents, there are not enough middle-status students in central city (and some suburban) school districts to allow for the possibility of a middle-class majority in every school. And the number of districts in this bind is increasing all the time as central cities lose middle-class population and the proportion of low-status students in their enrollment climbs inexorably by 1 to 5 percent each year.

One major reason this rise has occurred so steadily in so many school districts is precisely because so little has been done—or seemed possible—to ensure parents that existing trends and/or desegregation plans would not result in their children's being forced to attend predominantly low-status (that is, "inner-city" or "slum" type) schools. Lacking such assurance, large numbers of middle-class parents withdraw their children in favor of nonpublic schools or move to the suburbs when the proportion of low-income or minority students (which many parents equate with low-income) reaches a "tipping point" at which local schools are perceived as having lost a stable, middle-status orientation. There are other factors, of course, that help generate and accelerate middle-class flight to the suburbs, but lack of confidence in the social class stability of public schools must be counted one of the most important.

Use of the term "tipping point" should not be interpreted, however, as implying that there is a single unvarying "point" (proportion of minority students) at which schools always change suddenly from mostly white to mostly black. As a matter of fact, two separate studies in Detroit (Wolf,

1963) and Baltimore (Stinchcombe, McDill, and Walker, 1969) have found that there was no consistently discernible turnover point unless one considered anything above zero a tipping point: as neighborhoods changed in these cities, schools that enrolled a small proportion of black students became increasingly black and then predominantly black. The main reason was that black families had limited housing opportunities, and the ghetto grew inexorably to take in more and more neighborhoods and schools.

On the other hand, many educators do feel they know of big-city schools that have "tipped" rapidly from majority white to majority black, particularly in neighborhoods where real estate "scare" tactics have been most in evidence. All in all, the tipping point phenomenon certainly does exist in the sense that schools with low-income black students tend to become increasingly black, and the process is accelerated as soon as middle-class parents believe local schools are beginning to manifest a predominantly low-status atmosphere. Though this point is not clearly delineated and varies from school to school, it seems to be located in the vicinity of about 25 to 40 percent low-income and 30 to 50 percent black.

In terms of district student composition, the result of the process of resegregation has been that in cities like Atlanta, the proportion of black students in the city schools has increased rapidly, from 30 percent in 1961 to 70 percent in 1971. During this same period, 34 schools changed from all-white to 90 percent or more black, and new schools built partly to increase integration were completely black (that is, "resegregated") before they even were ready to open their doors. At the same time, an indeterminate but substantial proportion of black students in big-city public schools come from economically and educationally disadvantaged families, especially since many middle-status and middle-class oriented black families take their children out of the public schools or, increasingly, move out of the central city school district if they can find reasonably priced housing elsewhere. In this situation, there is little hope of stabilizing or counteracting the social processes that lead to the creation of more inner-city schools and general decay in the central city unless social class and racial integration of public education is sought on a metropolitan basis.[14] For as Stinchcombe, et al. (1969) concluded in their study of resegregation in Baltimore:

> From a practical point of view, ... a policy of setting quotas for a
> certain percentage of Negroes in desegregated schools [in a big city
> like Baltimore] is not a rational policy. Wherever the quota point is
> set, it will tend to be undermined by other causal forces. The only
> way that a quota system would work would be if it would make
> other forces non-operative. One way, for example, would be rede-
> fining of the social unit in such a way that most redistribution of

*the population occurs within the unit rather than across the unit.
In large urban areas this would mean setting a quota for a
metropolitan school system rather than for a city school system
separately. The effect this would have would be that wherever a
white student enrolled in a public school, suburban or city, the
same percentage of Negro students would be encountered. (p. 135)*

Partly as a result of failure to approach integrated education intelligently on a metropolitan basis which takes account of neighborhood stability and social or racial "tipping points," the schools have become an important force in accelerating the deterioration of metropolitan areas. As long as families have no assurance that their children will attend schools in which conditions favor rather than undercut learning, it hardly seems possible to halt or reverse the process of racial and social class turnover of neighborhoods and concomitant decay in the tax base of the central city accompanied by urban sprawl in the suburbs and deterioration in the overall quality of life in the metropolitan area (Levine, 1971).

THE COURTS AND METROPOLITAN INTEGRATION

The federal courts and the Supreme Court recently considered several suits which might have resulted in a nationwide effort to integrate metropolitan area schools. The following three cases were the most important:

Denver

Argued before the Supreme Court in October of 1972, the Denver case was concerned with *de facto* segregation. The case came to the Supreme Court after a federal district judge concluded that neither compensatory education nor integrated education alone constituted an adequate remedy for previous segregation, and ruled that maintenance of *de facto* segregated facilities for minority students (black and Mexican) in Denver was unconstitutional in itself. This was the first major case to reach the Court since the April, 1972 ruling in *Swann* v. *Charlotte-Mecklenburg Board of Education* obligating that school board to reverse the effects of past discrimination, and the first to deal so clearly with *de facto* segregation in the North (U.S. Congress, Senate, *Congressional Record*, June 23, 1973, S11781).

While the Denver case did not deal directly with integration on a metropolitan basis, the Supreme Court decision ruling *de facto* segregation to be unconstitutional as it exists in Denver (that is, originating at least partly in school board actions) could result in widespread integration in big cities which include a substantial proportion of their respective metropolitan areas and/or have a high proportion of white students. It remains to be seen whether legal suits challenging *de facto* segregation will be filed in many cities which fit this description.

Detroit

On September 27, 1971, U.S. District Court Judge Stephen J. Roth issued a "Ruling on the Issue of Segregation" (*Bradley* v. *Milliken*) which determined that both the state of Michigan and the Detroit Board of Education had engaged in practices that helped cause segregation in the Detroit public schools. Because the resulting denial of equal educational opportunity could no longer be corrected solely within the limits of the Detroit public schools, and because the state government is legally responsible for the delineation of school district boundaries, Judge Roth subsequently accepted an integration plan that included cross-busing of students between Detroit and 52 surrounding school districts. The heart of the plan was the arrangement of the 53 school districts into 16 clusters in which about 330,000 students would be bused (compared with 230,000 already bused for other reasons) to paired schools providing integrated education in a nearby school for at least half of each student's elementary career.

Responding with a vote-catching non sequitur to the effect that "blacks don't learn anything by riding buses," Governor Milliken decided to appeal Roth's decision. On December 8, 1972, a three-member panel of the Sixth U.S. Court of Appeals upheld Roth's finding that no plan limited to Detroit could effectively desegregate the schools but returned the case to his court on the grounds that all 53 school districts should have had an opportunity to be represented in court hearings on the plan. On February 8, 1973, however, the full nine-member court reopened the case and reviewed the arguments anew. A decision upholding Roth's findings was announced on June 11, 1973. The case then went to the U.S. Supreme Court.

In a 5 to 4 decision delivered on July 25, 1974, the Supreme Court voided Roth's decision and ruled that the integration plan for Detroit need not include other school districts in the metropolitan area. The majority opinion, delivered by Chief Justice Warren E. Burger, was based on the conclusion that, "Before the boundaries of separate and autonomous school districts may be set aside . . . it must first be shown that there has been a constitutional violation within one district that produces a significant segregative effect in another district." Large-scale busing across school district lines "would give rise to an array of other problems in financing and operating this new school system . . . [which] would impose on the outlying districts, not shown to have committed any constitutional violation, a wholly impermissible remedy."

The immediate effect of this precedent-setting ruling by the Supreme Court was to return responsibility for preparing and executing a district-wide integration plan to school officials in Detroit. Since two-thirds of the students in the Detroit schools are black, it is not possible to provide anything like an even racial balance in every school; school officials there may be forced (by the courts or the federal executive) to reassign and bus pupils so that the percentage of black students in each school varies from roughly fifty to eighty percent. Such a plan, in turn, probably will result in an additional exodus from the district of white and black middle-class students whose parents fear that their local schools thereby will become predominantly low-status in socioeconomic composition.

The consequences of the Supreme Court decision, however, will not be limited to the Detroit metropolitan area. Suits requesting interdistrict integration in Indianapolis and several other cities probably will be withdrawn or rejected by federal courts, and similar suits are unlikely to be filed in other metropolitan areas. As in Detroit, many other big city school districts with a high proportion of minority pupils are likely to experience a continuing or accelerating decline in percentage of white students and/or middle-class students, particularly where school officials may be required to carry out integration plans which "tip" additional schools in the direction of a predominantly minority and/or working-class student population. Most suburban school districts, on the other hand, will remain predominantly white, except in the few cases where evidence can be obtained showing that segregation in central city schools followed from an overt act by suburban or state school officials as contrasted with a "natural" outgrowth of segregated housing patterns. Socioeconomic and racial segregation in many metropolitan areas, in other words, not only will not be reduced but probably will become still more ingrained.

Southern and Border States

In February, 1973, U.S. District Court Judge John H. Pratt ruled that HEW must promptly move to enforce desegregation in 17 southern and border states which once legally mandated segregation. Pleading lack of manpower, HEW appealed the ruling, but on June 11, 1973, Pratt ordered the department to institute proceedings against 200 school districts in the 17 states. Judge Pratt's decision eventually may spur city-wide desegregation in a number of cities which have a large proportion of disadvantaged or minority students.

As of 1971, about 59 percent of the 3,585,000 black students in the continental United States outside the South were in schools 80 to 100 percent black. Many of these students attend segregated schools in cities like Washington, D.C., Philadelphia, Baltimore, Atlanta, and Chicago which had a black majority in enrollment (93, 60, 67, 68, and 54 percent, respectively) in 1972. As of 1970, 72 percent of the black students in the nation's 100 largest school districts and 52 percent of the Spanish-surnamed students in the 31 largest districts were in schools which enrolled 80 percent or more minority students. Not much could be done to overcome *de facto* segregation effectively in many of these districts in the absence of action leading to metropolitan integration. And, even if the courts continue—as in the Denver and Detroit cases—to rule out *de facto* segregation in big cities, developments likely will follow much the same pattern as in the past. That is, assuming that Congress did not overrule the courts with a constitutional amendment, court cases will be initiated in many cities, school officials will be required to submit and carry out large-scale desegregation plans, little attention and fewer resources will be given to preparing teachers, students, and others to implement integration successfully, and the whole sad scenario will be acted out thoughtlessly as the buses roll and social conflict reaches the boiling point both outside and inside many schools. Some academic gains may be registered by minority students in some locations, but ultimately the nation may be left more fractured and bleeding than before.

CONCLUSION

No one can foretell for sure what will happen in the future, but in a general sense the number of directions in which movement can occur in the next five or ten years is limited.

One possible direction is to develop and carry out long-range plans that take into account the difficulties of implementing school desegregation and to encourage careful and intelligent responses to the underlying issue of segregation in metropolitan society. A proposal for movement in this direction was offered in Senator Ribicoff's metropolitan education amendment discussed in the U.S. Senate in April 1971. The purposes of Ribicoff's amendment would have been:

> *to require State and local educational agencies in metropolitan areas throughout this country to develop and implement plans which will reduce and eliminate minority group isolation in our public schools, whatever the cause of such isolation; and to provide financial assistance to assist state and local educational agencies to develop and implement such plans.* (U.S. Congress, Senate, Congressional Record, *April 19, 1971, S5062–S5065)*

The amendment would have provided $1 billion between July 1973 and July 1975 and $2 billion a year thereafter to launch plans that would result in metropolitan-wide integrated education by 1985. If enacted, the amendment would have required that an agency be established in each Standard Metropolitan Statistical Area (SMSA) to develop "a plan to reduce minority group isolation. . . . [so that] no later than July 1, 1985, the percentage of minority group children in each school of the SMSA shall be at least 50 percentum of the percentage of minority group children enrolled in all the schools of that SMSA." With provisions for annual review of progress and cutoff of all federal education funds to noncomplying school systems, local plans could have included "the use of techniques, as appropriate in local circumstances, such as redrawing school boundaries, creating unified school districts, pairing schools or school districts, establishing educational parks and magnet schools as well as other techniques designed to end as soon as possible minority group isolation" (U.S. Congress, Senate, *Congressional Record*, April 19, 1971).

Ribicoff's plan for metropolitan integration had several major virtues that made it the most promising proposal for solving race-related problems of metropolitan schools and society and until now have received little public attention. First, the plan explicitly recognized the metropolitan basis and nature of problems arising from and associated with social class stratification and racial segregation. Second, it provided for step-by-step implementation over more than a decade rather than questionable "instant" solutions for pervasive and deepseated problems. Third, it provided for substantial funding to realize its objectives. Fourth, it identified specific government agencies that would be responsible and accountable for progress and implementation. Fifth, it applied equally to the North and the South, thus eliminating what many southerners perceived as a double standard that mandated integration in the South but not the North.

On the other hand, the approach embodied in Senator Ribicoff's proposal was open to criticism on several grounds (in addition to the specious attack of knee-jerk opponents and demagogues). For example, it did not provide adequate consideration to the social class aspects of integration, to the danger of an overly wide dispersal of handfuls of minority students, or to the relationship between metropolitan housing changes and school integration. (However, legislation Ribicoff had previously proposed unsuccessfully did provide for a coordinated, long-range pattern of housing and school desegregation.) As Strickman has suggested, an approach such as Senator Ribicoff's would have been stronger if it emphasized large financial incentives to middle-class schools receiving significant numbers of economically disadvantaged students (Strickman, 1972). Nevertheless, it did at least represent one of the few times a branch of the federal government almost recognized that metropolitan problems associated with poverty and urban decay can only be solved with systematic solutions on a metropolitan scale.

A different alternative we may follow—and the most likely one—is to continue in the direction events have been carrying us for the past few decades. Basically, this is a direction in which we deal with segregated schooling and society in the metropolis either by pretending it does not exist or by sporadic, piecemeal attempts to treat one or another symptom in an isolated part of the metropolitan area.

Following this approach, it may be of little consequence whether or not the Supreme Court rules that *de facto* segregated education in the North is unconstitutional and/or that a proper remedy requires the obliteration of existing school district boundaries in many metropolitan areas. In the long run, *pro forma*, court-ordered desegregation on a city-wide or metropolitan basis might not accomplish much other than to further generate and exacerbate social dissatisfaction and political conflict. Ultimately, little would be "gained" except an increase in the potential for still further deterioration in the structure of metropolitan society in the United States.

In truth, we already are entering a second period of reconstruction in which disadvantaged minorities are being forced back into their "place" as a separate underclass (that is, caste) in our society. Movement toward this Second Reconstruction recently has been greatly hastened by federal practices which—to greatly abbreviate a very long story—increasingly end up reflecting the notion that every family deserves to live in a decent, safe neighborhood only as long as it can afford an expensive house in the suburbs.

To be sure, there are important differences between the period after the Civil War which established a caste system in place of slavery and the present era when another type of caste structure is replacing the older one. Today, many minority families are escaping or have escaped into the mainstream of society where they have real opportunities for social, economic, and cultural advancement; those locked in slum ghettos constitute a much smaller percentage, proportionately, than did the victims of the First Reconstruction. On the other hand, the new underclass in our metropolitan areas constitutes a much larger concentration of increasingly bitter people, and they are in a much more strategic position to redirect their despair toward the larger society than was true one hundred years ago.

Located primarily in racial or ethnic central city ghettos, the members of this underclass tend to grow up in low-income, female-headed families in which poverty and social disorganization are being handed down from one generation to the next. Between 1958 and 1968, for example, the number of female-headed families below the poverty level in central cities increased by 45 percent (U.S. Bureau of the Census, *Current Population*

Reports, 1969, p. 8). By 1969, a staggering 49 percent of the nearly 300,000 female-headed black families in central cities were officially classified as below the poverty level, and approximately 68 percent of the persons below 18 years of age in these families were below the poverty level. Related to this, between 1959 and 1969 there was no decline in the number of below-poverty-level black citizens (1.8 million) in central cities in metropolitan areas with one million or more people, even as the number of citizens in poverty in the nation as a whole was falling from 38.8 million to 25.4 million (U.S. Bureau of the Census, *Current Population Reports*, 1970, pp. 80, 33). By 1970, children under 18 accounted for 54 percent of all black persons below the poverty level, as compared with 36 percent for whites (U.S. Bureau of the Census, *Current Population Reports*, p. 1).

To cite a high incidence of female-headed families in poverty as evidence of the formation of an underclass in big cities is not, of course, to say that low-income mothers in these households are not trying to help their children acquire skills needed for mobility, or that all of them fail. But it would be unrealistic to forget that female-headed families in inner-city neighborhoods face a multitude of special problems in raising children, as well as in merely earning enough money to make ends meet; for it is black women who head families, as Schuster (1968) has pointed out, who "bear the heaviest burden in all Big City ghettos: the longest periods of unemployment; the lowest pay when and if employed; the largest number of dependents; the lowest skilled jobs; the fewest opportunities for training; the least coverage by unemployment insurance; the most serious health problems; the greatest emotional burdens of family life" (p. 28). Not surprisingly, an extremely high proportion of such families in an urban community nearly always indicates that crime, low school achievement, delinquency, and other manifestations of social disorganization also are extremely high.

It is possible that, given a few carrots and enough repression, we can succeed in imposing and maintaining the new caste system without setting off large explosions that will reverberate throughout the country. But it would not be wise to bet on it.

NOTES

1. Parts of this chapter appeared in modified form as, "Integration in Metropolitan Area Schools: Issues and Prospects," *Phi Delta Kappan*, 54: 651–59 (May 1973).

2. Of course, unmanaged "negative" contact can also increase stereotypes in some situations.

3. This conclusion is meant to include "positive" stereotypes, which sometimes can be ultimately as harmful as negative ones.

4. A well-publicized study in which David Armor claimed he had disproved arguments regarding the desirability of integrated education is largely invalid due to extremely serious flaws in methodology and interpretation. See David Armor. "The Evidence on Busing," *The Public Interest*, Summer 1972, pp. 90–126, and an analysis of Armor's paper by Thomas Pettigrew and others, along with Armor's defense in the Winter 1973 issue of the same journal.

5. It should be noted that some observers believe there is evidence for a racial integration effect apart from or beyond achievement gains attributable to social class integration. Thomas F. Pettigrew, for example, concluded in 1971 that the evidence "tentatively point[s] to the operation of both social class and racial composition factors on Negro achievement" (U.S. Congress, Senate, *Congressional Record*, 92d Cong., 1st sess., April 19, 1971, S5071). Our own reading of the data is that racial factors generally have little or no important achievement effect beyond those associated with social class mixture.

6. There is some reason to believe that if such an effect exists, it may be smaller or less frequently detectable in urban areas in the South than is true in urban areas elsewhere in the country. See Department of Program Evaluation, 1972, *Evaluation of Desegregation—1970–1971*.

7. In a report released late in 1972, the U. S. Senate Select Committee on Equal Educational Opportunity submitted its report to Congress and registered agreement with Christopher Jencks's conclusion that racial-socioeconomic integration alone will reduce the gap in achievement test scores between black and white children and rich and poor children by 10 to 20 percent. The committee also pointed out that "compensatory education programs are most likely to produce significant and lasting gains when special educational efforts are combined with socioeconomic integration," and concluded that "where carefully designed educational programs provide for focused remedial services within a racially and socially integrated setting, substantially more dramatic gains [than 20 percent] can be expected" (p. 24).

8. For examples, see *Phi Delta Kappan* articles by Richard Lonoff, Seymour Fliegel, and William W. Wayson on "The Reform of Urban Education" (1971).

9. Of course it also should be kept in mind that integration and compensatory education are not completely exclusive. Rather, compensatory services definitely are necessary as part of any worthwhile integration plan.

10. For examples of programs that might be funded under the act, see Levine (1972).

11. For an extended discussion on this point, see Cohen (1968).

12. For examples, see Gilbert and Sessions (n.d.).

13. Such plans have been proposed in Wichita and several other cities but have not been accepted by the respective boards of education in these districts.

14. Recognizing this, the Atlanta NAACP in March of 1973 accepted a plan which—to the surprise of some observers—called for only a relatively small degree of additional integration in the city's public schools.

15. Some veteran Supreme Court observers concluded, however, that the present court is unlikely to mandate metropolitan desegregation if only because of the danger inherent in issuing so controversial and difficult (to implement) a decision on a divided basis.

16. In its brief to the Supreme Court during the hearings on this case, the

Justice Department noted that experts disagree about the effects of racial segregation in the schools and argued that an "appropriate remedy" for racial imbalance attributable to segregated housing could include (1) "evenhanded" application of resources, (2) identification of special needs of schools which provided inferior opportunities in the past, and (3) plans for designing and implementing a remedial program to meet these needs (U.S. Congress, Senate, *Congressional Record*, Cong., sess., October 17, 1972, S18461).

REFERENCES

Amir, Yehuda. 1969. "Contact Hypothesis in Ethnic Relations." *Psychological Bulletin* 71: 319–342.

Armor, David. 1972. "The Evidence on Busing." *Public Interest* (Summer): 90–126.

Averch, Harvey, et al. 1971. *How Effective is Schooling? A Critical Review and Synthesis of Research Findings.* Santa Monica, Calif.: Rand Corporation.

Bash, James H. and Roger L. Long. 1968. *Effective Adminstration in Desegregated Schools.* Bloomington, Ind.: Phi Delta Kappa.

Beker, Jerome. 1967. *A Study of Integration in racially Imbalanced Urban Public Schools.* Syracuse, N.Y.: Syracuse University Youth Development Center, May.

Chesler, Mark, et al. 1970. *Integrating the Desegregated School: Planning Educational Change.* Vol. 3. Washington, D.C.: U.S. Government Printing Office.

Cohen, David K. 1968. "Compensation and Integration." *Harvard Educational Review* 38: 114–137.

Cohen, Elizabeth G. and Susan S. Roper. 1972. "Modification of Interracial Interaction Disability: An Application of Status Characteristic Theory. *American Sociological Review* 37: 543–647.

Coleman, James S., et al. 1966. *Equality of Educational Opportunity.* Washington, D.C.: U.S. Government Printing Office.

Department of Program Evaluation. 1972. *Evaluation of Desegregation—1970–1971.* Miami, Fl.: Board of Education of Dade County, June.

Devries, David L. and Keith J. Edwards. 1972 *Student Teams and Instructional Games: Their Effects on Cross-Race and Cross-Sex Interaction.* Baltimore, Md.: Center for Social Organization of Schools, the Johns Hopkins University, September.

Fliegel, Seymour. 1971. "Practices that Improved Academic Performance in an Inner-City School." *Phi Delta Kappan* 52: 341–343.

Foster, Gordon. 1972. "School Desegregation: Problem or Opportunity for Urban Education?" *Urban Review* 6: 16.

Gilbert, Albin R. and Robert Paul Sessions (eds.). n.d. *Updating Intergroup Education in Public Schools. A Study-Action Manual*. Buckhanon, W.V.: West Virginia Wesleyan College. Mimeographed.

Hawkridge, David C., G. Karsten Tallmadge, and Judith K. Larsen. 1968. *Foundations for Success in Educating Disadvantaged Children*. Palo Alto, Calif.: American Institute for Research.

Integrated Education. 1970. "Chronicle of Race and Schools." 8: 22–23.

Integrated Education. 1972. "Chronicle of Race and Schools." 10: 18–19.

Lambda Corporation. 1971. *School Desegregation with Minimum Busing*. A Report to the Assistant Secretary for Planning and Evaluation, U.S. Department of Health, Education, and Welfare. Arlington, Va.: Lambda Corporation, December 10.

Levine, Daniel U. 1971. "The Inner City Disadvantaged and the Metropolitan Bind." Pp. 3–12 in R. C. Doll and M. Hawkins (eds.), *Educating the Disadvantaged, 1970–1971*. New York: AMS Press.

Levine, Daniel U. (ed.) 1972. *Models for Integrated Education*. Worthington, Ohio: Jones.

Lonoff, Richard. 1971. "Supervisory Practices that Promote Academic Achievement in a New York City School." *Phi Delta Kappan* 52: 338–340.

Mayeske, George, et al. 1970. *A Study of Our Nation's Schools*. Washington, D.C.: U.S. Government Printing Office.

Moss, Ruth. 1972. "The Integrated School and the Double Standard." *Chicago Tribune Magazine*, pp. 72–80. Reprinted, courtesy of the Chicago Tribune.

O'Reilly, Robert (ed.). 1970. *Racial and Social Class Isolation in the Schools*. New York: Praeger.

Pettigrew, Thomas F., et al. 1973. "Busing: A Review of 'The Evidence.'" *Public Interest* (Winter): 99.

Report on Education Research, vol. 1, April 29, 1970. p. 5.

St. John, Nancy H. 1972. "Desegregation: Voluntary or Mandatory?" *Integrated Education* 10: 7–16.

Schuster, Arnold. 1968. *White Power/Black Freedom*. Boston: Beacon.

Smith, Marshall B. 1972. "Equality of Educational Opportunity: The Basic Findings Reconsidered." Pp. 230–342 in F. Mosteller and D.P. Moynihan (eds.), *On Equality of Educational Opportunity*. New York: Random House.

Spady, William G. 1973. "The Impact of School Resources on Children." Pp. 135–177 in F. Kerlinger (ed.) *Review of Research in Education*. Itasca, Ill. Peacock.

Stinchcombe, Arthur L., et al. 1969. "Is There a Racial Tipping Point in Changing Schools?" *Journal of Social Issues* 25: 127–136.

Strickman, Leonard B. 1972. "Desegregation: The Metropolitan Concept." *Urban Review* 6: 18–23.

U.S. Bureau of the Census, *Current Population Reports*.
1969 Series P-60, No. 68, 1958 to 1968.
1970 Series P-23, No. 33.
1971 Series P-60, No. 71, in 1970.

U.S. Commission on Civil Rights. 1972 a. *The Diminishing Barrier: A Report on School Desegregation in Nine Communities*. Washington, D.C.: U.S. Government Printing Office.

U.S. Commission on Civil Rights, 1972 b. *Five Communities: Their Search for Equal Education*. Washington, D.C.: U.S. Government Printing Office.

U.S. Congress, Senate, *Congressional Record*, 92d Cong., 1st sess., April 19, 1971, S5062–S5065, S5071.

U.S. Congress, Senate, *Congressional Record*, 92d Cong., 1st sess., April 20 and 21, 1971, S5203–S5307.

U.S. Congress, Senate, *Congressional Record*, 92d Cong., 2d sess., October 17, 1972, S18461.

U.S. Congress, Senate, *Congressional Record*, 93d Cong., 1st sess., June 23, 1973, S11781.

U.S. Congress, Senate, Select Committee on Equal Educational Opportunity. 1972. *Toward Equal Educational Opportunity*. Washington, D.C.: U.S. Government Printing Office.

Vargo, Michael J., et al. 1971. *Further Examination of Exemplary Programs for Educating Disadvantaged Students*. Palo Alto, Calif.: American Institute for Research.

Wayson, William W. 1971. "Organizing Urban Schools for Responsible Education." *Phi Delta Kappan* 50: 344–347.

Weinberg, Meyer. 1972. "Comment on the St. John Article." *Integrated Education* 10, no. 1: 16–17.

Wolf, Eleanor P. 1963. "The Tipping Point in Racially Changing Neighborhoods." *Journal of the American Institute of Planners* 27: 217–222.

Index of Authors

Index of School Systems